Alternatives to Piaget

CRITICAL ESSAYS ON THE THEORY

Alternatives to Piaget

CRITICAL ESSAYS ON THE THEORY

Edited by

LINDA S. SIEGEL
Department of Psychiatry
McMaster University Medical Centre
Hamilton, Ontario, Canada

CHARLES J. BRAINERD
Department of Psychology
University of Western Ontario
London, Ontario, Canada

ACADEMIC PRESS   New York   San Francisco   London
A Subsidiary of Harcourt Brace Jovanovich, Publishers

ACADEMIC PRESS, INC.
111 Fifth Avenue, New York, New York 10003

United Kingdom Edition published by
ACADEMIC PRESS, INC. (LONDON) LTD.
24/28 Oval Road, London NW1

Library of Congress Cataloging in Publication Data

Main entry under title:

Alternatives to Piaget.

Includes bibliographies.
1.   Cognition in children—Addresses, essays, lectures.
2.   Piaget, Jean,   Date   —Addresses, essays,
lectures.   I.   Siegel, Linda S.   II.   Brainerd, Charles J.
BF723.C5A48   155.4'13'0924   77-75575
ISBN 0−12−641950−7

Contents

Contents

List of Contributors

Numbers in parentheses indicate the pages on which the authors' contributions begin.

Helene Borke (29), Hay Associates, Pittsburgh, Pennsylvania

Charles J. Brainerd (69), Department of Psychology, University of Western Ontario, London, Ontario, Canada

Edward H. Cornell (1), Department of Psychology, University of Alberta, Edmonton, Alberta, Canada

Robert H. Ennis (201), Department of Educational Policy Studies, College of Education, University of Illinois at Urbana–Champaign, Urbana, Illinois

Vernon C. Hall (153), Department of Psychology, Syracuse University, Syracuse, New York

Adrienne E. Harris (131), Department of Psychology, Glendon College, York University, Toronto, Ontario, Canada

Frank H. Hooper (169), Research and Development Center for Cognitive Learning, University of Wisconsin, Madison, Wisconsin

Daniel B. Kaye (153), Department of Psychology, Syracuse University, Syracuse, New York

Joseph T. Lawton (169), Division of Child Development, School of Consumer Sciences, University of Wisconsin, Madison, Wisconsin

Timothy E. Moore (131), Department of Psychology, Glendon College, York University, Toronto, Ontario, Canada

Richard D. Odom (111), Department of Psychology, Vanderbilt University, Nashville, Tennessee

Linda S. Siegel (43), Department of Psychiatry, McMaster University Medical Centre, Hamilton, Ontario, Canada

Preface

For more than a half-century now, Jean Piaget and his collaborators have written prodigiously on the development of human intelligence. Since his very first book appeared in 1926, Piaget's works have been widely discussed and quoted. When it comes to the study of children's intelligence, his theory dominates the landscape. Although a few studies on children's intelligence are conducted within other theoretical frameworks, the current literature has become virtually synonymous with the analysis of age-related changes in children's performance on Piagetian tasks. With such a massive amount of Piaget-oriented research and theorizing going on, it was only a matter of time before major inconsistencies began to appear between what the theory says about the way intelligence develops and what the research actually shows.

This book is about Piagetian theory and the ideas and experiments that have developed out of this theory. The papers in this book are all concerned with problem areas in the theory. Basic Piagetian hypotheses and stages are examined in light of current empirical findings and an analysis of the structure of the theory itself. The inconsistencies between empirical data and the theory's predictions are very serious. At the same time, analysis of the theory itself has revealed hitherto unsuspected logical problems with some of Piaget's key explanatory constructs. For these reasons, it now appears that a comprehensive reassessment and revision of the theory is in order. We believe that this book is the first real step in that direction.

The chapters in the book deal with the Piagetian analyses of the development of the object concept, perceptual development, the relationship of language and thought, social development, logical thinking, the role of learning in concept development, and the application of Piagetian theory to education. The book was written with developmental psychologists and educators especially in mind, but it will be of interest to all people who work with children.

Although the present volume contains discussions of diverse areas, there are nevertheless some general themes that unite the essays. Far and away the most important of these themes, because it enters into every essay in one way or another, is the so-called performance–competence problem. The problem itself is easily stated: When a child fails a certain Piagetian test that is supposed to tap some given underlying concept, what does this mean? Of course, it could mean that the child does not possess the concept. This interpretation is known as a "competence explanation", and is the sort of interpretation favored by Piaget. However, failure on a Piagetian test can also mean (and frequently does mean) that the test is too difficult. A Piagetian test invariably measures many other things than what it actually is supposed to measure. Therefore, it is always possible that failure on a Piagetian test results from these other things rather than from absence of the underlying concept. This second interpretation is known as a "performance explanation."

The performance–competence problem is most especially prominent in the papers by Borke, Ennis, Cornell, Odom, Moore and Harris, and Siegel. Piaget maintains that preschool children are egocentric—i.e., they do not realize that there are points of view other than their own. Borke argues that previous reports of egocentric behavior on the part of preschoolers may be an artifact of the excessive difficulty of standard Piagetian perspective-taking tasks. Piaget maintains that infants do not understand that objects have existences which are independent of their own actions until the second year of life. However, Cornell argues that Piaget's original findings may have resulted from, among other things, the attentional demands and the reinforcement contingencies operating in his object permanence tests. Cornell reports that, with newly devised object permanence tests, infants younger than one year are capable of Stage V and Stage VI object permanence. Piaget maintains that elementary school children cannot handle propositional logic. But, Ennis concludes that this claim is either false or untestable or not about logic at all. Piaget maintains that the conservation concepts of middle-childhood develop in an invariant sequence because different concrete contents are differentially resistant to the application of logical operations. Odom, however, argues that this *décalage* may be entirely attributable to the varying perceptual demands of conservation tests. Piaget maintains that preschool children do not possess a broad range of numerical and quantitative concepts. However, Siegel argues, on the basis of recent experiments, that Piaget's earlier results are primarily a consequence of the linguistic demands of his concrete-operational tests. Moore and Harris demonstrate that traditional Piagetian concrete operational tasks do not adequately tap the cognitive functions implicit in language comprehension and production.

Another underlying theme in the essays concerns the role of learning in cognitive development. This theme is most clearly evident in the papers by Brainerd, Cornell, Hall and Kaye, and Lawton and Hooper. Piaget's ideas about learning are best characterized as a classic readiness model in which learning is subordinated to development. In other words, it is assumed that the usual learning processes can operate only when children are developmentally ready to learn. This normally means that some incipient competence (concept, operation, structure, etc.) is supposed to develop before learning occurs. These ideas lead to some rather definite predictions about what sorts of learning experiences are most effective and how much learning is possible. Brainerd examines evidence bearing on these predictions gleaned from learning research on concrete-operational concepts. Hall and Kaye examine some related findings derived from experiments designed to extinguish concepts such as conservation. Both Brainerd and Hall and Kaye conclude that the available evidence tends to disconfirm Piaget's model of learning. Hall and Kaye argue that traditional learning theory provides a much better explanation of extinction data than does Piaget's model. Cornell explores the question of whether a straightforward reinforcement analysis is capable of explaining infants' performance on object permanence tests and the question of whether simple learning experiences alter performance on such tests. Finally, it is obvious that any theory of learning must have profound implications for instruction—especially elementary school instruction. The instructional implications of Piaget's views on learning are examined in the essay by Lawton and Hooper.

A third and final unifying theme is the consideration of theoretical viewpoints other than Piaget's. When Piagetian theory cannot explain a particular set of findings, it is obvious that other theories must be considered. Even when Piagetian theory does appear to explain certain findings, it may be that some other theory works just as well. Although the present contributors discuss theories other than Piaget's, no one theory predominates. Borke invokes the ideas of George Herbert Mead as alternatives to Piaget's claims about egocentrism during the preschool years. In Cornell's, Siegel's, and Hall and Kaye's papers, traditional S–R analysis is used to test for the presence of Piagetian cognitive operations and to explain performance on Piagetian tests. In Moore and Harris' paper, the inadequacy of the Piagetian model for language development is outlined. The theories of Chomsky are suggested as a useful alternative. In Odom's paper, perceptual-salience theory is invoked in conjunction with conservation *décalage*. Lawton and Hooper compare

Piaget-inspired instructional guidelines with those of more traditional curricula, especially those which stress self-discovery. Thus, while it is apparent from these essays that, in specific instances, alternative theories work as well or better than Piaget's, no single alternative has yet emerged.

These essays are designed to stimulate critical reassessments of Piagetian theory in light of the available data. They are also designed to encourage steering a middle course between throwing out the baby with the bath water and maintaining the infallibility of the theory in the face of all manner of disconfirming evidence.

We believe that the more prudent middle course lies somewhere between totally rejecting the theory and refusing to recognize its weaknesses. At a minimum, this intermediate approach involves recognizing the existence of disconfirmatory data and attempting to assess the specific implications of such data for the theory. This approach involves receptivity to theories other than Piaget's, but not a dogmatic rejection of the Piagetian viewpoint. It is in the hope of generating such an approach among those who study children's intelligence that we present this work. Under no circumstances is it intended to provide the last word on anything. In this book, we ask the questions; definitive answers will have to await those who come after us.

Linda S. Siegel
Charles J. Brainerd

1

Learning to Find Things: A Reinterpretation of Object Permanence Studies

EDWARD H. CORNELL
University of Alberta, Canada

> We say that a newborn baby knows how to cry, suckle, and sneeze. We say that a child knows how to walk and how to ride a tricycle. The evidence is simply that the baby and child exhibit the behavior specified. Moving from verb to noun, we say that they possess knowledge, and the evidence is that they possess behavior [Skinner, 1974, p. 137].

Introduction

In Piaget's theory *object permanence* is described as a concept, the concept that an object is solid and exists in three-dimensional space (Piaget, 1954). After becoming familiar with an object, we maintain that it is permanent even on those occasions when we are not in a position to perceive the object. Piaget suggests that this is knowledge attained during the first 18 months of life, knowledge that is certainly

Preparation of this chapter and the author's research reported herein were supported in part by the General Research Fund of the University of Alberta and by Grant A0267 from the National Research Council of Canada.

1

one of the cornerstones of intelligence (Piaget, 1952). Piaget also suggests that the object concept is *constructed;* that is, during his interactions with objects the infant organizes cognitive structures, which are described as different stages of knowledge about the permanence of things. The cognitive structures are actually inferred from the different ways infants interact with objects, and thus the stages of the object concept ultimately are defined in terms of patterns of behavior.

Piaget's observations of infant responses to the movement, occlusion, and disappearance of objects seem to be accurate (see reviews by Harris, 1975; Gratch, 1975, 1976). However, researchers have raised a number of questions concerning the *interpretation* of these observations. Are there situations in which the very young infant behaves as if objects are permanent? Are there meaningful, qualitatively different stages in the infant's performance? If so, what are the mechanisms of transition from one mode of response to the next? To introduce these issues, I will discuss the heuristics involved in studying the object concept and then summarize some of the approaches researchers have used to elucidate Piaget's theory. The remainder of the chapter puts forth a new approach: I intend to argue that learning theory can account for major aspects of infants' performance in object permanence tasks.

Heuristic Approaches and Errors

In his theory of intellectual development, Jean Piaget rejects the notion that empirical, associationistic learning is of primary importance as the infant comes to know the world. First, as Flavell (1963) has summarized, "[Piaget] emphatically rejects the notion that the subject is in simple and direct contact with the 'real' external world, either at the beginning of development or at any time thereafter [p. 68]." Second, whereas experience is seen as necessary to the development of intelligence, experience does not owe its value to the inherent structure of the objects and events in the world nor to the habits and associations that may be passively acquired in contact with these structures (Piaget, 1952). Instead, intellectual development and knowledge evolve as the child actively constructs his experience by modifying his activity to the special properties of the object or event *(accommodation)* and by structuring or restructuring his interpretation of the environment in accord with existing intellectual organization *(assimilation).* Piaget has dissociated these hypothetical adaptive processes from traditional notions of learning and, as will be illustrated herein, has neglected the possibility that learning affects performance in tasks in which cognitive development is explicated and assessed.

Perhaps the principal development of the sensorimotor stage in Piaget's theory of intellectual growth involves the object concept (Flavell, 1963). Piaget characterizes the young infant's knowledge of the world as a state of chaotic undifferentiation. At first the environment consists of a flux of perceptual images centered about the infant's personal activity. The young infant does not distinguish objects and events as external to himself or as independent of his activities, and he does not distinguish himself and his activities as placed among other things in space and time. Expressed in the form of a null hypothesis, Piaget maintains that the young infant has no knowledge of the solidity and objectivity of things.

The accepted heuristics of measurement hold that in assessing this hypothesis we are subject to two basic forms of error. An error of Type I involves rejecting the null hypothesis when in fact it is true. That is, following the infant's successful performance at some task, we could assert that the infant knows that objects are permanent when in fact he does not know. For example, the study of visual recognition memory indicates that infants as young as 5–6 months of age, when presented with two photographs of faces, spend relatively less time looking at that photograph that had been shown to them 2 weeks earlier (Fagan, 1973). We could argue that during the initial exposure some aspects of the familiar photograph had been encoded and stored and that the subsequent differential response indicates recognition of the constancy of the photograph. However, accepting performance on a recognition task as indicative of object permanence may lead to Type I error. According to Piaget's argument, recognition may occur as a result of associations between features of the object, subjective impressions of satisfaction or familiarity, and reflex-like motor acts. According to this point of view, the infant may be merely recognizing his own reaction before he recognizes the object as such. Piaget argues for a more rigid criteria: The infant must dissociate the object from old modes of reacting and must demonstrate that the object is represented in space and time by means of a new activity. Thus, for Piaget, the basic evidence for knowledge of the permanence of objects is the infant's search for the object, either by manually removing obstacles or by changing his visual perspective. Adopting a more rigid criteria in assessing the null hypothesis increases the probability of a Type II error—accepting the null hypothesis when in fact it is false. Thus, by requiring that the infant initiate search behaviors to obtain a missing object, we are more likely to observe inadequate performance and may conclude incorrectly that he has no knowledge of the constancy and permanence of things.

Unfortunately, developmental psychology can provide little information as to the correct criteria for assessing an epistemological concept such as object permanence. However, the methods of developmental psychology can be useful to describe the development of the child's response to objects as a function of both maturation and experience. In addition, developmental research can be directed to the purpose of empirical determinism, that is, specifying the conditions which exist when the child interacts with objects in particular ways. With this in mind, let us examine some of the approaches researchers have used in the study of the object concept.

Recent Approaches to the Study of Object Permanence

During the 1960s, Western investigators began systematic study of Piaget's description of the development of the object concept (Gratch, 1976). Since the early studies, which served to replicate his basic observations, there have been serious questions concerning Piaget's interpretation of structures, stages, and transitions. One rather fundamental approach is illustrated by the work of Moore (1973). Moore demonstrated that there exist several manual search tasks in which the infant's performance is intermediate between the developmental stages reported by Piaget. Since active search is considered sine qua non in defining the infant's cognitive competence, it is interesting that Moore describes not three but nine sequential developments in the solution of manual search tasks. His work supports the argument that descriptions of stages can be either selective or incomplete. Note that when more stages are discovered the development of the object concept appears to be more continuous.

Another approach aims to demonstrate infant competence in situations that are different from the standard Piagetian tasks. For example, Bower and Wishart (1972) tested 5-month-old infants in a manual search task in which an attractive toy was hidden underneath a cup. All of the infants failed to do anything to remove the occluding cup. The toy was then tied on the end of a string dangling in front of the baby. Before the baby could reach out for the toy, the room lights were extinguished, and the baby was left in total darkness. Nevertheless, all of the infants were able to obtain the toy while in the dark, and infrared videotape records indicated that their reaching was not random. Obviously, for these young infants out of sight was not out of mind.

Bower has summarized much of his work in this regard under the rubric of infant object *perception* (Bower, 1974, Chapter 5; 1975). In certain respects his approach can be considered similar to that of Yonas and Pick (1975) and Gratch (1975, 1976). These investigators have suggested that in studying the infant's representation of objects and space it may be instructive to determine what the infant perceives. This approach shifts the emphasis of study from what is inside the infant's head to what is out there, in the stimulus array, when the infant behaves as if objects are permanent. For example, J. J. Gibson (1966) has suggested that adult perceptual systems are particularly attuned to edges, surfaces, shadows, textures, drop-offs, and a number of other ecological invariants. In other words, Gibson maintains that we are sensitive to the inherent structure of objects and events in the world. Since there seems to be good evidence that the young infant is capable of perception of depth and form (Gibson, 1969; Fantz, Fagan, & Miranda, 1975), developmental psychologists have discussed the possibility that the infant can simply *see* that objects are solid in space. To date, this notion has received equivocal empirical support (Decarie, 1969; Gratch, 1975; Yonas & Pick, 1975; Dodwell, Muir, & DiFranco, 1976). In the future the approach may shift from the study of direct perception to how the infant learns to attend to the stimulus information that reveals that objects exist.

Butterworth (1976a) and Harris (1976) have presented an explanation of infant search behaviors that uses descriptive language different from that of Piaget. They maintain that an object's position can be specified relative to the self, by an egocentric code, or relative to the spatial surround, by an allocentric code. That is, an infant may represent an object as "to my left" or "on the table." Harris maintains that the use of cues in the external framework is relatively slow to develop, and he attempts to explain the errors in infants' search as a consequence of conflict between egocentric and allocentric codes. The theory can be used post hoc to account for infants' responses in situations where there exist both kinesthetic and external cues for successful search (Butterworth, 1975; 1976b). However, by postulating internal codes, the explanation tends to emphasize what the infant has rather than what the infant responds to.

A discrimination-learning theory has described a similar issue in terms of response versus place learning. In reviewing the animal studies, Restle (1957) concludes that performance in mazes depends upon many cues, in all available modalities and from all sources. The animal studies

did not support the notion that kinesthetic cues are the primary discriminative cues for maze learning for either adult or younger rats.
However, young human infants, when responding to objects and events
in space, may respond more on the basis of kinesthetic cues than do
older human infants (Cornell, 1976). The design of Cornell's study was
similar to Tolman's test of place learning versus response learning in
rats (Tolman, Ritchie, & Kalish, 1946). During training, in the experimental procedure, 4- and 8-month-old infants were presented with
novel visual patterns in one location over 20 trials. This could be either
90° to their left or right, and a repeated pattern was always presented
in the opposite location during the same trials. In the control procedure, infants of the same ages received exposure to the same patterns,
except the left–right positions of the repeated and novel patterns were
randomized over trials. Only the directional head-turning by the experimental groups indicated learning and anticipation of the location of
the repeated and novel patterns (Figure 1.1). In an immediate transfer
test, all infants were observed when rotated 180° in the room. In the
transfer task the east or west location of the repeated and novel pat-

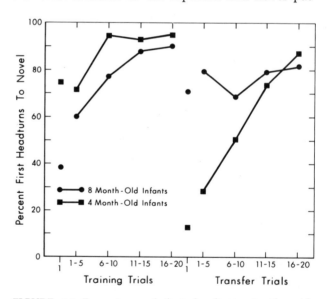

FIGURE 1.1 Percentage of first headturns to the side
of the room where novel visual stimuli were presented is
plotted as a function of presentation trials during training
and when the infant was rotated 180° following training.
The data were obtained from eight 8-month-old infants
and eight 4-month-old infants in the experimental condition.

terns remained the same for the experimental group. The 4-month-old infants in the experimental group persevered with their previously learned head-turning response for a number of trials. That is, after being rotated, they directed their first few looks toward the familiar side. However, they quickly shifted to looking to the side screens in a back-and-forth manner, and within 11–15 trials their first head-turns were to the novel side. Following rotation, the 8-month-old infants continued to look to the place where the novel stimuli appeared.

The results suggest the hypothesis that young infants attend more to response-produced kinesthetic cues than do older infants. Regardless of the nature of cues used by infants of different ages, Cornell's results are consistent with the interpretation that infants acquire and transfer spatially directed behavior in accord with the contingencies that exist in the environment. This is a learning approach to the study of object permanence, and in developing this approach, it may be useful to describe some of the contingencies that exist in common search situations.

Search Situations

An object clearly can only be in one place at one time. But objects in the world are often displaced, and some objects are displaced more often than others. In a situation where objects are moved about, a child can learn the characteristic displacements of a particular object—how often, if ever, it is displaced, and where it is located following displacement. If an object is novel in appearance, or can be eaten, or is pleasant to manipulate, or interests or stimulates the child in some other way, the opportunity to experience, use, or interact with the object can be the reward for search.

Consider the four situations illustrated in Figure 1.2. A and B represent loci where interaction with an object has occurred. The arrows indicate displacements of the object to a locus.

In Situation 1, the reward always occurs following search at the first locus where the object is experienced, the locus where the object is most often experienced, and the last locus where the object has been experienced. Situation 1 represents the most elementary contingency because the object is fixed at a locus.

In Situation 2, the reward often occurs following search at the first locus where the object has been experienced and sometimes at another locus where it has been experienced. This is the next most difficult

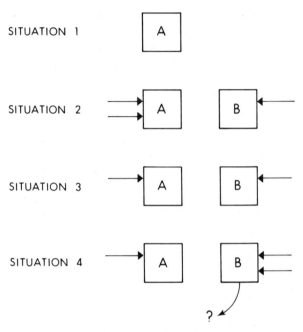

FIGURE 1.2 Hypothetical search situations.

contingency. Situation 3 is a different and perhaps more difficult version of Situation 2; that is, in Situation 3, reward for search occurs equally often in both loci where the object has been experienced.

Situation 4 is the most difficult contingency. The reward for search does not occur following search at the first locus where the object has been experienced (at A), nor at the locus where the object has been experienced most frequently (at B). The previous contingencies are not in effect because the object has been displaced to a locus that has never been experienced with the object.

It is easy to discover these and similar situations in everyday commerce with our environment. In situations where the displacements of an object are made by an animate agent, the contingencies of search may be very complex. For example, consider the following situation. The infant is seated across a table from an adult. The adult has a variety of colorful, odoriferous, multishaped objects of different textures and sizes arranged on a plate. The adult proceeds to pick up some objects and place them in a cavity. The opening of the cavity is then closed and, when reopened, the objects have disappeared. The procedure is repeated until the plate is cleared, and the procedure may be repeated two or three times a day. It seems obvious that the infant is exposed to many such situations in which, in fact, objects are *not* permanent. One of the facets of learning about objects must involve learning what behaviors are appropriate in particular situations. In new situations the child may rely on sequences of behavior that are successful in previous situations but not useful in the new task. However, learning theory predicts that if the responses are within his repertoire and successive training procedures are established, the child should learn to obtain an object when it does remain at a location.

The Competence–Performance Issue

A child interacts with an object at locus A, and then, in his presence, the object is displaced to locus B. What does the child's failure to search, or his errors in search, indicate? Some theorists (e.g., Piaget, 1954) explain futile search behaviors in terms of the absence of an underlying concept about objects—the concept that objects exist independent of ourselves and our experiences with the object. Thus, without the concept of permanence of objects, search behaviors are either unnecessary or directed to where our previous interactions have materialized the object. Such a theory is a competence theory, since it assumes that the behaviors of the child provide a measure of his knowledge about the permanence of objects. Other theorists believe that the child may know this fact about objects, and that we have not yet developed adequate situations in which this knowledge can be expressed. A performance explanation of an apparent concept deficit is that either the child is unable to perform certain aspects of the task or the researcher is incompetent in posing tests of the concept to the child. In fact, recent advances in the methods of studying infants have tended to substantiate that, in the past, investigators have underestimated the perceptual, learning, and cognitive capacities of young children (Kessen, Haith, & Salapatek, 1970).

Piaget's (1954) competence theory of object permanence emphasizes *egocentricity* because, as mentioned above, it is presumed that the infant first believes the location of an object is dependent on his own interactions with the object. Piaget is, no doubt, correct in assuming that previous interactions with an object are important for later search behaviors. But the more parsimonious interpretation is that *experience results in the coordination of abilities to the contingencies of search*, not that, during the course of development, the infant comes to differentiate the existence and location of the object and his own previous actions.

A learning approach to object permanence would emphasize the contingencies in search tasks and how they affect performance. It is assumed that errors in search would not necessarily imply concept deficiencies but, rather, behaviors that are inappropriate for obtaining the object. The first requirement for successful learning is that the child have the motor ability to perform all of the overt responses necessary to obtain the object. Then, if the object is not obtained in particular situations, we can seek explanations by further analyzing the requirements of the situation.

Response Requirements

For the most part, investigators have been careful to devise search tasks for which the infant has the ability to perform all of the motor components of the task. For example, Bower and Wishart (1972) used a simple procedure to demonstrate that most 5-month-old infants can remove a cover that serves to hide an attractive object. They covered the object with a transparent cup so that the target object remained visible, and they found that although infants had difficulty in removing the transparent cup, many more infants failed the test when an opaque cup was used. Thus, an explanation in terms of a motor deficit was not sufficient to account for the infants' inappropriate responses when the opaque cover was used. However, Bower and Wishart point out that picking up a cup for its own sake and picking up a cup to get at another object are two different tasks. The latter task involves the ability to conjoin actions, for example, pick up the cup, move it aside, then return to pick up the object. An analysis by Bruner (1970) suggests that in addition to the ability to coordinate such actions, there must be a capacity to delay responding so that the intent to manipulate is not directed to the occluding object at hand. Of course, performance at such tasks may have little bearing on whether the infant knows the hidden object is permanent.

The more subtle problem is the interpretation a researcher assigns to a particular response (or lack of response) as regards the infant's presumed competence. As Gratch (1975) has succinctly put it, "Seeking a hidden object, here or there, may occur for a variety of reasons, only some of which have to do with object representation [p. 18]." Some response interpretations are quite imaginative. For example, Bower (1971) reports an experiment in which he monitored the looking behavior of 3-month-old infants. The target object was a toy train which started at one position, A, then moved to a new position, B, stopped, and then returned to its original position, A, stopped, and continued in this to-and-fro manner. After a number of cycles, and following its last stop at a location, the train was moved to a completely new location, C. Bower found that when confronted with this new displacement, the infants looked to the empty location where the train had stopped on previous trials. Bower interpreted this error as evidence that the infant fails to recognize the identity of a moving object and the same object standing still. This interpretation presumes that for the infant viewing the original to-and-fro cycle of displacements, the cycle involves four separate objects: one at A, one at B, one moving from A to B, and one moving from B to A! A more straightforward interpretation is that the infants' error in looking for the object at a previous location is due to the learning that occurred in the cyclical trials. That is, the to-and-fro looking response which was successful in providing visual interaction with the object has persisted in the test situation with the new displacement.

The results obtained in a more complex tracking task (Bower, Broughton, & Moore, 1971, Experiment III) can be accounted for by a similar learning interpretation. In this study there were four displays of object movement, as schematized in Figure 1.3. In the first, the object

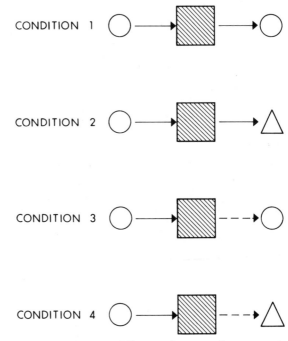

FIGURE 1.3 Displays of different objects and movements in Experiment III of Bower, Broughton, & Moore (1971).

moved behind one side of a screen and then reappeared on the other side of the screen as if moving in a continuous trajectory. In the second, the object traveled behind the screen and then a different object reappeared in the same trajectory. In the third and fourth displays, as the object moved behind one edge of the screen, instantaneously, at the other edge, either a physically identical or a different object appeared. The latter two displays specify a discontinuous trajectory of movement. Groups of infants were presented with one of these four displays for a number of trials; then each display was intermittently modified so that the target object would remain behind the screen or would stop before it went behind the screen. Bower *et al.*, interpreted the infant's visual gaze as either anticipatory or nonanticipatory; that is, if the object stayed behind the screen in Condition 1 and the infant looked to where it previously had reemerged, the response was anticipatory. To Bower *et al.*, anticipation should properly occur only when the object was behind the screen in Condition 1, for if the object stopped in view, there would be no need for anticipatory "search" behaviors. However, the young infants in Condition 1 showed anticipatory looking to the same extent regardless of whether the object stopped in view or behind the screen. Bower *et al.*, interpreted this as a failure for the young infant to integrate stationary objects as termini of moving objects. The young infants in Condition 2, seeing a different object emerge on the same trajectory, also showed anticipatory looking whether the target object was stopped in view or behind the screen. This response was interpreted as indicating the insensitivity of young infants to changes in the featural characteristics of a moving object. In Conditions 3 and 4 hardly any anticipations were made; that is, the young infants did not continue to look when the trajectory was discontinuous regardless of whether the target object stopped in view or not. Surprisingly, in Conditions 3 and 4, the infants' failure to continue looking for the target object was not interpreted as perception that the discontinuous trajectory specified at least two objects. Instead, the overall conclusion was that young infants can detect a change of motion, but do not respond to other featural changes of an object and do not identify a moving object with itself when stationary.

Such a perplexing state of affairs is unnecessary if one does not burden the anticipatory-looking response with mentalistic interpretations. Such head–eye responses function primarily to track movement in the visual array. During pretest trials there is movement successively occurring from one side of the screen to the other in all four conditions. A simple interpretation of the results is that it is easier for the infant to learn a sequence of looking responses to a display when it involves a continuous movement rather than discontinuous movements. Thereafter, during test trials in which a target object has stopped, the previously learned responses may persevere.[1]

Attention Requirements

As search situations include more displacements and complex sequences of displacements, the infant encounters more places and events and must maintain attention longer in order to observe the last displacement. We would not expect the infant to perform very well on such a search task if he does not attend to the last displacement of the target object. The fact that the infant watches the final hiding but does not search at this locus seems to indicate absentmindedness. But what are the cues that specify that the object has finally come to rest? In most hidden-object situations the infant must learn to discriminate that locus from which the empty vehicle of displacement was withdrawn last. The inexperienced infant may be attending solely to the vehicle of displacement and its movements, rather than intermittent stopping-off points. This means that before we can evaluate the infant's ability to represent objects at loci, there must be some overt evidence that the infant has selectively attended to the loci. One obvious indication that the infant has attended to the last of a series of loci is search at this locus. Another often-noted behavior is that the infant holds an orientation to the last hiding place, if the infant does not first direct his responses to the vehicle of displacement (Gratch, 1975). This would also constitute overt evidence that the final locus in the series of displacements has been attended.

Gratch, Appel, Evans, LeCompte, and Wright (1974) have provided evidence that successful manual search is related to the infant's attentiveness and direction of gaze after an object is hidden. In their procedure 9-month-old infants were assigned to one of four delay groups, with either 0, 1, 3, or 7 seconds duration between the last displacement and when the baby was allowed to search. During the first delay trials, the object was consistently hidden in one of two places, A, and an alternative locus, B, remained covered. The infant had to succeed on five consecutive A trials before the object was hidden at B. During the delay between hiding and search, the infant's behavior was rated as

---

[1] Several of my colleagues have argued that such interpretations are not attractive because they are mundane. As an alternative, they suggest Dr. Edward Start's (1976) brilliant analysis of the neonatal burp, "Is politeness innate?"

to degree of attentiveness to the two loci and direction of gaze (i.e., to which locus the attention was most directed).

The results obtained during B trials indicated that 11 of the 12 infants who experienced no delay between hiding and search found the object on the first trial. This provides strong evidence that the last locus was attended. When there was even a short delay between hiding and search, the majority of infants erred by searching at A. For these infants it was discovered that their performance was a function of both attentiveness and pattern of gaze during the delay period. It was found that when infants were attentive, they were very likely to err when they directed their gaze to A either while the object was in view or shortly after it was hidden at B. Infants who were attentive and looked at B or both A and B were not likely to err. Less attentive infants were likely to err irrespective of where they looked when they looked at the hiding places. Younger infants tended to adopt an A pattern of gazing, and the authors pointed out that Gratch and Landers (1971), in a longitudinal study, found the pattern of gazing to shift from A to AB to B. To summarize, the careful observations of Gratch et al. (1974) indicate that infants who must wait before search, infants who err in search, and younger infants—all show more persistence in attending to a location previously associated with successful search.

The attention requirements of manual-search tasks became apparent in a recent demonstration at the University of Alberta infant laboratory. We were attempting several training procedures aimed at facilitating infants' performance on the object permanence scale of the Albert Einstein Scales of Sensorimotor Development (Corman & Escalona, 1969). Two 7–8-month-old infants were repeatedly trained and tested; each was seen for four 1-hour sessions over the course of two weeks. At the beginning of the first session both infants were able to retrieve an attractive object when it was placed in the experimenter's hand and the hand was closed, rendering the object invisible. However, at this time neither of the infants was able to successfully retrieve the object when it was hidden behind one occluder, then visibly displaced to a second occluder. We were able to repeatedly train and test these infants until they achieved an arbitrary performance criterion. The performance criterion was successful search in three differing tasks, administered at different times during the final test sessions, but all involving invisible displacements at three loci. The criterion tasks differed as to whether flat pads, pillows, or vertical screens served to occlude the target object. Successful search was defined by two or more successive trials in which the infant moved a barrier and touched the object or exposed it out of reach and stared at it.

Analysis of videotape records of the test sessions indicated two hypotheses. The first hypothesis is that repeated attempts at successive search tasks lead to successive performance increments. This seemed especially true when, following a failure at a more complex search task, the infant was allowed to find the toy several times in a simple search situation. In effect, we felt we were training the infants to persevere in *attempting* to search. Sometimes we would introduce search situations that we considered intermediate between the successive tests indicated on the object permanence scales. For example, the infant might have had three round pillows in front of him but the target object was only moved beneath one of them, which would be a single visible displacement. This procedure was intended to familiarize the infant with successful search when there was more than one possible locus. Another training technique was attempted to facilitate the infant's attention to the last hiding place following a series of invisible displacements. The experimenter would leave his open hand on top of, or near, the occluder where the object had last been hidden. After several such training trials using different horizontal and vertical occluders and different locations of the object, the infant would then be tested when the empty hand was withdrawn. Using these and similar informal techniques, both infants were able to attain the performance criterion following 200–230 varied training and test trials.

The second hypothesis was obtained from the videotape records when we scored the infants' performance during each test trial. If the baby was judged to look away from the test situation on the table during any displacement, the performance was scored as nonattended. When the baby did not attend, he was not permitted to search or play with the object, and the next trial was initiated. Attention to all displacements and a first-attempt retrieval was denoted as a pass, and attention and a first-attempt error was denoted as a failure. Table 1.1 indicates the scored performance combined for both babies in all sessions as a function of search tests. It is apparent that there is very little difference in the proportion of failures at search in tasks involving visible and invisible displacements. One hypothesis is that the lower overall proportion of successful search in tasks involving invisible displacements is due to the infant's tendency to show poor attention during these situations. Regardless of the number of hiding places on the table, we frequently noticed that immediately after the target object disappeared in the experimenter's hand, the baby would refuse to track movements of this vehicle and would gaze at either the experimenter's face or twist to look toward his mother. It appeared that following disappearance of the target object, attention was commanded by the next

TABLE 1-1
*Proportion of Pass, Fail, and Nonattend Responses
in All Sessions as a Function of Search Tests*

Displacement	Number of tests	Proportion of responses		
		Pass	Fail	Nonattend
1-place visible	39	.64	.26	.10
2-place visible	17	.59	.29	.12
3-place visible	26	.92	.04	.04
1-place invisible	39	.46	.23	.31
2-place invisible	20	.40	.20	.40
3-place invisibe	41	.51	.12	.37

most attractive object in the experimental situation, a face. An attention deficit hypothesis is also suggested by the responses on the criterion task, scored within sessions. Figure 1.4 indicates that within-session fatigue or satiation may decrease attention to a three-place series of invisible displacements. The difference between the proportion of successes and failures on attended tests appears to be stable. If such performance analyses are included in assessing the object concept, we are less likely to conclude that the young infant has incomplete knowledge of the constancy and permanence of things, and we will have some indication of what conditions affect successful search.

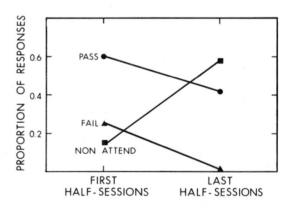

FIGURE 1.4 The change in proportions of Pass, Fail, and Nonattend responses that occurred during the first and last halves of test sessions on the tests involving a three-place invisible displacement. The data were collapsed to include both infants' performance during sessions 3 and 4. The first half-sessions included 20 tests of the three-place invisible displacement, and the last half-sessions included 21 of these tests.

Memory Requirements

Different studies have indicated that memory capacities limit the infant's performance on object concept tests. For example, Bower (1967, Experiment III) monitored the sucking behavior of 2-month-old infants in relation to the presence of a sphere. Whenever the sphere disappeared, sucking was suppressed, and this change was taken to indicate anticipation of the object's reappearance. If the sphere reappeared within 5 seconds, sucking rate increased to its predisappearance level. However, if the object reappeared after a longer delay, sucking did not recover, which was taken to indicate that the infants perceived a completely new event. Similarly, in tasks in which slightly older infants visually track an object as it moves behind a screen, several researchers have found that infants anticipate reemergence beyond increasingly wider screens with age (Gratch, 1975). And, as has been discussed in reference to manual-search tasks, if there is even a minimal delay between hiding and search, infants perform less ably than when there is no delay. Since successful search in delayed reaction tasks is known to develop continuously throughout infancy (see, e.g., Hunter, 1913), performance on object concept tests may reflect the systematic difficulty of memory requirements.

After finding an object placed at locus A and then attending while the object is displaced to locus B, why do some infants sometimes search at locus A? Some investigators have interpreted the failure to search at the locus as another instance of a memory deficit. Such an error could indicate that the information about the last displacement was not completely consolidated or was forgotten.

Harris (1973) has suggested that a tendency to search at an inappropriate previous location is evidence for proactive interference of memory for where the object was last located. In three experiments, infants were given pretest training at one of two loci, A, until they searched three times correctly in succession. In Experiment I, Harris found that 10-month-old infants made few errors in finding an object when they were permitted to immediately search its new location, B. In Experiment II, when a 5-second delay was introduced between displacement and search, a relatively large number of incorrect choices occurred because infants searched in the first location where the object was hidden, A. In Experiment III, four test conditions were used, as illustrated in Figure 1.5. Again there were two locations, A and B, and the object was always hidden at location A for pretest trials. In Figure 1.5 the arrows indicate displacements of the object for test trials, that is, for half of the test conditions the object was last hidden at B,

17

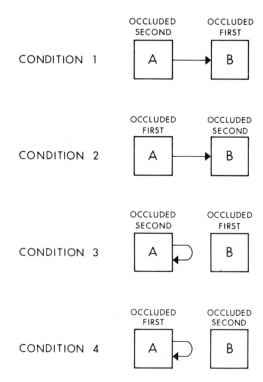

FIGURE 1.5 Conditions of displacement and occlusion in Experiment III of Harris (1973).

and for half of the conditions the object was last hidden where it also was first hidden, at location A. In Figure 1.5 the information above locations A and B indicates the temporal order in which the locations were occluded, regardless of whether the object was present at the location. Harris hypothesized that proactive interference was maximal in Condition 1 since the first location was last to be occluded and, presumably, the act of occlusion called the infant's attention to cues associated with this previous location. There would not be proactive interference in Condition 4 since the object had never been experienced in the last occluded location. As expected, a relatively large number of incorrect searches occurred in Condition 1, and infants made virtually no errors in search in Conditions 2, 3, and 4. The interpretation was that the more recent occlusion at a previous locus produced proactive interference of short term memory for the more recent locus.

In reexamining Harris's results (1973), Experiments I and II indicate another alternative to either the attention or memory deficit hypotheses. We can induce that the 10-month-old infant is operating under two contingencies in these first two search tasks, as indicated by the presence or absence of a delay between displacement and search. The first contingency is indicated by the behaviors in Experiment I: Given no delay between displacement and search, reward follows search at the last location. It happens that the contingency is appropriate in Experiment 1. The second contingency is indicated by some of the behaviors in Experiment II: If there is a delay between displacement and search, reward follows search at the first location. The latter is inappropriate in the particular search situation of Experiment II. Now let us examine Figure 1.5 to see if these two hypothetical contingencies can account for the observed performance in Experiment III. There is a relatively short delay between the object occlusion and search in Conditions 2 and 3, which specifies search at the last location. In Conditions 1 and 4 there is a longer delay between occlusion of the object and search, the time needed to occlude the other location. To some infants the delay may specify search at the first location, which would be an error in Condition 1 and appropriate in Condition 4.

Although it is possible to account for the obtained data within a learning interpretation, like the memory interference hypothesis, the explanation is speculative. Further study must be done to see if the presence or absence of delay serves as a discriminative stimulus for particular search behaviors by infants.

In a follow-up study, Harris (1974) found that 10-month-old infants approach a prior location even when the object is visible at the last location! This finding raises additional difficulties for the attention and memory deficit hypotheses, since the infant can see where the object is during search tests. Harris (1974, 1975) revised his mnemonic hypothesis to state that interference obtains for both perceived and stored locations and that the infant must develop rules to delete from memory all but the last location of the object. However, it may be unnecessary to hypothesize memory interference mechanisms or rules. The perseverance of search activity at an apparently empty place reaffirms the potency of the infant's previous learning (see also Harris, 1974, 1975). In short, it may often be the case that the infant fully registers the object at a new location, but reveals exploratory behavior controlled by cues previously associated with successful search.

There is evidence to support the latter interpretation. Webb, Massar, and Nadolny (1972) studied the performance of 14- and 16-month-old infants in a series of three-choice delayed reaction problems. The problems differed in that the infant was allowed to search for an object hidden in one of three places after a delay of either 5, 10, or 15 seconds. The infant watched as the experimenter hid the object, and, if there was any doubt about the infant's attention, the hiding was repeated in the same location. After the object was out of view, the infant was turned away from the display of loci until the delay had elapsed. The infants were tested with several hidings in each problem. The test procedure was unique in that the infant was permitted to search for the object until it was uncovered or searching ceased. Thus, the data included a record of performance during initial search trials and of where the infant searched if the initial search was futile. The results indicated that regardless of the length of delay, the first time the object was hidden the vast majority of the 16-month-old infants searched and showed correct first choices. Six of the 14-month-old infants ceased to search immediately after the first hiding, but the proportion of correct first choices of the 14 subjects who did search (.86) was comparable to the proportion of correct first choices by the older infants. When the infants were first presented the second and third hidings within a problem, successful search was at chance levels. In general, most infants returned to the location used on the initial hiding. However, the majority of the 16-month-old infants found the target object with their second choice. That is, during the second and third hidings 50 out of a total of 71 (.70) second searches attempted by the older infants were correct. These data indicate that the hiding was attended and registered, and that it remained in memory even while the infant was searching another location.

Webb *et al.* suggest that the cues to act at a previously successful location may be more potent in determining the young infant's search behaviors than the visual cues present during the new hiding. Their results are consistent with the interpretation that the infant must first attend to the final displacement of the object and then must learn that the cues associated with the last locus specify successful search.

Response Perseverance

In several instances in the preceding discussion, response perseverance has been suggested as an explanation for performance, especially when attention and memory variables cannot account for an inappropriate response. Response perseverance can be defined as the behavioral remnants of a previously experienced search contingency. This requires that the infant has learned something from events that can be specified in the past. The infant need not have performed the response in the past, although some theorists maintain that a reinforced overt behavior would more likely persist (see discussion in Landers,

1971). The infant can observe contingencies in the environment, and this may affect the probability for emitting a response.

Perhaps the most frequently occurring contingency is that reward follows search at the first place an object is experienced. This is because most objects in the environment are relatively static, and those objects that are displaced are usually seen first in their most frequent locus, the locus where the object is most often returned following a displacement. This line of reasoning seems to have ecological validity, and may sometimes explain why the "first-place error" is committed by children and adults. In addition, there are a few studies that experimentally vary pretest search contingencies, and the results indicate that response perseverance is an important phenomenon in infant search tasks.

In a longitudinal study, Gratch and Landers (1971) presented a sequence of search tasks during each session with each infant. Following a warm-up procedure, the sequence consisted of A trials in which a toy was consistently placed in one of two hiding wells until the infant found it twice in succession. During this phase the alternative locus was visible, but its well remained covered during hiding. No hiding manipulations were directed to this covered well, and if the infant lifted the cover to search there, he was allowed to correct his error or was corrected by the experimenter. After performing to criterion at A, the toy was consistently hidden on the B side. During these B trials the A hiding place remained covered, and the toy was hidden on the B side until the infant found it twice in succession or refused to search for the toy. The infant was not permitted to correct his mistakes, but the experimenter uncovered the toy for the infant to view. The next phase of the sequence consisted of AB trials. The AB trials were a ten-trial series in which the toy was hidden on either side in the pattern ABAABBAABB. Note that the pattern of AB hidings starts at locus A and that directly preceding AB trials the infant has been presented with a series of search tasks at B. On the first AB trial, a first-place response would be to search at locus A. A response in accord with the most recent contingency would be to search at locus B.

The authors tested 13 6-month-old infants biweekly for approximately 6 months. They did not report the number of infants who initially erred and then successfully searched on B trials within a single session. However, on the first AB trial, 8 subjects searched at B. This observation is consistent with the idea that when the probabilities for reward are approximately equal at two loci, the infant either responds according to chance or is guided by the most recent successful searches.

On the nine subsequent AB trials Gratch and Landers (1971) found that infants typically searched first at locus A. This result reflects the fact that performance in B trials was poorer than performance in A trials. Preceding the AB trials, after infants passed A trials for the first time, 10 of the 13 infants searched at locus A on the first B trial. Following this initial error there was a relatively long sequence of A errors on B trials, and seven infants refused to search during B trials. Remember, refusal to search was followed by the experimenter exposing the toy, and two successive refusals marked the end of the B trials for a session. Thus, the perseverance of responses at locus A in the AB task may simply indicate that A learning was more complete.

A direct study of the effects of differential experience on infants' search behaviors was reported by Landers (1971). Infants between the ages of 7½ and 10½ months were assigned to one of three conditions. In one condition a toy or object was consistently hidden in one of two wells, the other well remaining covered throughout these trials. The hiding at the initial locus, A, was continued until the infant successfully searched for two consecutive trials. In a second condition, the procedure was similar, except that the second group of infants was required to successfully search 8 or 10 times in succession at A. For a third group of infants the pretest trials consisted of 8 to 10 demonstrations of hiding at A in which the infants were only allowed to observe, followed by two active search trials. Thus, the three groups had different experiences with the object at locus A, with infants in the second condition actively reaching in A most frequently and with the most success.

The effects of the different experiences were tested in subsequent B hiding trials. On these trials the object was hidden in the previously covered well, and the A well remained covered. The B hiding trials were administered to subjects in each group until the infant found the object twice in succession or refused to search. The results indicated that on the first test trial the majority of the infants in all three conditions searched at A. The second group of infants, who had the most experience searching and finding an object at A, made significantly longer error runs at this position than did the other two groups, whose error runs were comparably short. Landers (1971) interpreted the results as supporting Piaget's argument that the young infant's behavior and object concepts are dependent on previous action within a context, rather than on the more recent visual input of a displacement. The interpretation offered here is that response perseverance is more likely to occur when the search behavior is repeatedly rewarded at one position.

It might be expected that younger infants show more rigidity or response perseverance than older infants (Cornell, 1976). Appel and Gratch (1969) have also demonstrated such a difference between the manual search behaviors of 9- and 12-month-old infants in a simple transfer test. There were five initial trials in one of two conditions. In one condition half of the infants in each age group saw a toy hidden beneath a cover. In the other condition the other infants saw or heard the experimenter direct attention to the hiding place, but no toy was hidden. The infants who saw a toy hidden searched after each trial, and the "no toy" infants did not attempt to search. Then, for five additional trials, the infants were switched to the alternate condition. All of the infants who formerly saw no toy hidden now appropriately searched on every trial. The 12-month-old infants who had previously seen a toy hidden did not search on any trial when a toy was not hidden. However, the 9-month-old infants who had previously seen a toy hidden continued to search for a number of trials even when a toy was not hidden. Such differential response perseverance may be a confounding factor in a number of findings in the object concept literature.

The obvious counterpart to the notion that inappropriate search behaviors are fostered by contingencies is that appropriate search behaviors can be learned. Unfortunately, because of the emphasis on understanding what may be artifactual discontinuities in performance, most investigators have not attempted to find procedures to teach the child to search. We have already discussed the possibility that close successiveness in task requirements is important for coordinating abilities and extending abilities. Simple practice at a single task may have positive effects as well (Bower & Paterson, 1972).

The latter approach is best illustrated in a paper by Nelson (1974), which reports one attempt to foster an appropriate search response with infants of 7 months of age. The response was anticipatory looking, and rather than using successively more difficult tracking tasks, Nelson simply repeatedly presented the infants with the same sequence of object movements. It should be noted that this technique, learning by repetition, may work against itself when orienting responses are assessed. Satiation may occur to the features of the object or to the redundant movement itself. Nevertheless, after observing 16 trials in which a man walked to and fro behind a screen, infants showed a significant improvement in their anticipatory looking. Moreover, the data indicated that anticipations were more frequent as the learning trials progressed, and the anticipatory looking generalized when a new object (a toy truck) or a new movement was used in subsequent to-and-fro tracking tests. The results of this novel experiment are straightforward: Nelson concludes that the infant's progress toward a general concept of object permanence may be based on similar instances of gradual acquisition and transfer of responses.

Conclusion

To extend the previous analyses of the infant research, it seems possible to describe different search tasks as different problems in discriminative learning. The cues for search behavior in any one task depend on the nature of the object and its locus. In order to respond appropriately, it may be necessary to discern the solidity of the object, whether it moves about, and where it was last located. When studied as a discrimination problem, the answer to how the infant attains the object concept will probably be found in a complete description of changes in attention. Currently there are two major developmental theories of learning as it affects attention. Perceptual learning theory emphasizes that as a result of perceptual experience with a class of stimuli the child is able to extract features that remain invariant and serve to differentiate the stimuli (Gibson, 1969). Traditional discrimination-learning theories tend to emphasize that external reinforcement increases the probability that appropriate responses will be emitted in the presence of the discriminative stimuli, and that among these are responses that could be considered attentional in nature (Stevenson, 1972). Because the learning approach has been neglected in the study of the object concept, the relative value of these two theories as explanations for infant search behaviors remains to be demonstrated.

Nevertheless, learning has always been of primary importance to experimental psychologists, and there is a rich legacy of theory from which to derive predictions for children's performance in search tasks. The learning approach may be particularly useful for teaching delayed infants how to find things (e.g., Dunst, 1976). Complex search contingencies can be analyzed in regard to the task requirements discussed in the preceding sections. Specific training procedures may be devised, and as a result of successes and failures, a continuum of subtasks can be induced. One prediction is that if the loci where an object may be found are made more distinguishable, the child's performance should be facilitated (Cornell, 1977). One might also predict that during a series of displacements the child should be better able to delay response until the last displacement following training at delayed response to a single displacement. I leave it to the reasoning and efforts of the interested reader to apply learning interpretations to new search situations. Obviously, many shortcomings of the approach will emerge as research issues. However, two advantages of learning theory should be apparent. First, there is no need to reify mental concepts, processes of cognitive assimilation, or the idiosyncratic search behaviors of the child in any particular situation. Second, we can complete the description of the situations in which the child behaves or learns to behave as if objects remain permanent in space.

REFERENCES

Appel, K. J., & Gratch, G. The cue value of objects. Paper presented at the meeting of the Society for Research in Child Development, Santa Monica, California, March, 1969.

Bower, T. G. R. The development of object permanence: Some studies of existence constancy. *Perception and Psychophysics*, 1967, 2, 411–418.

Bower, T. G. R. The object in the world of the infant. *Scientific American*, 1971, 225, 30–47.

Bower, T. G. R. *Development in infancy*. San Francisco: Freeman, 1974.

Bower, T. G. R. Infant perception of the third dimension and object concept development. In L. Cohen & P. H. Salapatek (Eds.), *Infant perception: From sensation to cognition* (Vol. 2). New York: Academic, 1975.

Bower, T. G. R., Broughton, J. M., & Moore, M. K. Development of the object concept as manifested in changes in the tracking behavior of infants between 7 and 20 weeks-of-age. *Journal of Experimental Child Psychology*, 1971, 11, 182–193.

Bower, T. G. R., & Paterson, J. G. Stages in the development of the object concept. *Cognition*, 1972, 1, 47–55.

Bower, T. G. R., & Wishart, J. G. The effects of motor skill on object permanence. *Cognition*, 1972, 1, 165–172.

Bruner, J. S. The growth and structure of skill. In K. J. Connolly (Ed.), *Mechanisms of motor skill development*. New York: Academic Press, 1970.

Butterworth, G. Object identity in infancy: The interaction of spatial location codes in determining search errors. *Child Development*, 1975, 46, 866–870.

Butterworth, G. Perception and cognition: Where do we stand in the mid-seventies? In P. Williams & V. Varma (Eds.), *Piaget, psychology and education: Papers in honor of Jean Piaget*. London: Hodder & Stoughton, 1976. (a)

Butterworth, G. Asymmetrical search errors in infancy. *Child Development*, 1976, 47, 864–867. (b)

Corman, H. H., & Escalona, S. K. Stages of sensorimotor development: A replication study. *Merill–Palmer Quarterly of Behavior and Development*, 1969, 15, 351–361.

Cornell, E. H. Learning by young infants: The localization of visual events in space. Unpublished manuscript, University of Alberta, Canada, 1976.

Cornell, E. H. The effects of distinctiveness of hiding places on infant manual search. Unpublished manuscript, University of Alberta, Canada, 1977.

Decarie, T. G. A study of the mental and emotional development of the thalidomide child. In B. Foss (Ed.), *Determinants of infant behavior* (Vol. 4). London: Methuen, 1969.

Dodwell, P. C., Muir, D., & DiFranco, D. Responses of infants to visually presented objects. *Science*, 1976, 194, 209–211.

Dunst, C. J. *Object permanence programs*. Unpublished manuscript, 1976. Available from Infant's Program, Western Carolina Center, Morgantown, N.C., U.S.A. 28655.

Fagan, J. F. Infant's delayed recognition memory and forgetting. *Journal of Experimental Child Psychology*, 1973, *16*, 424–450.

Fantz, R. L., Fagan, J. F., & Miranda, S. B. Early visual selectivity. In L. Cohen & P. Salapatek (Eds.), *Infant perception: From sensation to cognition* (Vol. 1). New York: Academic, 1975.

Flavell, J. H. *The developmental psychology of Jean Piaget.* New York: Van Nostrand, 1963.

Gibson, E. J. *Principles of perceptual learning and development.* New York: Appleton-Century-Crofts, 1969.

Gibson, J. J. *The senses considered as perceptual systems.* Boston: Houghton Mifflin, 1966.

Gratch, G. Recent studies based on Piaget's view of object concept development. In L. Cohen & P. Salapatek (Eds.), *Infant perception: From sensation to cognition* (Vol. 2). New York: Academic Press, 1975.

Gratch, G. On levels of awareness of objects in infants and students thereof. *Merrill–Palmer Quarterly of Behavior and Development*, 1976, *22*, 157–176.

Gratch, G., Appel, K. J., Evans, W. F., LeCompte, G. K., & Wright, N. A. Piaget's Stage IV object concept error: Evidence of forgetting or object conception? *Child Development*, 1974, *45*, 71–77.

Gratch, G., & Landers, W. F. Stage IV of Piaget's theory of infants' object concepts: A longitudinal study. *Child Development*, 1971, *42*, 359–372.

Harris, P. L. Perseverative errors in search by young children. *Child Development*, 1973, *44*, 28–33.

Harris, P. L. Perseverative search at a visibly empty place by young infants. *Journal of Experimental Child Psychology*, 1974, *18*, 535–542.

Harris, P. L. Development of search and object permanence during infancy. *Psychological Bulletin*, 1975, *82*, 332–344.

Harris, P. L. Subject, object and framework: A theory of spatial development. Unpublished manuscript, University of Lancaster, England, 1976.

Hunter, W. S. The delayed reaction in a child. *Psychological Bulletin*, 1913, *24*, 75–87.

Kessen, W., Haith, M. M., & Salapatek, P. H. Human infancy: A bibliography and guide. In P. Mussen (Ed.), *Carmichael's manual of child psychology* (Vol. 1), New York: Wiley, 1970.

Landers, W. F. Effects of differential experience on infants' performance in a Piagetian Stage IV object-concept task. *Developmental Psychology*, 1971, *5*, 48–54.

Moore, M. K. The genesis of object permanence. Paper presented at the biennial meeting of the Society for Research in Child Development. Philadelphia, 1973.

Nelson, K. E. Infants' short-term progress toward one component of object permanence. *Miller–Palmer Quarterly of Behavior and Development*, 1974 *20*, 3–8.

Piaget, J. *The origins of intelligence in children.* New York: International Universities Press, 1952.

Piaget, J. *The construction of reality in the child.* New York: Basic Books, 1954.

Restle, F. Discrimination of cues in mazes: A resolution of the "Place-vs-Response" question. *Psychological Review*, 1957, *64*, 217–228.

Skinner, B. F. *About behaviorism.* London: Jonathan Cape, 1974.

Start, E. Is politeness innate? *New Scientist*, 1976, *71*, 585–587.

Stevenson, H. W. *Children's learning.* New York: Appleton, 1972.

Tolman, E. C., Ritchie, B. F., & Kalish, D. Studies in spatial learning: II. Place learning versus response learning. *Journal of Experimental Psychology*, 1946, *35*, 221–229.

Webb, R. A., Massar, B., & Nadolny, T. Information and strategy in the young child's search for hidden objects. *Child Development*, 1972, *43*, 91–104.

Yonas, A., & Pick, H. L. An approach to the study of infant space perception. In L. Cohen & P. Salapatek (Eds.), *Infant perception: From sensation to cognition* (Vol. 2). New York: Academic, 1975.

2

Piaget's View of Social Interaction and the Theoretical Construct of Empathy

HELENE BORKE

Hay Associates, Pittsburgh, Pennsylvania

Although Piaget is best known for his theories of cognitive development, many of his writings contain references to the significance of social influences. Piaget (1950) states, "the human being is immersed right from birth in a social environment which affects him as much as his physical environment [p. 156]." When discussing the structures that organize mental activity, Piaget (1967) identifies "motor or intellectual" structures on the one hand and "affective" structures on the other. Intellectual and affective structures are organized along two dimensions—"intrapersonal" and "social or interpersonal" (p. 5). Piaget (1967) describes affectivity and intellectual functions as "two indissociable aspects of every action" (p. 33) and sees both as being influenced from earliest childhood by socialization. According to Piaget, there is never a purely intellectual act that is unaffected by emotion, and, similarly, there is never a purely affective act totally devoid of comprehension. Piaget's concern with egocentrism, the growth in children's ability to play cooperatively with one another, and the moral development of the child all reflect his awarenes of the importance of social factors.

In discussing the interdependence of social and intellectual development, Piaget (1930) differentiates among three separate but interre-

29

lated processes that are closely synchronized with one another: "All three begin very early, . . . remain uncompleted at the close of childhood, and survive throughout the intellectual development of the adult [p. 252]." The first process is primarily social. It reflects the transition from an *egocentric view*, in which the young child is unaware of the existence of anyone else's perspective, to *reciprocity*, in which the same value is attributed to the other person's point of view as to one's own. The second process is primarily intellectual and describes the transition from *absolutism*, or the acceptance of each perception as a separate and independent entity, to *relativism*, where all concepts and objects are thought of in relation to one another. The third process stems from an interaction between intellectual and social factors. It involves the gradual change from *subjectivity*, with the expectation that everything comes from, or is somehow related to, the self, to *objectivity*, where the individual is able to distinguish between what originates from within and what is part of external reality as observed by everybody.

Piaget's Theory and Empathy

If Piaget's ideas concerning reciprocity, relativism, and objectivity are applied to a model based strictly on social interaction, then human beings have the capacity for being aware of other people's perspectives, for relating these perspectives to their own and other individual's life experiences, and for understanding these varying perspectives within the framework of external reality. This description of the most advanced stage of social interaction is very similar to current thinking about adult empathic awareness.

When Lipps (1909) first introduced the word *Einfühlung* to explain social reactions such as sympathy, he defined it as the human capacity for experiencing the feelings of another. Most social psychologists (Allport, 1937; Murphy, 1937) continued to regard empathy primarily as a potential for emotional responsiveness until the late 1940s, when Cottrell and Dymond (1949) proposed an operational definition of empathy in terms of social interaction. These psychologists defined empathy as the ability to understand the world from another person's perspective by "imaginatively transposing oneself into the thinking, feeling and acting of another [Dymond, 1950, p. 343]." This shift in emphasis from feeling to role-taking for the first time placed empathy firmly within the tradition of social psychology. Early social psychologists such as Cooley (1902/1922) and Mead (1934) had long recognized the central importance of role-taking for early development. The use of the term empathy to describe the type of social sensitivity which involves the accurate interpretation of the attitudes and intentions of others also closely parallels Piaget's thinking concerning reciprocity, relativism, and objectivity.

Parameters of Empathy

According to Cottrell and Dymond (1949), empathy is central to the development of the social self and provides the basis for all social communication. If, as Cottrell and Dymond suggest, empathy reflects a necessary and uniquely human capacity for social interaction, then the ability to empathize with another individual can be viewed as an evolutionary advance in the interpersonal sphere comparable to abstract thinking in the intellectual sphere. Although the early stages of these potentials are present to some extent in other species, especially the higher apes, it is only in human beings that empathy and abstract thinking reach their highest level of development and become central mediating forces in adaptation.

Once empathy is thought of as an innate potential, some of its general characteristics can be identified. Individual capacities for empathy, as for intelligence and language, appear to be influenced by the interaction of both genetic and environmental factors. The significance of the environment for the development of empathic awareness is supported by two studies (Van Lieshout, Leckie, & Smits-Van Sonsbeek, 1975; Yarrow, Scott, & Waxler, 1973) in which preschool age children were given training in social-perspective-taking behavior. Following this training the youngsters demonstrated a significant increase in their role-taking ability. In several instances the children also showed more spontaneous expressions of sympathetic concern and a greater sensitivity to the inferred needs of other people.

While empathy itself is neutral and has no innate ethical or moral directives, the ability to understand the thoughts and feelings of others helps to explain the emergence in human relationships of such positive interpersonal responses as sympathy, altruism, and love. It is difficult to imagine the intensive caring over time displayed by most human parents for their children without the capacity for empathy. Both the social interaction definition of empathy and Piaget's conceptualization of adult social development closely resemble Fromm's (1956) description of mature love as active caring, responsiveness to the other's needs, knowledge about the other's thoughts and feelings, and respect for the other's unique individuality.

Research on Perspective Role-Taking

From observations of children's language, social interaction, and perspective role-taking ability, Piaget (1950) concluded that young children are primarily egocentric and, therefore, not capable of empathy. The young child reduces all social and physical influences "to his point of view and therefore distorts them without realizing it, simply because he cannot yet distinguish his point of view from that of others [p. 160]." According to Piaget, it is only after the child reaches 7 or 8 years of age that sociocentric thought first appears. The sharing of ideas and feelings with other children results in the reexamining of the child's own concepts in relation to those of others. This leads to greater awareness of the self as distinct and separate, and to the growing realization that each person perceives reality from a different perspective.

Piaget's view of the development of a sense of self as the outgrowth of social contact is very similar to Mead's (1934) theory that the self "arises in the process of social experiences [p. 135]" and that self-awareness results from the perception that the other has thoughts and feelings differing from one's own. Mead observed evidence of the beginnings of the social self at a much earlier age than did Piaget in the imaginary play of young children. According to Mead, when children 2 and 3 years of age pretend to be mothers feeding and rocking their babies or fathers going to work, they demonstrate an awareness of the difference between the self and the other by taking the role of the other in its simplest form of "being another to oneself [p. 151]."

Until fairly recently there has been relatively little research investigating the development of perspective role-taking behavior. The best known and most frequently cited study is Piaget and Inhelder's (1956) mountain experiment. Subjects between 4 and 12 years of age were shown a model representing three mountains and asked to predict how a doll would view these mountains from various perspectives (see Figure 2.1). The subjects communicated their role-taking ability by selecting one picture from a group of pictures that best showed what the doll saw, by using cardboard replicas of the mountains to reconstruct the doll's viewpoint, or by selecting a picture and placing the doll in an appropriate position for taking an identical snapshot. Piaget and Inhelder reported that all of the 4- and 5-year-old subjects responded egocentrically by giving their own perspective. Between 6½ and 7 years

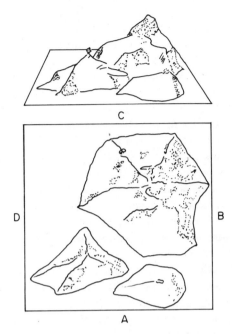

FIGURE 2.1 Piaget and Inhelder's Three Mountains. [From *The Child's Conception of Space*, by J. Piaget and B. Inhelder. London: Routledge & Kegan Paul, 1956.]

of age some subjects began indicating an awareness that the doll's viewpoint differed from their own by making some attempt to vary their responses to show the doll's perspective. Despite their efforts, they were still unsuccessful in reproducing the doll's view. From 7 to 12 years of age, the subjects showed "a progressive discrimination and coordination of perspectives [p. 213]." Piaget and Inhelder interpreted their results as indicating that young children are basically egocentric because they "fail to realize that different observers will employ different perspectives and . . . regard their own point of view as the only one possible [p. 213]."

A number of investigators interested in studying perspective role-taking ability have used adaptations of Piaget and Inhelder's basic experimental design. Flavell, Botkin, and Fry (1968) presented a series of four geometric configurations of increasing difficulty to subjects between 7 and 17 years of age. The subjects were given an identical set of geometric shapes and asked to reconstruct each model to look the way the examiner saw it from various positions. The results indicated that the youngest subjects had difficulty with even the easiest display and that the majority of 17-year-olds were unable to reconstruct the most difficult configurations correctly. Flavell and his colleagues concluded that while all of their subjects were aware of what the task required, "they differed widely in their ability to cope with these demands—differed as a function of age, task and doubtless many other variables [p. 70]." Flavell and his co-workers also designed a series of tasks specifically for children between 3 and 6 years of age. Although a significant number of the 3- and 4-year-old subjects succeeded on the two easiest tasks (e.g., orienting a picture for the examiner to look at upside down and predicting which of two pictures the examiner was viewing) the overall variation in the younger children's performance as compared to the 5- and 6-year-olds led Flavell to conclude that Piaget was correct in describing very young children as primarily egocentric.

Fishbein, Lewis, and Keiffer (1972) used Piaget and Inhelder's research as a model to study the effects of complexity of stimulus task and the type of response required on the perspective role-taking behavior of children between 3½ and 9½ years of age. These researchers found that the ability to coordinate perspectives was a function of both stimulus complexity (e.g., three toys were more difficult than one toy) and the mode of responding (e.g., turning the toys was easier than selecting a photograph). Even their 3½-year-old subjects made significantly fewer errors when asked to rotate a display than when asked to indicate another person's perspective by selecting a picture.

In studying rotation and perspective problems with third grade and fifth grade children, Huttenlocher and Presson (1973) observed that their subjects made many more egocentric errors on perspective role-taking tasks than on rotation tasks. Since Huttenlocher and Presson found no relationship between children's egocentric responses and age, they attributed these error differences to the greater difficulty of the perceptual task rather than to an "egocentric approach unique to childhood [p. 299]."

Recent studies by Hoy (1974) and Eliot and Dayton (1976) have systematically investigated the relationship between perspective role-taking and characteristics of the stimulus task. Hoy found that the ability of 6-, 8-, and 10-year-old subjects to predict another person's perspective depends on both the type and number of dimensions that must be considered simultaneously (e.g., before–behind, right–left, variations in shape) and the type of response required (e.g., constructing the other's perspective with blocks or selecting an appropriate picture). The younger children had the greatest difficulties with the right–left dimension and with indicating the other person's perspective by selecting a picture. Elliot and Dayton also observed a significant relationship between stimulus characteristics and the tendency to give egocentric responses. These investigators found no direct relationship between egocentric errors and age and reported that their adult subjects gave a significantly greater number of egocentric responses on the more difficult tasks. Based on these results, Eliot and Dayton concluded that "egocentric errors are more a function of task complexity and experience with ambiguous perceptual tasks than an inability to take another's viewpoint [p. 16]."

In a series of studies, Borke (1971, 1973, 1975) investigated early egocentrism by presenting subjects between 3 and 6 years of age with simple, age-appropriate, role-taking tasks. The first study (1971) used middle class American children as subjects. The second investigation (1973) was a cross-cultural study comparing American and Chinese youngsters from middle and lower class backgrounds. In both investigations the subjects were told a series of short stories and asked how another child might feel in various situations. One set of stories presented general situations that might make a child feel happy, afraid, sad, or angry. The second set of stories presented situations in which the subject behaved in a way that might cause another child to feel happy, afraid, sad, or angry. Before hearing any of the stories, the subjects were asked to identify drawings of faces representing these four basic emotions. After helping the children identify each of the faces, the examiner presented the first set of stories. Each story in this set was accompanied by a picture of a child with a blank face engaged in the described activity. The children were asked to complete the pictures by selecting the face that best showed how the child in the story felt. The faces were presented in random order, and with each presentation the examiner again identified the emotions for the subjects. The same procedure was followed for the second set of stories involving peer interactions, except that a single picture of a standing youngster was used for all of the stories. These studies indicated that by 3 to 3½ years of age, even children from very different cultural and socioeconomic backgrounds can accurately identify happy and unhappy responses in other people. The ability to recognize sad and fearful situations appears to be influenced to some extent by social class and cultural factors. Chinese youngsters between 3 and 4 years of age correctly identified sad situations to a significantly greater extent than American children in this age group. Chinese middle class children also recognized fearful situations at a much earlier age than either Chinese lower class children or American children, regardless of social class background. These results suggest that rather than being egocentric, children as young as 3 years of age show an ability to take another person's perspective.

Chandler and Greenspan (1972) replicated and confirmed Borke's results but took serious exception to the conclusion that young children's ability to anticipate other people's emotional reactions indicates a capacity to respond empathically. These investigators argued that a response can only be considered empathic if it involves taking the perspective of someone who's thoughts and feelings differ from one's own. When Chandler and Greenspan used a task requiring a shift in perspective (subjects were first asked to anticipate the emotional reaction of someone after they were shown a series of events in cartoon form and then were asked to describe the perspective of a late comer who had only limited knowledge about the situation), their results supported Piaget's findings that true empathic responses do not develop until middle or later childhood. Borke (1972), in responding to Chandler and Greenspan, pointed out that the task these investigators used to measure empathy not only required advanced verbal skills but also was far too complex for younger children to be able to comprehend. Chandler and Greenspan obtained the same results as Piaget because they made the same error of confounding empathic development with cognitive-development.

In a later study, Borke (1975) specifically tested the hypothesis that young children are capable of taking perspectives that differ from their own by adapting Piaget and Inhelder's original mountain experiment to insure the age-appropriateness of the task for very young children. The two main changes consisted of using familiar objects as the stimulus material and having the children communicate their awareness of the other person's perspective by rotating a three-dimensional model. The 3- and 4-year-old subjects were first shown a practice display consisting of a large red fire engine. An exact duplicate of the fire engine appeared on a revolving turntable to the subject's left. Each youngster was then introduced to Grover, a character from Sesame Street. The examiner moved Grover to various points around the display. Whenever Grover stopped to look out of his car, the subject was asked to rotate the fire engine on the turntable so that it looked just the way Grover saw it. If a subject incorrectly predicted how the fire engine looked to Grover for any of the three positions, the examiner took the subject over to where Grover was parked. The subject was then asked to go back and move the turntable so that the fire engine appeared the way Grover saw it. If the subject again gave an incorrect response, the examiner moved the turntable to the correct position explaining that this was the way Grover saw the fire engine from where he was parked.

After completing the practice trial with the fire engine, each subject was shown the three experimental displays one at a time (see

Figure 2.2). Display 1 consisted of a small lake with a toy sailboat (1), a miniature horse and cow (2), and a model of a house (3). Display 2 was a papier-mâché replica of Piaget and Inhelder's three mountains: the mountain with a cross on top (1), the mountain with a snow cap (2), and the mountain with a small house on top (3). Display 3 contained a wide variety of miniature people and animals in natural settings: cowboys, Indians, and trees (1), a lake with ducks (2), a windmill (3), cows pulling a wagon (4), a dog and a doghouse (5), a barn with farm animals and a farmer (6), a woman feeding chickens (7), two rabbits and a pigpen with pigs (8).

The procedure for these three displays was similar to that used in the practice task except that the child was not given any further opportunity to look at the scene from Grover's point of view. If the subject gave an incorrect response, it was simply accepted and the experimenter moved Grover to the next position. For every display, Grover parked in turn at each of the three sides that presented a view different from that of the subject. The sequence of stops was varied randomly for

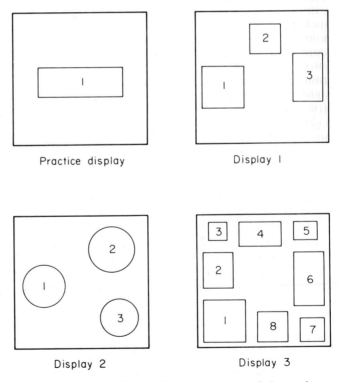

FIGURE 2.2 Displays as viewed from above.

the three scenes. A subject's response was scored as correct if the revolving display was turned so that it matched Grover's perception and scored as egocentric if the display conformed to the subject's own view.

All subjects accurately predicted Grover's perceptions on the two scenes containing familiar toy objects over 80% of the time. On Piaget and Inhelder's scene the 3-year-old subjects gave only 42% correct responses, and the 4-year-old subjects gave 67% correct responses. These results support the findings of previous investigations that the nature of the task is a significant variable in young children's ability to demonstrate perspective role-taking. Discrete, easily differentiated objects provide more cues for young children to identify and remember than essentially similar configurations such as Piaget and Inhelder's three mountains. The 4-year-old subjects were even able to achieve some degree of success on Piaget and Inhelder's three mountains when asked to rotate an exact duplicate of the scene. This is in sharp contrast to the completely egocentric nature of responses reported by Piaget and Inhelder when subjects under 7 or 8 years of age were asked to indicate their awareness of someone else's perspective by reconstructing a model or by selecting a two-dimensional picture. The results of this study suggest that when presented with tasks that are age-appropriate, children as young as 3 and 4 years of age are capable of taking another person's perspective. These findings, together with other recent research on perspective role-taking, support the hypothesis that previous conclusions regarding early egocentrism resulted from children's inability to perform on tasks which were cognitively too difficult for them, rather than from any inherently egocentric orientation on the part of young children.

Observations of social interaction behavior in children 1½ to 2 years old provide evidence that the ability to take the role of the other can occur in children even younger than 3 or 4 years of age. In one incident described by Borke (1972) a 15-month-old boy inadvertently knocked over a younger playmate. The child first hugged the crying youngster and then tried to pick him up. When neither of these actions succeeded in comforting the playmate, the boy looked around the room, found the younger child's bottle, and handed it to him. In another incident reported by Hoffman (1975) a 20-month-old youngster offered a friend his beloved teddy bear to take home when the friend started crying because her parents were away. The child insisted that his playmate take the teddy bear even after his parents pointed out that he would probably miss his stuffed companion very much. Although the children's actions in both incidents are imitative of adult behavior, it would be difficult to account for their motivations without hypothesizing some awareness of the other person's feeling and some capacity for role-taking.

Stages of Empathic Development

If current research and observations no longer support Piaget's conclusions regarding early childhood egocentrism, neither does Piaget's own theory. According to Piaget, development proceeds in hierarchical stages with each stage firmly rooted in the experiences of the one preceding it. This would lead to the expectation that empathy, like cognition, develops in a gradual and orderly sequence. Evidence for this hypothesis comes directly from Piaget's own carefully documented observations. In his writings, Piaget identifies the appearance of object permanence during the second half of the first year as one of the first steps in the development of abstract thinking. Piaget (1950) also recognizes that at this time an equally significant advance occurs in the interpersonal sphere: "From the affective point of view, it is no doubt only at the stage at which the notion of an object is formed that there is a projection of affectivity onto people conceived as similar centers of independent action [p. 158]." What later became obscured by other evidence which Piaget interpreted as pointing to egocentrism, is that this "projection of affectivity" onto other people represents one of the earliest stages in the development of social awareness.

With the transition to abstract thinking, which Piaget identifies as occurring between 1½ and 2 years of age, the young child acquires the intellectual capacity for mentally representing the other. This ability to visualize the other results in increased awareness of the separate individualities of the self and others. Piaget (1967) and Mead (1934) both observed sympathetic reactions in children of this age. While Piaget attributed little significance to these responses, Mead recognized that sympathy involves taking the attitude or role of the other. The appearance of role-taking or empathic behavior between 1½ and 2 years of age can be attributed to the integration of the child's capacity for emotional responsiveness with the newly acquired capacity for mental representation.

The potential for role-taking during the preoperational period is obviously limited by the child's cognitive capabilities at this stage of development. The young child's ability to take the perspective of the other is confined to immediate, simple situations that fall within the realm of each child's own life experiences. The significant point is that contrary to Piaget's (1967) assertion that young children show "a lack of differentiation between [their] own view and that of others [p. 29]," even children as young as 1½ years of age appear capable of perspective role-taking behavior. What Piaget recognized so brilliantly in the cognitive area he failed to see in the social realm. Just as mental representation at this early age constitutes the first tentative step toward adult capabilities for abstract reasoning and formal operations, empathic awareness during this stage of development represents the rudimentary beginnings of the empathic abilities of the adult.

During the period of middle childhood significant transformations occur in both the cognitive and social spheres. Piaget has extensively documented how children between 7 and 12 years of age learn to relate experiences over time and to think in terms of general concepts and principles. This advance in intellectual capabilities makes possible equally significant changes in the child's capacity for role-taking and empathic awareness. A number of investigators (Dymond, Hughes, & Raabe, 1952; Flapan, 1968; Gollin, 1958; Rothenberg, 1970) have reported a significant increase in the accuracy of perception of other people's feelings, thoughts, and motives between 6 and 12 years of age. Older youngsters interpret and infer feelings and motives to a greater extent than younger children and also show more tendency to give explanations of other people's reactions and behavior in psychological terms. As Piaget (1967) observed, the child during this stage develops the capability "both to dissociate his point of view from that of others and to coordinate these different points of view [p. 39]." This is the beginning of reciprocity, which strengthens the autonomy of the individual and at the same time enhances the individual's ability to relate to the group. With the transition to formal operational thinking during adolescence, the individual for the first time is intellectually capable of the reciprocity, relativism, and objectivity which, in Piagetian terms, represents the most advanced stage of socal development. Growth in these processes continues throughout adulthood, but their earliest manifestations can be seen in the very young child, provided one uses appropriate methods to identify them.

Summary and Implications

Piaget's long-standing conceptualization of adult human social interaction closely resembles current definitions of empathy. While Piaget's insights into the later stages of social development are consistent with other people's observations, his insistence on the predominantly egocentric orientation of children under 7 years of age has recently been seriously challenged. Research on role-taking ability during the pre-school years (Borke, 1971, 1973, 1975) and observations of young children's interactions (Borke, 1972; Hoffman, 1975) fail to support Piaget's premise that very young children are completely unaware of any perspective other than their own. The persistence of egocentrism throughout early childhood is also inconsistent with Piaget's own view of the interrelationship between cognitive and social development. If, as Piaget maintains, cognitive and social development are two sides of the same coin, then one would expect that some awareness of the other's perspective would first occur with the appearance of abstract thinking and mental representation between 1½ and 2 years of age. Just as the child's initial attempts at abstract thinking bear only the slightest resemblance to the formal operational thought processes of the adult, the child's understanding of the subjectivity of the other resembles adult empathy primarily in the awareness that the other's viewpoint exists.

If empathy, like intelligence, represents an evolutionary advance, we can hypothesize that in addition to aggressive drives human beings also have a built-in potential for understanding the other person's perspective. While socialization in human societies has been far more effective in encouraging the development of aggressive tendencies than empathic awareness, this imbalance on the side of aggression is becoming increasingly untenable from a survival point of view (Lorenz, 1966). One alternative is to cultivate the human capability for empathy. Just as early stimulation from the environment is essential for the growth of human intellectual potential, the development of social understanding must also be nurtured from a very early age if the human potential for reciprocity, relativism, and objectivity in social interaction is to be realized. Biological evolution may have given human beings the capacity for adaptive social interaction many millennia ago, but it is becoming increasingly evident that this potential will only be realized through social evolution that emphasizes empathic development as an integral part of the socialization process.

REFERENCES

Allport, G. W. *Personality: A psychological interpretation.* New York: Henry Holt, 1937.

Borke, H. Interpersonal perception of young children: Egocentrism or empathy? *Developmental Psychology*, 1971, 5, 263–269.

Borke, H. Chandler and Greenspan's "ersatz egocentrism"; a rejoinder. *Developmental Psychology*, 1972, 7, 107–109.

Borke, H. The development of empathy in Chinese and American children between three and six years-of-age: A crosscultural study. *Developmental Psychology*, 1973, *9*, 102–108.

Borke, H. Piaget's mountains revisited: Changes in the egocentric landscape. *Developmental Psychology*, 1975, *11*, 240–243.

Chandler, M. J., & Greenspan, S. Ersatz egocentrism: A reply to H. Borke. *Developmental Psychology*, 1972, 7, 104–106.

Cooley, C. H. *Human nature and the social order.* New York: Scribner, 1902/1922.

Cottrell, L. S., Jr., & Dymond, R. F. The empathic process. *Psychiatry*, 1949, *12*, 355–359.

Dymond, R. F. Personality and empathy. *Journal of Consulting Psychology*, 1950, *14*, 343–350.

Dymond, R. F., Hughes, A. S., & Raabe, V. L. Measurable changes in empathy with age. *Journal of Consulting Psychology*, 1952, *16*, 202–206.

Eliot, J., & Dayton, C. M. Egocentric error and the construct of egocentrism. *Journal of Genetic Psychology*, 1976, 128, 275–289.

Fishbein, H. D., Lewis, S., & Keiffer, K. Children's understanding of spacial relations: Coordination of perspectives. *Developmental Psychology*, 1972, 7, 21–33.

Flapan, D. *Children's understanding of social interaction.* New York: Teachers College Press, 1968.

Flavell, J. H., Botkin, P. T., & Fry, C. L., Jr. *The development of role-taking and communication skills in young children.* New York: Wiley, 1968.

Fromm, E. *The art of loving.* New York: Harper and Row, 1956.

Gollin, E. S. Organizational characteristics of social judgment: A developmental investigation. *Journal of Personality*, 1958, *26*, 139–154.

Hoffman, M. L. Developmental synthesis of affect and cognition and its implications for altruistic motivation. *Developmental Psychology*, 1975, *11*, 607–622.

Hoy, F. A. Predicting another's visual perspective: A unitary skill? *Developmental Psychology*, 1974, *10*, 462.

Huttenlocher, J., & Presson, C. Mental rotation and the perspective problem. *Cognitive Psychology*, 1973, 4, 277–299.

Lipps, T. *Leitfaden der Psychologie.* Leipsig: W. Engelman, 1909.

Lorenz, K. Z. *On aggression.* New York: Harcourt, Brace and World, 1966.

Mead, G. H. *Mind, self and society.* Chicago: University of Chicago Press, 1934.

Murphy, L. B. *Social behavior and child personality.* New York: Columbia University Press, 1937.

Piaget, J. *The child's conception of physical causality.* London: Kegan Paul, 1930.

Piaget, J. *The moral judgment of the child.* London: Kegan Paul, 1932.

Piaget, J. *The psychology of intelligence.* New York: Harcourt Brace, 1950.

Piaget, J. *Six psychological studies.* New York: Random House, 1967.

Piaget, J., & Inhelder, B. *The child's conception of space.* London: Routledge & Kegan Paul, 1956.

Rothenberg, B. Children's social sensitivity and the relationship to interpersonal competence, intrapersonal comfort, and intellectual level. *Developmental Psychology*, 1970, *2*, 335–350.

Van Lieshout, C. F., Leckie, G., & Smits-Van Sonsbeek, B. The effect of social perspective-taking training on empathy and role-taking ability of preschool children. In K. F. Riegel & J. A. Meacham (Eds.), *The developing individual in a changing world* (Vol. 2). The Hague: Mouton, 1975.

Yarrow, M. R., Scott, P. M. and Waxler, C. Z. Learning concern for others. *Developmental Psychology*, 1973, *8*, 240–260.

3

The Relationship of Language and Thought in the Preoperational Child: A Reconsideration of Nonverbal Alternatives to Piagetian Tasks

LINDA S. SIEGEL

McMaster University Medical Centre

The Piagetian model of cognitive development is a comprehensive and general theory of the growth of children's understanding of the world around them. It is a basic premise of this system that in the course of development the child passes through an invariant sequence of stages, each of which represents a unique level of analysis, internal organization, and understanding of environmental information and events. The purpose of this chapter is to examine the evidence for the existence of one of these stages, the preoperational stage, which corresponds approximately to the period between 2 and 6 years. In this connection, we will deal with the following issues: (a) the role of language in measuring the existence and structure of logical operations as defined by the Piagetian system; (b) the theoretical relationship between cognitive operations and language and the empirical evidence concerning this relationship in the preoperational child; (c) the implications of this

This research was partially supported by Grant MA-3773 from the Medical Research Council of Canada. The author wishes to thank Jon Baron, Daphne Maurer, Betty Ann Levy, and John Gibbs for their helpful comments and suggestions on earlier drafts of this chapter.

43

relationship for the measurement and analysis of preoperational thought; *(d)* issues concerning the operational definitions of Piagetian structures; and *(e)* the role of nonverbal tasks in assessing cognitive functioning. This discussion will concentrate on the preoperational stage because, as will be shown, the issue of the language–thought relationship is critical at this period.

In the Piagetian system, preoperational thought has egocentric and transductive qualities, but the preoperational stage as a unique stage of development is inferred from the *absence* of certain cognitive operations, such as seriation, conservation, transitivity, and class inclusion, among others. All these operations are defined by tasks that have two critical features: *(a)* they require that the child comprehend language related to relative and absolute quantity (e.g., *more, same, put things in order, larger than)*; and, perhaps more importantly, *(b)* they define successful performance in terms of the production of some appropriate verbal responses or explanation by the child. If there is some reason to suspect linguistic competence, then failures on these tasks may be due to either the lack of the cognitive operation being tested or the inability to comprehend and produce the required language or, of course, both.

In regard to the language typically used in these tasks, there is a substantial body of evidence showing significant deficiencies in the young child's understanding of relational terminology. Studies such as those of Clark (1973a,b), Donaldson and Balfour (1968), Griffiths, Shantz, and Sigel (1967), LaPointe and O'Donnell (1974), Lawson, Baron, and Siegel (1974), Palermo (1973, 1974), Rothenberg (1969), Siegel and Goldstein (1969), Townsend (1974), Weiner (1974), and Willoughby and Trachy (1971) have shown that 3- to 6-year-old children evidence difficulty in comprehending terminology such as *more, longer, less,* and *same.* Also, children in this age range often make errors indicating an incomplete understanding of words such as *big, bigger, small (wee),* and *little* (Clark, 1970; Donaldson & Wales, 1970; Lumsden & Kling, 1969; Lumsden & Poteat, 1968; Maratsos, 1973, 1974; Phye & Tenbrink, 1972; Poteat & Hulsebus, 1968; Siegel, 1977). Not only do children fail to understand this relational language, but their errors reveal some systematic misinterpretations of these terms. For example, Donaldson and Balfour (1968) found that 3- to 5-year-old children interpret *less* as meaning *more;* and Lawson, Baron, and Siegel (1974) found that 3- to 5-year-old children confuse terminology related to number *(more)* with that related to length *(longer),* especially in situations in which these cues are in conflict. These confusions make it especially difficult to assume that the child understands the language of the task. On the basis of the findings of these studies, it is clear that the young child is deficient in his understanding of the language of relational comparisons. Therefore, there seems to be no way of determining, with the traditional Piagetian tasks, the relative contributions of cognitive or linguistic deficiencies when the child fails to achieve the correct solution.

Furthermore, not only do young children have difficulty in understanding relational terminology, a number of studies have shown significant differences between children in certain dimensions of language use and understanding as a function of the child's problem-solving ability. Sinclair-de-Zwart (1969) found differences between conservers and nonconservers in the use of comparative numerical terminology. Conservers were more likely than nonconservers to use relational terms to describe objects of differing size and sets of different numbers. The conservers also showed more discrimination than the nonconservers in their use of terminology for different dimensions. For example, the conservers would use *fat* to describe width, and *big* and *little* to indicate height, while the nonconservers would use a single term (such as *big* or *little*) to describe both height and width. Peters (1970) found that the understanding of relational terminology was related to conservation performance, in that children who correctly solved conservation of area, numerical equality, and difference problems had significantly higher scores on a language comprehension task. Harasym, Boersma, and Maguire (1971) found that conservers' semantic differential ratings showed a clearer differentiation of *more* and *less* than the ratings of nonconservers. Bruner and Kenney (1966) found that children who failed a multiple-ordering task produced more undifferentiated relational terminology than did children who were able to solve the task. In this study, children who failed the matrix task, as opposed to those who passed it, were more likely to employ confounded or mixed dimensional usage ("that one is tall and that one is little"), rather than using terms usually associated with opposite ends of a single dimension (e.g., *tall* and *short* or *big* and *little*). Farnham-Diggory and Bermon (1968) also found differences between conservers and nonconservers in the production of relational terminology; that is, children who were able to pass a conservation of liquids task were more likely to adequately describe differences in objects that differed simultaneously in two dimensions (e.g., height and width) than those who did not pass the task. If children's problem solution is correlated with their linguistic ability, then observed differences in cognitive functioning may be a reflecton of the differences in language ability. In any case, this correlation between language use and problem solution makes it difficult to draw conclusions about cognitive processes when they are assessed by linguistic methods.

The form of verbal material in questions designed to elicit logical responses can be shown to influence whether a child will be able to give a correct response. In the case of conservation, Goodnow (1973) has shown that differences in the form of the question in postjudgment inquiries are related to the child's rationale for his judgment (Goodnow, 1973). She asked two types of questions to independent groups of children who were able to understand the conservation of liquids; that is, that pouring a quantity of liquid into a container of a different shape does not change the amount. First- and second-graders who were asked "Can you tell me how you know?" were more likely to give identity arguments ("Because you didn't add anything") than children from the same grade levels who were told "But look, this one comes up to here"; the latter were more likely to give compensation arguments ("Because this one's taller but that one's fatter"). Therefore, the structure of the question can influence the reason given, and Goodnow notes "the need for caution in inferring processes leading to conservation from the types of reasons given." Cohen (1967) was able to elicit correct conservation of quantity responses by asking questions that involved the equitable sharing of candy and orangeade. Many children were able to conserve quantity and liquid when they had to imagine a situation in which it was very important that each child receive the same amount of candy or orangeade or a "terrible quarrel" would ensue. Larsen and Flavell (1970) found that children's understanding of the concept of compensation in relation to the conservation of liquids depended on the form of the question. The question, "If I poured this water into here, how high would it come up to?" elicited more correct judgments than a question that emphasized *same amount*, "If I put the same amount of water in here, how high would it come up to?"

In the case of class inclusion, Markman (1973) showed that certain changes in the structure of the class inclusion question facilitated the solution to this problem by 6- to 8-year-old children. She found that with comparisons of classes, using the word *family* for superordinate class, and *parents* and *children*, which cannot individually be labeled family for the subordinate classes, the children were more likely to give the correct answer than when more traditional forms of the question were used. We have shown that 3- and 4-year-old children can solve a class inclusion problem when some of the confusing language is removed from this task (Siegel, McCabe, Brand, & Matthews, 1977). In order to do this, we showed 3- and 4-year-old children an array that included two kinds of candy, smarties and jelly beans (more smarties than jelly beans). We asked the child whether he or she would rather eat the candy or the smarties. Many 3- and 4-year-olds could make a correct class inclusion response in this case (they chose to eat the candy—jelly beans and smarties) although they could not do so when asked the more traditional form of the question ("Are there more smarties or more candies?").

In the area of logical operations, Odom and Coon (1967) found that the form of the question influenced the child's ability to solve transitivity problems. The children were more likely to solve problems in which the relational terminology was consistent throughout the problem. For example, the child was told A is smaller than B, B is smaller than C, and then was asked either "Which is bigger, A or C?" or "Which is smaller, A or C?" The latter question was much easier. With older subjects, Ward and Pearson (1973) found that problems testing the understanding of formal logical operations were more easily solved when the materials with a reduced verbal content were used. All of these studies lead to the conclusion that linguistic factors are important in problem solution and that failure to solve traditional Piagetian problems may reflect linguistic, rather than cognitive, deficits.

Aside from whether or not the child understands the language used in the task, there is another important problem when studying the absence or presence of cognitive operations in the young child, and one which is based on the fundamental assumptions of the Piagetian system itself. Within the Piagetian system, language is not the cause of the emergence of cognitive operations; they emerge and develop independently of language (Inhelder & Piaget, 1964; Sinclair-de-Zwart, 1969). Therefore, it would seem to be a paradox to postulate the independence of language and thought, and then to rely on language to infer the existence of certain kinds of thought. If, in fact, thought is not necessarily dependent on language, then it would seem that nonverbal methods should serve as the *only* appropriate test of Piagetian theory. Brainerd (1973) has outlined a similar argument in discussing whether judgments or explanations are the appropriate criteria for the classification of conservation and nonconservation responses. It may in fact be true that certain critical features of thought in the Piagetian system can be assessed only by linguistic methods (a point we will discuss in detail later), but if this is the case, the need to use language as part of the measurement techniques makes it difficult to establish distinctly cognitive operations, apart from language. If language is necessary to the measurement of a cognitive operation, the absence of such an operation cannot logically be inferred in a child in the preschool age range, whose language production and comprehension is immature and inadequate for the task. For such a child, the existence of a preoperational stage becomes, at best, indeterminate.

The use of nonverbal methods of assessment of cognitive operations in the young child seems essential on two grounds: (a) in relation to certain quantity concepts, it can be shown that thought and language exist independently in the preschool child, and, as a corollary, thought develops prior to language for these concepts; and (b) nonverbal methods that contain the critical features of these cognitive operations can be designed, although representing different operational definitions of the classical Piagetian concepts.

Evidence for the independence of language and thought in the young child comes from studies that have examined the sequence of development of a particular concept and those linguistic abilities that are assumed to be analogous to this concept. In general, these studies have found that concepts develop prior to, and independently of, related language. For example, in the area of quantity concepts, Beilin and Kagan (1969) found that children's performance on a task involving the discrimination of one from two subjects was superior to their ability to produce the correct plurals of nouns, possessives, and verbs. Koff and Luria (1973) found that children were able to learn the concept of middle size before they could comprehend and produce comparatives expressing the relationship between objects of different sizes. Saravo and Gollin (1969) found that children could learn oddity discriminations, but did not necessarily understand the labels *same, not the same,* or *different.* Similarly, in the area of logical concepts, Pascual-Leone and Smith (1969) found that children's ability to convey information about class membership was determined by the logical structure of the task, not by the language available to them. The development of time concepts precedes the ability to understand the past progressive tense and terminology such as *before* and *after* in relation to a sequence of events (Weil, 1970).

We have found examples of this language and thought independence in the preschool child in our studies of the development of quantity concepts (Siegel, 1976). The particular concepts examined were the child's understanding of numerical equality and relative size. We used tasks designed as nonverbal tests of these basic concepts and compared performance on these tasks with the development of language abilities. To test the understanding of numerical difference, a "magnitude task" was used. The task is a concept attainment paradigm, described in detail in Siegel (1971). Basically, the child is shown a stimulus with a set of alternatives and told that if he picks the right one he will get a candy (or play money or some other reinforcer). After each correct choice he or she is rewarded with the reinforcement. In this particular magnitude task, the stimulus for each trial contains two sets of unequal numbers of dots, the particular combination selected randomly from the numbers 2–9. A representative stimulus for this task is shown in Figure 3.1. The child is reinforced for selecting the larger (or, for counterbalancing, smaller) group of dots. The corresponding language task tested the child's understanding of the words *big* and *little* when applied to discrete objects. For this language task the child was asked, for each of the stimuli used in the magnitude concept tasks, "Which is the *big* (*little*, if the smaller set size was reinforced in the concept) one?"

For the concept of numerical equality, called equivalence, the child had to select from four choices the set with the same number as the sample. A representative stimulus is shown in Figure 3.2. For the corresponding language task, the child was asked to select the stimulus with the same number as the sample. Identical stimuli were used for the concept and language tasks in each case, magnitude and equivalence, to minimize task differences that might inflate the possibility of finding a discrepancy between the acquisition of the concept and the relevant language. For both these concept tasks, stimuli differed on every trial so that a specific stimulus response association was not being tested, but rather the understanding of the concept "bigger," "smaller," or "same number" (depending on what was being reinforced). A within-subjects design with counterbalanced orders of concept and language task administration was used to examine the sequence of emergence of language and thought in an individual child.

As shown in Table 3.1, the concepts clearly develop before the relevant language. Children can understand basic concepts of numerical

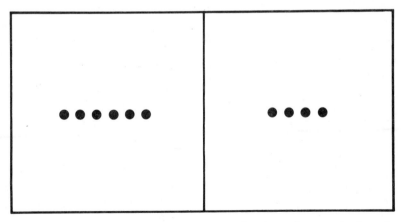

FIGURE 3.1 A stimulus from the magnitude task.

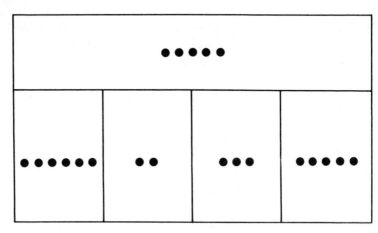

FIGURE 3.2 A stimulus from the equivalence task.

equality and difference before they can respond appropriately to the words, *big*, *little*, and *same* in reference to sets of discrete objects. The large number of children who failed the language but passed the concept tasks and the small number who failed the concept but passed the language tasks illustrate this thought and language asynchrony. For the magnitude task, 44% of the 3-year-olds and 30% of the 4-year-olds passed the concept task and failed the language comprehension task. For the equivalence task the percentages were 9% for the 3-year-olds and 14% for the 4-year-olds. The young children's concepts, defined in the present manner, exist independently of, and prior to, even the simplest language used to refer to these parameters.

TABLE 3.1
Concept and Language Performance

Group	Pass language pass concept	Fail language pass concept	Pass language fail concept	Fail language fail concept
Magnitude				
3-year-olds***	15	20	2	8
4-year-olds***	37	17	1	2
Equivalence				
3-year-olds*	7	4	0	34
4-year-olds**	40	8	0	9

NOTE: The table figures represent the number of subjects.
* $p < .06$.
** $p < .004$.
*** $p < .001$.

If language and thought exist independently, there are certain implications of this dichotomy. The following predictions, among others, follow from this assumption of independence: *(a)* the addition of verbal cues should not influence concept acquisition and *(b)* there should be no necessary relationship between a child's ability to solve a problem and his ability to describe the solution by producing the appropriate language. These predictions require a complete independence of language and thought. Obviously some dependence would allow for existence of these relationships, but a strong case for independence would require that at least these conditions exist. The following two experiments were designed to test these specific hypotheses for the basic quantity concepts described previously.

To determine whether or not language could facilitate the acquisition of these concepts, several variations of magnitude and equivalence tasks were administered to two independent groups of children. Representative stimuli for each of these tasks are shown in Figure 3.3. These tasks are described in detail in Siegel (1976). For one group, called the cue condition, the task instructions contained a verbal cue to the nature of the solution (specifically, the children were told to select either the *big* or *little* sets, or the one with the *same number* as the sample). Con-

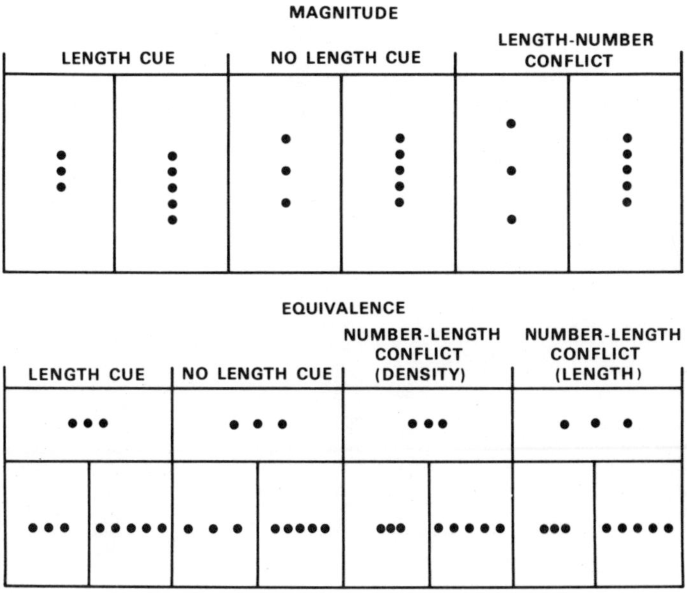

FIGURE 3.3 Stimuli from the set of magnitude and equivalence tasks.

trol groups (no-cue condition) received no verbal cue to the nature of the solution. The results of this study are shown in Figure 3.4. For the 3-year-olds, the verbal cue did not facilitate concept attainment. For the 4-year-olds, the verbal cue resulted in a significant difference in the number of errors between the cue and no-cue conditions. The cue condition was obviously easier for these children. These effects were found for both the magnitude and the equivalence tasks. For the 3-year-olds, there appears to be a language–thought independence; language is not mediating their concept formation. For the 4-year-olds, an externally presented language cue facilitated performance, an effect suggesting that language is beginning to serve some function in relation to thought for children of this age.

Within the context of this study, we also examined the child's ability to produce language about quantity and the relationship of this language to his ability to arrive at the correct solution to these tasks. After the concept task was administered, we asked the child, "How did you know which one to pick? Which one got the candy?" Responses

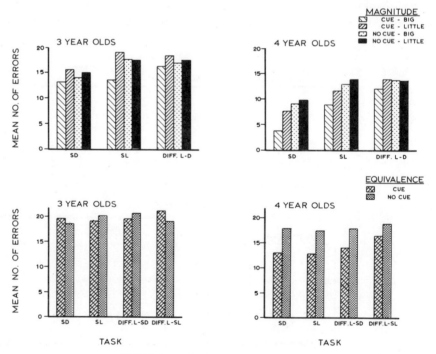

FIGURE 3.4 Performance on the tasks as a function of the presence or absence of a verbal cue.

to this question were scored for the absence or presence of a correct quantity response. Correct quantity responses were statements such as "The big (little) one," "The one that was more big," "One was bigger and one was little," "It's the same" (equivalence). Incorrect responses were statements such as "I like it," "I wanted to," "My mommy told me," "I know the numbers in the alphabet," "I knowed it in my brain." The relationship between success and failure on the concept task and the ability to give a correct quantity response was calculated using the McNemar test. In most of the cases, concept attainment occurred prior to the production of the appropriate language. On the basis of their ability to produce an adequate verbal description of the solution once they have solved the problem, there is strong evidence for the independence of language and thought in these children.

In addition, there were substantial numbers of children who were unable to verbalize the solution in any way. These percentages are shown in Table 3.2. These children can reliably categorize instances in terms of some general concept, and yet their language behavior gives no indication that they understand the concept. Even children who are able to comprehend relational language are often not able to verbalize the critical dimension of stimulus variation. Siegel (1977) tested children's comprehension of relational terminology and then asked them how they knew which was the right answer. Many could respond significantly better than chance to the word *(big, little,* or *same number)*

TABLE 3.2

Proportion Passing Concept Attainment Task and Failing Language Production Task

	Magnitude		
Group	Length cue	No length cue	Length/ number conflict
3-year-olds	.69	.65	.78
4-year-olds	.32	.40	.52

	Equivalence		
Group	Length cue	No length cue	Length/ number conflict (density)	Length/ number conflict (length)
3-year-olds	1.00	.50	1.00	.50
4-year-olds	.79	.87	.85	.70

yet could not produce any language in relation to quantity. Thus, even adequate comprehension does not insure successful production of an appropriate response.

These results are consistent with findings from a number of studies that have demonstrated that children can evidence successful problem solution without being able to produce appropriate language. LaPointe and O'Donnell (1974) found that among preschool children who could give conservation responses, few could produce correct explanations. Dimitrovsky and Almy (1972) found that young conservers (5-year-olds) had more difficulty in producing explanations than did older ones. Estes (1976) reports that quantity concepts mediated the young child's choice in discrimination-learning tasks and transfer tasks, yet the children could not always verbalize their reasons for choice, nor did their verbalizations about the correctness of a stimulus control their choice behavior. Stern and Bryson (1970) have shown that 4-year-olds understood comparative concepts but could not produce the appropriate labels, and Martin (1951) and Deal (1969) found that the understanding of numerical concepts was not necessarily reflected in measures of quantitative language ability. Pratoomraj and Johnson (1966) found a discrepancy between correct judgment responses and explanations for a conservation of substance response.

The results of all these experiments indicate that attainment of concepts can in no way be inferred from verbal responses. In summary, there is a strong suggestion of the independence of language and thought for the younger children, and for many of the older ones, in these studies. In the early stages of the development of these concepts, there is ample evidence of this independence, but the area of overlap of language and thought increases as the child gets older. Many of the children could not (or did not) use externally given linguistic cues, verbalize the concept, or associate a word with a concept, yet they were well able to demonstrate through nonverbal means the presence of concepts. Therefore, a meaningful analysis of the structure of the child's intellect in this period would seem to require methods that are not dependent on language to convey critical information to the child about what is required of him or to define successful problem solution. Investigators of cognitive development should be wary of using language as a dependent variable to study thought. Language skills are not completely correlated with cognitive development, but, more important, this relationship changes with age. Thought cannot be inferred from the language of a young child, although it may be from that of an older child. This developmental shift means that the measurement error will be greater with younger children.

Thus, nonverbal tasks would seem to be the appropriate mode of analysis of thought. Braine (1959, 1962) made the initial attempt to deal with this problem for the development of logical concepts; our discussion here attempts to extend Braine's original analysis and to argue for a nonverbal approach, both on the basis of the assumptions of the Piagetian theory and on empirical demonstration of the lack of relationship between language and thought in the young child.

This language–thought dichotomy in the young child would suggest that, unlike the traditional Piagetian tasks, nonverbal measures of cognitive processes would be able to tap the abilities of the child to understand certain quantity and logical concepts. The nonverbal tasks we will discuss here were designed as analogues to the traditional Piagetian tasks. They are tests of operational abilities and have the feature, critical to concepts, that an instance which has never been specifically defined can be properly categorized or assimilated into the system. Thus, we are not studying stimulus–response associations in which the child learns to respond properly to a single stimulus, as in a typical discrimination learning paradigm; we are studying more complex concepts. The other characteristic of these tasks is that the solution to the problem is not dependent on the child's comprehension of language or on the production of verbal explanations about the solution to the problem. Although words may be used in the instructions, they are not necessary to the solution, since the child can arrive at the correct solution by a process of learning. These tasks make no a priori assumptions about the development of a child's linguistic skills. The question is whether he is capable of learning the concept within the conditions of the experiment. What we are proposing is a new paradigm that we think more appropriately taps cognitive operations.

Let us consider how some of the Piagetian cognitive operations can be translated into nonverbal tasks. The Piagetian conservation of number task is designed to answer the question of whether the young child can recognize numerical invariance. "A set or collection is only conceivable if it remains unchanged irrespective of the changes occurring in the relationship between elements [Piaget, 1965, p. 3]." "As long as optical correspondence exists, the equivalence is obvious; once the first is changed, the second disappears, which brings us back to nonconservation of the whole [Piaget, 1960, p. 132]." The Piagetian conservation of number task typically involves altering the length of one of two numerically equivalent rows and requiring the child to recognize the numerical identity despite this transformation. Below age 5 or 6, children typically fail this task (Gelman, 1972; Rothenberg, 1969; Siegel & Goldstein, 1969). However, there is evidence that these young children do have concepts of numerical invariance when it is assessed in other ways. Gelman (1972) found that children could treat small numbers as invariant in that they were surprised by surreptitious addition or subtraction of elements but not by changes in spatial arrangement. Bryant (1972) found that children could retain a concept of invariance despite certain kinds of transformations. We have devised a task called non-linear equivalence that requires the child to select a stimulus identical in number to the sample when the dots are arranged in random arrays. For this task, the set sizes used for the sample and the four alternatives were selected from the population one to nine. The set size of the sample and the alternatives varied randomly on every trial. The random arrangement of the arrays removed spatial cues to number. Thus the child had to learn the concept of numerical equivalence but had to ignore spatial arrangement. A representative stimulus is shown in Figure 3.5. Many 4-year-olds and most 5-year-olds can learn to select the correct stimulus, indicating that they have a concept of cardinal number that is not dependent on the spatial relationship between the elements (Siegel, 1973). The relationship between this task and performance on a Piagetian conservation task is shown in Table 3.3. The percentages of children who passed the nonverbal conservation task and failed the

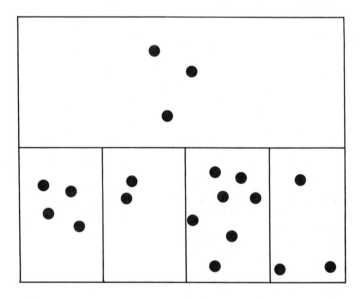

FIGURE 3.5 A stimulus from the nonlinear equivalence task.

TABLE 3.3

Number of Subjects in Each Category

	Age				Total
	4	5	6	7	
Pass Piagetian conservation, pass nonverbal conservation	1	17	40	53	111
Fail Piagetian conservation, pass nonverbal conservation	18	25	16	5	64
Pass Piagetian conservation, fail nonverbal conservation	3	1	2	5	11
Fail Piagetian conservation, fail nonverbal conservation	42	21	6	1	70
	9.33*	20.35**	9.39*	.10	36.05**

* $p < .01$.
** $p < .001$.

Piagetian conservation task were as follows: 4-year-olds, 28%; 5-year-olds, 39%; 6-year-olds, 25%; and 7-year-olds, 8%. Note that this discrepancy is particularly apparent with the younger children; in fact, the nonverbal task may impede the performance of the oldest ones. However, the inherent differences between the nonverbal and the verbal tasks (feedback, language, number of trials) can never be reconciled. Any direct comparisons only serve to emphasize the differences. A seemingly more important question involves structuring the situation so that the abilities of the young child are assessed in an appropriate manner. Children do or do not have a concept in an absolute sense. What one concludes about the abilities of a child depends on the operational definition of the concept. We are arguing here for one set of operational definitions that we feel tap the child's abilities in an age-appropriate manner.

What other evidence is there that children understand numerical invariance? Young children can also learn to recognize the numerical identity of heterogeneous arrays when shape and color of the object is irrelevant to the numerical size of the group (Siegel, 1973). We call this task heterogeneous equivalence. A typical stimulus for this task is shown in Figure 3.6. Again, the ability of the child to solve this type of problem demonstrates a concept of numerical equivalence, independent of the perceptual characteristics of the array. Many 4- and 5-year-olds solve this problem easily. Another task required the child to coordinate length and number and select a stimulus identical in number but different in length, as opposed to one that is identical in length to the sample

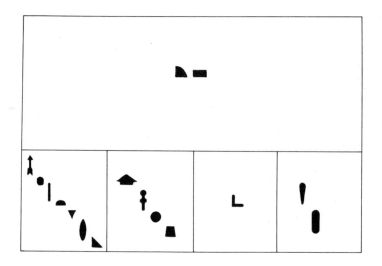

FIGURE 3.6 A stimulus from the heterogeneous equivalence task.

(Siegel, 1977). Again, children can learn this task. Siegel (1971) found that after learning to match sets of dots of equivalent numerical sizes, preschool children could select the correct alternative when spatial configuration was no longer a cue to numerical size. For this test of conservation-like ability, children were given 20 trials of equivalence training; they were trained to match sets on the basis of some number with a spatial cue to set-size correspondence. The next 5 trials were test trials; there was no spatial cue to set sizes. Of the children who passed the equivalence part, 30% of the 3-year-olds and 40% of the 4-year-olds passed the "conservation test" (5 out of 5 correct responses). What we have shown here is that even in the face of what Piaget calls lack of optical correspondence, a child can make a conservation, or identity-preserving, response.

One objection might be that these tasks do not require the child to witness a transformation; therefore, they are removing a critical source of failure to conserve. We have some evidence concerning quantity judgments after transformation. Lawson, Baron, and Siegel (1976) have found that when children are asked to judge the relative numerosity and length of arrays after they had been transformed or when they remained unchanged, there are no diffences between these conditions in the number or type of errors. Thus the transformation of the stimulus appears not to be the critical source of errors in failure to make correct conservation judgments. All of these tasks suggest that young children do, in fact, possess concepts of numerical invariance which are not apparent when a traditional conservation of number task is administered to them.

The Piagetian seriation task requires the child to be able to demonstrate his recognition of the reciprocal relationships between a group of objects that differ in a particular dimension (usually size). The instructions usually involve asking the child to "put the sticks in order from the biggest to the littlest," or some variation of this. Nonverbal alternatives to this task exist, and they demonstrate that a young child can order objects in relation to size. Siegel (1972), Gollin, Moody, and Schadler (1974), and Marschark (1976) used tasks in which the child was shown a series of configurations like those shown in Figure 3.7 and asked to select either a terminal (biggest or smallest) or nonterminal (next to the smallest, next to the largest) size line. The stimuli used for each trial were randomly selected from vertical bars of nine possible heights. Children of 3, 4, and 5 years can learn to do this task. The only way that they could be making these correct responses is to seriate the lines. Blackstock and King (1973) have shown that young children can discriminate a seriated sequence from a nonseriated one. Both these types of tasks show that the preschool child is capable of

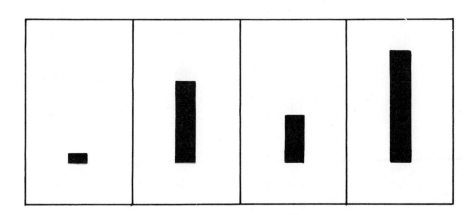

FIGURE 3.7 A stimulus from the nonverbal seriation task.

some type of seriation operations, although not necessarily the Piagetian seriation task.

All of these nonverbal measures suggest that the so-called preoperational child has certain quantity and logical concepts that are not apparent when assessed with the traditional Piagetian tasks. Assessment with the Piagetian tasks appears to be producing many "false negatives." Systematic biases in the Piagetian tasks prevent the child's logical abilities from emerging. The nonverbal tasks enable the control of variables which are irrelevant to the operations being tested, the availability and comprehension of language. The tasks presented are part of a growing body of literature that represents dissatisfaction with Piagetian assessments on a number of grounds. There have been several investigations of nonverbal alternatives to a variety of Piagetian cognitive operations. Braine and Shanks (1965a,b) used nonverbal techniques to produce successful conservation of shape and size properties in young children. King (1971) used feedback procedures to produce successful conservation of length in young children. Mehler and Bever (1968) proposed a nonverbal alternative to conservation, but it has been criticized on theoretical grounds (Piaget, 1968; Beilin, 1968), and the findings have not been replicated (Beilin, 1968; Rothenberg & Courtney, 1969; Willoughby & Trachy, 1971). When certain probability concepts are assessed nonverbally, 4- and 5-year-old children evidence the understanding of probability (Yost, Siegel, & Andrews, 1962). Bryant and Trabasso (1971) demonstrated transitivity in young children through the use of a training procedure that controlled the possible influence of memory in tasks measuring transitivity. Mermelstein and Shulman (1967) examined the understanding of conservation of continuous quantity with a nonverbal task that tested the child's surprise reaction to the surreptitious addition of water to a container. The children were surprised and puzzled when each of two identical beakers filled a third container (to which water had surreptitiously been added) to different levels. Many of these same children failed a conservation of liquid task administered in the traditional Piagetian manner. Children of 4 and 6 years have been able to solve matrix problems when they are presented in a nonverbal choice situation (Odom, Astor, & Cunningham, 1975).

It should be noted that in a recent review of the literature, Miller (1976) concluded that most of the available evidence indicates that performance on nonverbal or less verbal versions of Piagetian tests is not very different from performance on traditional Piagetian tests. There are, however, several problems with this conclusion. First, few studies directly compared nonverbal and verbal task performance. Second, in many cases, the alternate, or nonverbal, tasks used complicated language in the instructions. Finally, there is enough suggestive evidence that reasoning processes may emerge earlier in young children to leave the question unresolved.

Certain questions can be raised about the validity of this whole area of nonverbal assessment. Probably the crucial one involves the issue of whether or not the nonverbal tasks are measuring abilities analogous to the ones tested by the Piagetian tasks. Bruner (1975, p. 44) calls the question "The game of true and pseudo." Do these nonverbal tasks produce false positives? That is, are we falsely concluding that Piagetian cognitive operations are present in children who can solve the nonverbal problems? There is no doubt that the nonverbal tasks are not identical to the Piagetian tasks, in that the operational definitions of the concepts are different. However, the nonverbal tasks have been chosen so that the child must possess what appear to be the same underlying abilities as those needed to solve the Piagetian problems. Thus, the critical features of the cognitive operation appear to have been maintained. At this point, the burden of specifying in which way these tasks fail to tap structures rests with the Piagetian system. We see these nonverbal tasks as different, but not inappropriate, definitions of cognitive structure in the preschool child. Perhaps, we need a test of the formal operational skills of investigators of cognitive development. Can they make a correct conservation of conservation response or a correct conservation of logical-abilities response? Can they recognize that the identical ability can be measured in different ways? The superficial features of tasks may be different, but the underlying processes may be the same.

A Piagetian might be tempted to call these nonverbal tasks "perceptual" in that they can be solved on perceptual cues and do not involve cognitive structures. Yet these tasks do involve the process of extracting a general concept and interpreting unique instances in terms of this concept. Gibson (1969) has argued that perception is in itself a process that involves extracting information from the environment, perceiving distinctive features, and selecting invariants, and that "higher-order structures" represent an outgrowth, perhaps not clearly distinct, of the development of these skills.

In one aspect these nonverbal tasks may fail; they do not appear to assess certain critical features of the Piagetian operations, specifically characteristics such as reversibility, reciprocity, and negation. The criterion for the existence of these abilities has been in the traditional assessments, the production of certain kinds of verbal responses. Some of these features are present, to a degree, in the nonverbal tasks. In the seriation task, there is a degree of reciprocity in that the child must judge the identical element "longer than" in some cases and "shorter than" in other cases. In some of the equivalence tasks, the child must recognize that changes in length result in changes in density but not numerosity. If, in fact, characteristics such as reversibility can only be assessed by verbal techniques, then some of the questions of genetic epistemology may reduce study of the young child's language. This is not an adequate solution if language and thought are not completely overlapping, and there is ample evidence to believe that they are not in the preschool child.

The tasks proposed here attempt to measure a child's cognitive abilities by examining his or her ability to *learn* certain relationships. It is impossible to know whether the child possesses the concept being examined when he or she starts the task or whether he or she acquires it in the course of learning the task. It is a question of what a child is capable of learning. This seems as valid a question as what he or she innately knows and may even be more appropriate than the typical structural analysis with children, especially at the age where there is a problem in conveying what the experimenter requires of them. W. Estes (1974) has argued that the direct measures of learning processes should be considered as a serious alternative to the traditional product-oriented methods of measuring intelligence. Estes suggests that consideration be given to the possibility of characterizing intelligence in terms of the learning process. What we are suggesting, with the use of these tasks, is that consideration be given to defining cognitive operations in terms of learning processes rather than by the presence or absence of structures. In the case of the young child, or the retarded child, or the deaf child, or any group about which there is reason to suspect nonoptimal language competence, measures that are not dependent on language for successful outcomes seem more appropriate to a process- rather than a product-oriented approach. As Bruner (1975) has noted, developmental psychologists have concentrated too long and too hard on the problem of what a child cannot do before a certain age instead of asking how a child uses his capacities, how he can benefit from instructions, and whether the child uses a concept in his or her natural environment. Of course, this formulation does not imply that the child learns about the world around him in a manner analogous to these tasks; it does imply that information about how abilities develop might be gained more fruitfully from the study of the acquisition of concepts than from their presence in the initial state.

On the basis of the child's performance on these nonverbal tasks, there is serious question of whether or not the young child is really preoperational. The child at this stage is clearly not linguistically mature and, what is more important, he cannot systematically apply language to his conceptual behavior. However, the child can incorporate the information from instances of a concept and respond to unique instances in terms of a systematic formulation that suggests he or she is not responding randomly to certain dimensions of quantity and that he understands certain logical concepts. In other words, there is a great deal of evidence for the presence of cognitive operations. This is not to say that the young child is completely logical; he or she has enough difficulty with some of these tasks to suggest that he or she certainly lacks mature concepts of quantity and logical relationships. However, the performance of children solving these tasks suggests that there is a gradual emergence of abilities. This emergence starts long before the child can solve any of the classical Piagetian concrete operational tasks. The verbal nature of these tasks may be the principal source of variance that yields asynchronous development, which is then interpreted as representative of stage differences. We must ask to what extent the differences between cognitive skills at different ages can be reduced to differences in language development. The exact determination of the young child's abilities awaits the development of more sophisticated comprehensive nonverbal techniques, because the mere use of the traditional Piagetian techniques with these young children assumes that one can gain access to the thought processes of a child through language. This assumption may be a fallacious one.

Piaget, himself, was not insensitive to this problem. Here is one of his comments on his own work (quoted in Evans, 1973, pp. 123–124):

> The first of these shortcomings consisted in limiting my research to language and expressed thought. I well knew that thought proceeds from action, but I believe then that language directly reflects acts and that to understand the logic of the child one had only to look for it in the domain of conversations or verbal interactions. It was only later, by studying the patterns of intelligent behavior of the first two years, that I learned that for a complete understanding of the genesis of intellectual operations, manipulation and experience with objects had first to be considered. Therefore, prior to study based on verbal conversations, an examination of patterns of conduct had to be carried out.

REFERENCES

Beilin, H. Cognitive capacities of young children: A replication. *Science*, 1968, *162*, 920–925.

Beilin, H., & Kagan, J. Pluralization rules and the conceptualization of number. *Developmental Psychology*, 1969, *1*, 692–706.

Blackstock, E. G., & King, W. L. Recognition and reconstruction memory for seriation in four- and five-year-olds. *Developmental Psychology*, 1973, *9*, 255–259.

Braine, M. D. S. Piaget on reasoning: A methodological critique and alternative proposals. In W. Kessen & C. Kuhlman (Eds.), Thought in the young child. *Monographs of the Society for Research in Child Development*, 1962, 27, (Ser. No. 82, Whole No. 2), 41–61.

Braine, M. D. S., & Shanks, B. L. The conservation of a shape property and a proposal about the origin of the conservations. *Canadian Journal of Psychology*, 1965, *19*, 197–207. (a)

Braine, M. D. S., & Shanks, B. L. The development of conservation of size. *Journal of Verbal Learning and Verbal Behavior*, 1965, 4, 227–242. (b)

Braine, M. D. S. The ontogeny of certain logical operations: Piaget's formulation examined by nonverbal methods. *Psychological Monographs*, 1959, *73*, (5, Whole No. 47).

Brainerd, C. J. Judgments and explanations as criteria for the presence of cognitive structure. *Psychological Bulletin*, 1973, *79*, 172–179.

Bruner, J. S. The objectives of developmental psychology. *Newsletter.* Division of Developmental Psychology–American Psychological Association, November, 1975.

Bruner, J. S., & Kenney, H. J. On multiple ordering. In J. S. Bruner et al. (Eds.), *Studies in cognitive growth.* New York: Wiley, 1966.

Bryant, P. E. The understanding of invariance by very young children. *Canadian Journal of Psychology*, 1972, *26*, 78–96.

Bryant, P. E., & Trabasso, T. Transitive inferences and memory in young children. *Nature*, 1971, *232*, 456–458.

Clark, H. H. The primitive nature of children's relational concepts. In J. R. Hayes (Ed.), *Cognition and the development of language.* New York: Wiley, 1970.

Clark, E. V. What's in a word? On the child's first acquisition of semantics in his first language. In T. E. Moore (Ed.), *Cognitive development and the acquisition of language.* New York: Academic Press, 1973. (a)

Clark, E. V. Non-linguistic strategies and the acquisition of word meanings. *Cognitive Psychology*, 1973, *2*, 161–182. (b)

Cohen, G. M. Conservation of quantity in children: The effect of vocabulary and participation. *Quarterly Journal of Experimental Psychology*, 1967, *19*, 150–154.

Deal, T. N. Longitudinal case study analysis of the development of conservation of numbers and certain sub-skills. Paper presented to the Society for Research in Child Deveopment, Santa Monica, 1969.

Dimitrovsky, A., & Almy, M. Language and thought: The relationship between knowing a correct answer and ability to verbalize the reasoning on which it is based. *Journal of Psychology*, 1972, *80*, 15–29.

Donaldson, M., & Balfour, G. Less is more: A study of language comprehension in children. *British Journal of Psychology*, 1968, *59*, 461–471.

Donaldson, M., & Wales, R. J., on the acquisition of some relational terms. In J. R. Hayes (Ed.) *Cognition and the development of language.* New York: Wiley, 1970.

Estes, K. W. Nonverbal discrimination of more and fewer elements by children. *Journal of Experimental Child Psychology*, 1976, *21*, 393–405.

Estes, W. K. Learning theory and intelligence. *American Psychologist*, 1974, *29*, 740–749.

Evans, R. I. *Jean Piaget: The man and his ideas.* New York: Dutton, 1973.

Farnham-Diggory, S., & Bermon, M. Verbal compensation, cognitive synthesis, and conservation. *Merrill–Palmer Quarterly of Behavior and Development*, 1968, *14*, 215–228.

Gelman, R. Logical capacity of very young children: Number invariance rules. *Child Development*, 1972, *43*, 75–90.

Gibson, E. J. *Principles of perceptual learning and development*. New York: Appleton-Century-Crofts, 1969.

Gollin, E. S., Moody, M., & Schadler, M. Relational learning of a size concept. *Developmental Psychology*, 1974, *10*, 101–108.

Goodnow, J. J. Compensation arguments on conservation tasks. *Developmental Psychology*, 1973, *8*, 140.

Griffiths, J. A., Shantz, C. A., & Sigel, I. E. A methodological problem in conservation studies: The use of relational terms. *Child Development*, 1967, *38*, 841–848.

Harasym, C. R., Boersma, F. J., & Maguire, T. O. Semantic differential analysis of relational terms used in conservation. *Child Development*, 1971, *42*, 767–780.

Inhelder, B., & Piaget, J. *The early growth of logic in the child*. New York: Harper & Row, 1964.

King, W. L. A nonarbitrary behavioral criterion for conservation of illusion-distorted length in five-year-olds. *Journal of Experimental Child Psychology*, 1971, *11*, 171–181.

Koff, E., & Luria, Z. Concept and language: The comparative relation. Paper presented at Society for Research in Child Development meeting, Philadelphia, 1973.

Larsen, G. Y., & Flavell, J. H. Verbal factors in compensation performance and the relation between conservation and compensation. *Child Development*, 1970, *41*, 965–977.

LaPointe, K., & O'Donnell, J. P. Number conservation in children below age six: Its relationship to age, perceptual dimensions and language comprehension. *Developmental Psychology*, 1974, *10*, 422–428.

Lawson, G., Baron, J., & Siegel, L. S. The role of number and length cues in children's quantitative judgments. *Child Development*, 1974, *45*, 731–736.

Lawson, G., Siegel, L. S., & Baron, J. Transformation and set size as factors in children's judgments of quantity. Unpublished manuscript, McMaster University, 1976.

Lumsden, E. A., & Kling, J. L. The relevance of an adequate concept of "bigger" for investigations of size conservation: A methodological critique. *Journal of Experimental Child Psychology*, 1969, *8*, 82–91.

Lumsden, E. A., & Poteat, B. W. S. The salience of the vertical dimension in the concept of "bigger" in five- and six-year-olds. *Journal of Verbal Learning and Verbal Behavior*, 1968, *7*, 404–408.

Maratsos, M. P. Decrease in the understanding of the word "big" in preschool children. *Child Development*, 1973, *44*, 747–753.

Maratsos, M. P. When is a high thing the big one? *Developmental Psychology*, 1974, *10*, 367–375.

Markman, E. The facilitation of part–whole comparisons by use of the collective noun "family". *Child Development*, 1973, *44*, 837–840.

Marschark, M. Lexical marking and the acquisition of relational size concepts. Unpublished manuscript, University of Western Ontario, London, Ontario, 1976.

Martin, W. E. Quantitative expression in young children. *Genetic Psychology Monographs*, 1951, *44*, 147–219.

Mehler, J., & Bever, T. G. Quantification, conservation, and nativism. *Science*, 1968. *162*, 979–981.

Mermelstein, E., & Shulman, L. S. Lack of formal schooling and the acquisition of conservation. *Child Development*, 1967, *38*, 39–52.

Miller, S. A. Nonverbal assessment of Piagetian concepts. *Psychological Bulletin*, 1976, *83*, 405–430.

Odom, R. D., Astor, E. C., & Cunningham, J. G. Effects of perceptual salience on the matrix task performance of four- and six-year-old children. *Child Development*, 1975, *46*, 758–762.

Odom, R. D., & Coon, R. C. A questionnaire approach to transitivity in children. *Psychonomic Science*, 1967, *9*, 305–306.

Palermo, D. S. More about less: A study of language comprehension. *Journal of Verbal Learning and Verbal Behavior*, 1973, *12*, 211–221.

Palermo, D. S. Still more about the comprehension of 'less'. *Developmental Psychology*, 1974, *10*, 827–829.

Pascual-Leone, J., & Smith, J. The encoding and decoding of symbols by children: A new experimental paradigm and a neo-Piagetian model. *Journal of Experimental Child Psychology*, 1969, *8*, 328–355.

Peters, D. L. Verbal mediators and cue discrimination in the transition from non-conservation of number. *Child Development*, 1970, *41*, 707–721.

Phye, G., & Tenbrink, T. Stimulus position and functional direction: Confounds in the concept of "bigger" in 5- and 6-year-olds. *Psychonomic Science*, 1972, *29*, 357–359.

Piaget, J. *Psychology of intelligence*. Paterson, NJ: Littlefield Adams, 1960.

Piaget, J. *The child's conception of number*. New York: Norton, 1965.

Piaget, J. Quantification, conservation, and nativism. *Science*, 1968, *162*, 276–281.

Poteat, B. W. S., & Hulsebus, R. C. The vertical dimension: A significant cue in the preschool child's concept of "bigger". *Psychonomic Science*, 1968, *12*, 369–370.

Pratoomraj, S., & Johnson, R. C. Kinds of questions and types of conservation tasks as related to children's conservation responses. *Child Development*, 1966, *37*, 343–353.

Rothenberg, B. B. Conservation of number among four- and five-year-old children: Some methodological considerations. *Child Development*, 1969, *40*, 383–406.

Rothenberg, B. B., & Courtney, R. G. Conservation of number in very young children: A replication of and comparison with Mehler and Bever's study. *Developmental Psychology*, 1969, *1*, 493–502.

Rothenberg, B. B., & Orst, J. H. The training of conservation of number in young children. *Child Development*, 1969, *40*, 707–726.

Saravo, A., & Gollin, E. G. Oddity learning and learning sets in children. *Journal of Experimental Child Psychology*, 1969, *7*, 541–552.

Siegel, L. S. The sequence of development of certain number concepts in preschool children. *Developmental Psychology*, 1971, *5*, 357–361.

Siegel, L. S. Development of the concept of seriation. *Developmental Psychology*, 1972, *6*, 135–137.

Siegel, L. S. The role of spatial arrangement and heterogeneity in the development of concepts of numerical equivalence. *Canadian Journal of Psychology*, 1973, *27*, 351–355.

Siegel, L. S. The development of number concepts: Ordering and correspondence operations and the rule of length cues. *Developmental Psychology*, 1974, *10*, 907–912.

Siegel, L. S. The relationship of language and thought in the young child. Unpublished manuscript, McMaster University, 1976.

Siegel, L. S. The cognitive basis of the comprehension and production of relational terminology. *Journal of Experimental Child Psychology*, 1977, *24*, 40–52.

Siegel, L. S., McCabe, A. E., Brand, J., & Matthews, J. Evidence for the understanding of class inclusion in the preschool child: Linguistic factors and training effects. Unpublished manuscript, McMaster University, 1977.

Siegel, L. S., & Goldstein, A. G. Conservation of number in young children: Recency versus relational response strategies. *Developmental Psychology*, 1969, *1*, 128–130.

Sinclair-de-Zwart, H. Developmental psycholinguistics. In Elkind, D., & Flavell, J. H. (Eds.), *Studies in cognitive development*. New York: Oxford University Press, 1969.

Stern, C., & Bryson, J. Competence versus performance in young children's use of adjectival comparatives. *Child Development*, 1970, *41*, 1197–1201.

Townsend, D. J. Children's comprehension of comparative forms. *Journal of Experimental Child Psychology*, 1974, *18*, 293–303.

Ward, J., & Pearson, L. A comparison of two methods of testing logical thinking. *Canadian Journal of Behavioural Scence*, 1973, *5*, 383–398.

Weil, J. The relationship between time conceptualization and time language in young children. Unpublished doctoral dissertation, The Graduate Center, City University of New York, 1970.

Weiner, S. L. On the development of "more" and "less". *Journal of Experimental Child Psychology*, 1974, *17*, 271–287.

Willoughby, R. H., & Trachy, S. Conservation of number in very young children: A failure to replicate Mehler and Bever. *Merrill–Palmer Quarterly of Behavior and Development*, 1971, *17*, 205–209.

Yost, P. A., Siegel, A. E., & Andrews, J. M. Nonverbal probability judgments by children. *Child Development*, 1962, *33*, 769–780.

4

Learning Research and Piagetian Theory

CHARLES J. BRAINERD
University of Western Ontario

Experiments in which children are trained to acquire concepts from Piaget's stages have been an abiding theme in the cognitive development literature for more than a decade. Most of the experiments have been conducted by North American researchers, but some by Genevan researchers have also appeared recently. Befitting their status as "the main symptoms of a budding system of operational structures" (Inhelder & Sinclair, 1969, p. 3), the conservation concepts of middle childhood have been the focus of most of the experiments. Smaller segments of this literature are concerned with training relational concepts (seriation, transitivity), classificatory concepts (double classification, class inclusion), and spatial concepts (projective imagery).

Several exhaustive reviews of the neo-Piagetian learning literature have been written during the past few years (e.g., Beilin, 1971; Brainerd, 1973a; Brainerd & Allen, 1971a; Glaser & Resnick, 1972; Hatano, 1971; Hooper, Goldman, Storck, & Burke, 1971; Strauss, 1972). For the most part (and quite properly so, in my view), these reviews deal with narrowly defined empirical issues, such as whether Piagetian concepts are in fact trainable, whether trained concepts can be extinguished, whether some training procedures are more effective than others, whether transfer of training occurs, etc. The available data provide reasonably clear answers to these and similar questions. In this chapter I break with the tradition of reviewing the neo-Piagetian learning literature in light of narrowly defined empirical issues and examine some rather more speculative questions. I shall stress the implications of this literature and selected specific findings from it for some key tenets of Piagetian theory. I do this because the literature seems to raise serious doubts about the theory's ability to explain the laboratory learning of Piagetian concepts.

We begin with a discussion of the Genevan perspective on learning research. We then consider Piaget's views on how learning takes place and what can be learned. These views appear in a series of papers by Piaget himself (e.g., Piaget, 1970a,b) and by some of his collaborators (e.g., Inhelder, 1968, 1972; Inhelder, Bovet, Sinclair, & Smock, 1966; Inhelder & Sinclair, 1969; Sinclair, 1973). The same basic ideas, along with eight ostensibly supportive experiments, also appear in a recent book by Inhelder, Sinclair, and Bovet (1974). By considering the Genevan position in some detail, I hope to clarify a question on which there seems to be endless confusion: What is the relationship between Piagetian theory and learning research? It has been widely held—largely, perhaps, as a consequence of Flavell's (1963) classic treatise—that the theory predicts negligible training effects. This interpretation, while correct in spirit, turns out to be something of an oversimplification.

Piaget's position on learning research is not, as is sometimes supposed, that stage-related concepts such as conservation, transitivity, class inclusion, and so on must evolve spontaneously and are not responsive to training. One of Piaget's co-workers states that any such interpretation "would go counter to the developmental theory that is resolutely interactionist and constructionist [Sinclair, 1973, p. 57]." Although the possibility of learning is acknowledged in an absolute sense, the thrust of Piaget's position is to impose constraints that he believes are quite foreign to the conception of learning promulgated by North American psychologists. These constraints deal with how learning takes place and what can be learned. Concerning the former, Sinclair (1973) asserts that training treatments conceived according to "strictly empirical epistemological tenets . . . whereby the subject has to accept a link between events because the link is imposed on him, do not result in progress [p. 57]." The training procedures that do promote learning of Piagetian concepts are those that are microscopic embodiments of the global Piagetian laws of cognitive growth. According to Sinclair (1973), self-discovery training methods are supposed to be especially efficacious because *"active discovery* is what happens in development [p. 58]." Turning to the question of what can be learned, Genevan authors argue that children cannot be taught a given concept unless it is already understood by them to a certain degree. Generally speaking, it is supposed to be impossible for a child functioning at one stage of cognitive development to learn concepts from a subsequent stage. A subject can be taught a concept belonging to some given stage if he is either already at that stage or in a transition phase between that stage and the preceding one. This is because learning a Piagetian concept is supposed to consist not of learning per se but of learning to generalize the mental structures appropriate to a given stage (Brainerd, 1976a, 1977a).

In brief, Piaget's position is that learning occurs when two conditions are met. First, the training treatment incorporates laws of spontaneous development. Second, the to-be-trained subjects already possess the to-be-learned concept to some measurable extent. Below, the meanings of these two conditions are explicated, and the lines of empirical evidence believed to support them are examined.

The How of Learning

Précis of Piaget's Views

If training is to be effective, then it should embody the laws of spontaneous cognitive development identified in Piaget's original cross-sectional studies of the to-be-learned concept. For example, Inhelder and Sinclair (1969) explain how this guiding philosophy affects the design of their learning experiments: "The choice of exercise items has been dictated by what we know of the spontaneous (that is, outside the laboratory) acquisition of the operations or concepts in question [p. 5]." Sinclair (1973) justifies the training procedures reported in a later paper by observing that "learning is dependent on development . . . in the sense that in learning—that is, in situations specifically constructed so that the subject has active encounters with the environment—the same mechanisms as in development are at work to make progress [p. 58]." Finally, Inhelder, Sinclair, and Bovet (1974) explain the choice of training procedures reported in their book on learning as follows: "We started with the idea that under certain conditions an acceleration of cognitive development would be possible, *but that this could only occur if the training resembled the kind of situations in which progress takes place outside an experimental set-up* [p. 24; italics added]." In these

71

and other Genevan tracts of learning, no empirical or logical rationale is offered as grounds for the assumption that children must learn Piagetian concepts in the laboratory in the same way that they learn them in everyday life. The assumption, which is more than slightly reminiscent of Werner's (1948) microgenesis principle, is simply advanced as though it were self-evident.

The general law presumed to govern mental growth outside the laboratory is *construction* (e.g., Piaget, 1967). The construction principle works roughly as follows. The child's own activity is supposedly the chief cause of progress. Children continually engage in manipulative motor behaviors which transform the objects in their environment. These manipulative and transforming behaviors lead to cognitive growth via a dissonance-like process. The general paradigm is simple: (*a*) the child holds some incorrect belief, *A*, that leads him to expect that his behavior will produce certain prescribed consequences in the environment; (*b*) the child *discovers* that the consequences of his behavior are not precisely what *A* leads him to expect, and this leads him to adopt a more appropriate concept, *A'*. The familiar concept of numerical invariance provides a classic illustration. The child of, say, 5 believes that the cardinal number of a set is affected by the spatial configuration of the elements that comprise the set. A collection of *N* tightly packed elements is believed to have a smaller cardinal number than a collection of *N* loosely spaced objects. It is possible for the child to discover the incorrectness of this belief via his own spontaneous behavior. Suppose he is playing with an aggregate of marbles which he arranges in several different configurations. Suppose he counts the marbles each time he rearranges them. Of course, he will discover that, contrary to his hypothesis, the cardinal number of the collection does not change. He might discover the same fact on other occasions about aggregates of pebbles, coins, etc. As a consequence of discoveries of this sort, he eventually acquires a generalized grasp of numerical invariance.

The principle of construction appears to have been borrowed without significant alteration from the philosophy of Henri Bergson.[1] Bergsonian irrationalism, like Piaget's theory, emphasizes that overt behavior is the sole basis for knowledge and is best understood as a reaction to certain tenets of classical empiricist epistemology. Bergson saw traditional epistemology—especially the empiricism of Locke, Berkeley, and Hume—as unacceptably passive. By *passive*, Bergson meant 'contemplative.' Knowledge, in the Bergsonian view, is not ac-

---

[1] Although Bergson is rarely mentioned in Piaget's scientific writings, his influence is acknowledged in Piaget's autobiography (1952).

quired via reflection and contemplation. Instead, it is won through a vigorous and creative struggle to wrest it from the environment. As might be expected, Bergson disparaged contemplative activities such as analysis, reflection, and pedagogy as bases for knowledge. For him, the indispensable element in knowledge was always the impulse to action.[2] So it is with Piaget's construction principle. The crucial fact to bear in mind about construction is the element of action-based self-discovery —that is, Step *b* above. If progress is to occur, the child must *discover for himself* the inconsistencies between his beliefs and the results of his behavior. Whether or not he makes use of such information is, of course, quite another matter. An important tenet is that cognitive progress is not supposed to result simply from showing the child that he is incorrect or telling him so. We saw above how numerical invariance is presumed to emerge via construction. However, suppose we simply tell children repeatedly that they are wrong to believe that configuration affects cardinal number. Or suppose we ask them to observe an expert model making correct judgments of numerical invariance. Or suppose that numerical invariance is demonstrated to children by repeatedly rearranging and counting collections of objects for them. According to Piagetian theory, numerical invariance is not originally acquired as a function of such experiences because in each case the element of self-discovery is lacking.

Insofar as learning experiments are concerned, the construction principle leads to a distinction between training treatments that incorporate a provision for self-discovery and those that do not. The latter treatments, which Piaget and his collaborators view as offshoots of North American learning theory, are called *tutorial methods* herein. Considerable emphasis is placed on this distinction by Inhelder and Sinclair (1969), Inhelder, Sinclair, and Bovet (1974), and Sinclair (1973). It may be taken as fundamental to the Genevan position on learning. Tutorial methods, of course, are not supposed to work very well. Sinclair (1973), for example, advances a strong indictment of such methods by observing that in training experiments in which they have been used, "almost universally the results were negative [p. 57]." We may group all of the familiar procedures from both classical learning theory and social learning theory—for example, operant conditioning, observational learning, learning set—under the heading of tutorial methods.

---

[2] Although Bergson advocated these views passionately, he never bothered to present reasons for believing them to be true (Russell, 1945, Chapter 28). To do so would presumably have been too contemplative and, worse, would have deprived the reader of discovering the truth of Bergson's ideas for himself.

In these latter procedures, self-discovery is treated more as a source of error than as an essential component of learning.

Two tutorial methods are singled out for special criticism in Genevan writings on learning: *prediction–outcome* conflict and *rule instruction*. The former was first used by Smedslund (e.g., 1961a). It consists of asking the child to predict the result of certain stimulus transformations and then providing information that confirms or disconfirms the prediction. To illustrate, consider the numerical invariance concept again and consider some child who believes that spatial configuration affects cardinal number. Suppose that an experimenter poses the familiar number conservation problem. The child is shown two rows of five pennies each and is asked what would happen if one of the rows is shortened. Since he believes that configuration affects manyness, the child replies that the shorter row will have fewer pennies than the longer row. The disconfirming information consists of the experimenter shortening one of the two rows and then counting both rows aloud. Rule instruction, on the other hand, consists of exposing children to algorithms that are relevant to the to-be-learned concept, either by stating them verbally or by demonstrating them perceptually or both. This method was introduced by Beilin (1965) and Wallach and Sprott (1964). Returning to the number conservation problem, there are several rules that may be used to generate correct solutions. One of them is that the cardinal number of an aggregate remains constant so long as elements are neither added nor subtracted. Another is that the shortening transformation could be reversed to give the original configuration. Another is that the decrease in the length of the transformed row is compensated by the increase in its density. We could train these rules by demonstrating them or by explaining them verbally or both. We could then readminister the number conservation problem to determine whether teaching these rules tends to lead to solution.

In place of tutorial methods, the construction principle suggests treatments in which "the subject himself is the mainspring of his development, in that it is his own activity on the environment or his own active reactions that make progress [Sinclair, 1973, p. 58]." Or, according to Inhelder *et al.* (1974) "in terms of successful training procedures . . . the more active a subject is, the more successful his learning is likely to be [p. 25]." It may not be easy at first to see how such statements translate into training procedures that differ in important respects from tutorial methods. Inhelder and Sinclair (1969) clarify matters by observing that although the fine details of self-discovery procedures differ from one concept to another, "in all of them we avoid imposing definite strategies on the child . . . the child is encouraged to make his

own coordinations . . . the child is asked to anticipate the likely outcome of certain transformations and then to observe the actual outcome
of the transformation. . . . In other cases, we aim at a step-by-step
circumscription of the problem destined to make the child aware of
contradictions in his arguments [pp. 4 and 5]."

It is perhaps not immediately apparent that self-discovery learning
differs in any fundamental way from the prediction-outcome method.
Not surprisingly, the key difference lies in the extent to which the child
is an active participant in prediction–outcome conflict. To illustrate, consider a procedure for training liquid quantity conservation reported by
Inhelder *et al.* (1974, Chapter 1). The apparatus, shown in Figure 4.1,
consists of a series of titration vessels of different diameters attached
to a stationary stand. The vessels are arranged vertically so that liquid
may be transferred from one vessel to another. The experimenter explains how the apparatus works. He encourages the child to manipulate
the apparatus and to observe the consequences of transferring liquid

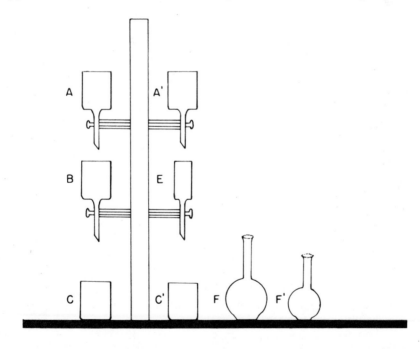

FIGURE 4.1 An apparatus used by Inhelder, Sinclair, and
Bovet (1974) to train liquid quantity conservation. [From
Inhelder, B., Sinclair, H., & Bovet, M. *Learning and the
Development of Cognition.* Cambridge, Massachusetts:
Harvard University Press, 1964. Reprinted by permission.]

from one vessel to another. The child also may be explicitly instructed to transfer liquid from a given vessel to another and to note the result. In contrast, the child is primarily an observer in the prediction-outcome method. It is the experimenter who carries out the liquid transferrals. The child is instructed to pay attention to what the experimenter is doing (he may be rewarded for doing so). The experimenter may verbalize the results of each transferral. The prediction-outcome method of training numerical invariance described above could be converted to a self-discovery procedure by having the child rearrange the elements and count them after each rearrangement. But the experimenter must rigorously avoid telling the child whether his responses are correct or incorrect: "'Such reasoning cannot, and for that matter should not, be eliminated by coercion [Inhelder *et al.*, 1974, p. 25].'"

In Genevan writings, two lines of evidence are used to support the views discussed up to this point. First, against the use of tutorial methods, a series of experiments conducted during the late 1950s and early 1960s by Smedslund (1959, 1961a,b,c) and Wohlwill (1959; Wohlwill & Lowe, 1962) are cited. (See also Inhelder, *et al.*, 1974, pp. 10–14.) In Smedslund's experiments, prediction-outcome procedures were used in unsuccessful attempts to train conservation concepts. To train conservation of weight, for example, the classic test of the concept (Piaget & Inhelder, 1941) was first administered. Children who failed the test proceeded to the training phase. Each training trial began by weighing two objects on a pan balance. After the child had noted the relative weight of the objects, the experimenter deformed one of them in some way and questioned the child about the relative weight of each. After the child had replied, feedback was provided by weighing the objects on the pan balance. The experimenter did not comment on either the predictions or the feedback. The classic weight conservation test was repeated following the training trials. Very few of the subjects learned to conserve. Wohlwill used feedback, rule instruction, and perceptual set to train number conservation. His subjects, like Smedslund's did not learn conservation as a result of such training. The negative fiindings of these early experiments are the only *empirical* grounds for eschewing tutorial methods cited in Genevan discussions of learning (cf. Brainerd, 1977b).

The second line of evidence is a series of experiments using self-discovering training that were conducted in Geneva. The designs of these experiments and some pilot data have been reported in several papers (e.g., Inhelder, 1968, 1972; Inhelder, Bovet, Sinclair, & Smock, 1966; Inhelder & Sinclair, 1969; Sinclair, 1973). A more complete report of the experiments appears in a recent book by Inhelder *et al.*

(1974). One self-discovery procedure, for training liquid quantity, has already been discussed. A very similar procedure is used to train length conservation (Inhelder *et al.*, 1974, Chapter 2). Children who passed a test for number conservation but failed a test for length conservation were trained to adopt a numerical strategy to solve length conservation problems. The children were asked to construct "roads" of various lengths using match sticks. The experimenter questioned the children about the relative lengths of the roads they constructed. It was hoped that this procedure would lead them to discover that continuous lengths may be thought of as fixed numbers of equal unit lengths. When conceptualized in this manner, two continuous lengths remain equal as long as the number of unit lengths is not altered. The emphasis was on the children discovering the principle for themselves: They constructed the roads by themselves, and although the experimenter posed questions, the children were not told which of their answers were correct and which were incorrect. In other words, feedback, in the usual sense, was absent. Inhelder and her colleagues (1974) report improvements in both conservation (Chapters 1, 2, 3, 6, 7, and 8) and class inclusion (Chapters 7 and 8) as a result of self-discovery training. By comparison with tutorial methods and subject to some qualifications discussed later on in this chapter, the investigators conclude that such methods are effective procedures for training Piagetian concepts.

Before discussing criticisms of these views about how learning takes place, some brief remarks are in order about what is meant by "improvement" in a Piagetian concept as a function of training. This question is usually termed the "criterion problem" in the literature, and it has been a source of continuous debate between Genevan and non-Genevan researchers (e.g., Braine, 1962; Brainerd, 1973b, 1974a, 1975, 1977c; Brainerd & Hooper, 1975; Gruen, 1966; Reese & Schack, 1974; Strauss, 1972). The problem is that, largely as a matter of principle, Genevan investigators maintain that the only acceptable improvement consists of *general advances* on several dependent variables. Specific improvement on the trained dependent variable is not viewed as credible evidence of learning. For example, to have learned conservation during training, a subject must (*a*) give correct answers on a repetition of the pretest for that concept; (*b*) give correct answers on a test for that concept that uses different stimuli than the pretest; (*c*) give logically acceptable explanations for the answers on *a* and *b*; (*d*) pass a test for at least one other conservation concept; and (*e*) continue to meet criteria *a–d* several days after training. The use of such an insensitive learning criterion—insensitive in that only massive changes in behavior can be detected by it—has been criticized on both theoretical and psychometric grounds by investigators outside Geneva. These latter investigators usually view *a, b,* and *c* as more than adequate evidence that learning has occurred.

In place of a detailed consideration of the various points at issue in the criterion debate, I should simply like to note that the debate is something of a straw man because there is a considerable difference between the criteria Geneva investigators advocate and those they actually employ. The length conservation experiment mentioned above provides a case in point. Inhelder and Sinclair (1969) reported that 65% of their subjects "profited from the learning procedure [p. 10]." Close inspection reveals that a minority of the subjects who "profited" were able to meet criteria *a–e*. For example, only 43% were able to provide explanations of their answers. Hence, although I certainly do not wish to minimize the significance of the issues involved in the criterion debate, it would seem, nevertheless, that the debate is somewhat academic. Methodological manifestos notwithstanding, there is little practical difference between the behavioral changes that Genevan and non-Genevan investigators accept as evidence of learning (see also Brainerd, 1973a).

Analysis of Piaget's Views

We now consider some objections to the preceding account of the conditions under which children learn concepts in the laboratory. Before examining these objections, it should be noted that detailed consideration will not be given to the various methodological anomalies that characterize Genevan experiments using self-discovery training. Two obvious anomalies are the lack of standardization of the training trials and the use of extremely small subject samples. Concerning standardization, the fact that the steps in the training trials vary from one subject to another means, among other things, that these experiments cannot be replicated with any precision. Concerning sample size, it is difficult to place much faith in the stability of findings from 5 or 10 subjects. While methodological problems such as these are not to be dismissed lightly, it seems unlikely to me that a detailed analysis of them will prove fruitful as a means of evaluating the views discussed above. I think such an analysis would lead to the conclusion that more research is needed. By considering other issues, a more definitive evaluation may be possible.

In place of a methodological analysis, we examine logical and empirical objections to, first, the general thesis that training treatments must reflect laws of spontaneous cognitive development and, second, the specific emphasis on self-discovery training. Concerning the former, this thesis rests on some Rousseauian predispositions whose validity is considerably less than obvious. Concerning the latter, existing experiments provide no support for the claim that the learning of Piagetian concepts takes place exclusively or primarily under conditions of self-discovery. It turns out that there are flaws in the designs of the early experiments on which Piaget and his collaborators base their rejection of tutorial procedures. Recent research indicates that these procedures are successful when the flaws are eliminated. But, more important, there are many other tutorial training methods that do not figure in the Genevan indictment of such procedures. The available data on these procedures suggest that they work at least as well as, and probably better than, self-discovery training.

IS MOTHER NATURE ALWAYS RIGHT?

The Genevan perspective on learning involves some distinctly Rousseauian biases that should be recognized for what they are; namely, assumptions rather than self-evident truths. These biases are especially apparent in the thesis that (a) there are important differences between what goes on in everyday ("spontaneous") cognitive development and laboratory learning; and (b) the latter should or must reflect the principles that operate in the former. Among other things, this thesis suggests that laboratory learning research has no unique contributions to make outside the context of spontaneous cognitive development. We developmental psychologists seem to be inexorably drawn to any doctrine that puts spontaneous development first and the laboratory study of learning second (cf. Brainerd, 1977a; White, 1970). Consequently, the Genevan assumption that training treatments should reflect the laws of spontaneous cognitive growth is never discussed in the literature and is rarely recognized as something other than a self-evident truth. However, the evidence for this doctrine is far from compelling, and I do not propose to leave it unexamined. Since the doctrine is Rousseauian in origin, we begin with a brief reprise of Rousseau's philosophy. This sketch, which strays considerably from our main theme, is intended to suggest that the "mother nature is always right" element in Piagetian learning theory is a dubious maxim. Later, near the end of this section, we return to the doctrine itself and examine it in light of the points raised in the discussion of Rousseau.

Historically, Rousseau's philosophy was a rebellion against the main social and intellectual currents of the Age of Reason. During the sixteenth and seventeenth centuries, memories of the barbarism and anarchy of the Middle Ages were still fresh in Europe. Philosophers busied themselves with the construction of systems of thought that would reinforce social stability. The two most influential philosophical schools of the Age of Reason, continental rationalism and British empiricism, are good illustrations. As everyone knows, one essential ingredient of a stable society is the capacity to delay gratification of present desires for the sake of future rewards. All civilizations are based on this principle, which is codified in the notion of law. Both rationalist and empiricist philosophers exalted prudence as the chief moral virtue—prudence embodies respect for man-made law, which in turn embodies the capacity to delay gratification. Reason was exalted as the source of prudence and was assigned the imposing task of creating order from the chaos of nature.

In politics, the goal of weaving a stable social fabric suggested both utilitarian ethics and the need to curtail individual liberties for the sake of social stability. To our minds, these doctrines may evoke the specter of authoritarianism. However, since rationalists and empiricists viewed the effects of civilization as almost entirely beneficial, they advocated both doctrines. Since they also believed that civilization exerted a perfecting influence on human nature, they greatly valued the intellectual traditions—especially science, mathematics, and technology—that make civilization possible. In their view, the functions of education were to transmit these traditions, reinforce civilized values, encourage restraint in the expression of strong emotion, and, above all, promote the use of reason and the exercise of prudence.

For various reasons, not the least of which was a longing for adventure and excitement, Rousseau rebelled against the proportionate and well-ordered world of the Age of Reason. Rather than cultivate reason and prudence, Rousseau preferred the antithesis, which was called *la sensibilité* in his day. According to the doctrine of *la sensibilité*, mankind should strive for passionate emotional expression rather than planned and measured lives. Knowledge and truth, according to this doctrine, are corrupted by reason; they are to be found instead in human emotion. In place of self-restraint, *la sensibilité* substituted the direct and violent expression of spontaneous feelings.[3] As might be expected, Rousseau rejected the principle that the liberty of individuals must be restricted to insure the stability of society. He set up rugged individualism in its place. Utilitarian values were also rejected, and aesthetic values substituted. Rousseau deplored science, mathematics, and technology because, although there is no doubting their utility, they are not aesthetically pleasing to a mind unaided by reason.

---

[3] There are some interesting parallels between *la sensibilité* and the modern encounter group movement in psychotherapy which have been discussed by my colleague Kellog Wilson (1975).

Rousseau argued that civilizing intellectual traditions promote immorality by leading men to desire things of which they have no need in their natural state. He expanded this theme in his *Discourses on Inequality*, in which he advanced the famous maxim that "man is naturally good and only by institutions is he made bad." Most of the philosophical doctrines for which Rousseau is remembered today were first introduced in the *Discourses*. The most important of these was the doctrine of natural law, which inspired the constitution and led to the French Revolution. The doctrine states that civilized institutions should not be governed by the need to promote artificial social goals such as peace, stability, and economic well-being. An "artificial" goal is one not to be found in man's natural state and, therefore, must be regarded as a social fiat. Instead, institutions should be governed by what we know of this natural state. Natural man, or the "noble savage," as Rousseau preferred to call him, is spontaneously virtuous. By creating stables societies, we run the risk of corrupting man and destroying his spontaneous virtue. However, if we remain determined to create such societies, we must study uncivilized man and determine the principles that govern his existence in the natural state. If we have more than our share of luck, we may be able to minimize the damage done by civilization. We may even be able to learn more about man's natural state and how to promote it. But we cannot hope to *improve* upon the natural state. Improvement is an illusion—or, more precisely, a delusion. Mother nature is always right. At the very most, we may be able to create institutions that promote the status quo of nature. Since the chances of doing so are not promising, Rousseau thought it wiser to abandon civilization altogether.

Upon reading Rousseau's *Discourses*, Voltaire wrote a letter that said in part: "One longs, in reading your book, to walk on all fours. But as I have lost that habit for more than sixty years, I feel unhappily the impossibility of resuming it. Nor can I embark in search of the savages of Canada because the maladies to which I am condemned render a European surgeon necessary . . . and because the example of our actions has made the savages nearly as bad as ourselves." Voltaire's defense of civilization is, I think, sufficiently eloquent to require no peroration.

Let us turn now from our forensic excursion into Rousseau's philosophy to the statements about learning presented earlier. There are some remarkable parallels between these statements and the doctrine of natural law. In fact, to my mind, the former reads like an application of the latter to laboratory learning experiments. For many years, Piaget has euphemistically termed learning research the "American question." He is not convinced that any benefits will accrue from such research for either the child or the scientist. In the first place, he argues that "teaching children concepts that they have not attained in their spontaneous development . . . is completely useless [1970b, p. 30]." Second, since these concepts are going to develop anyway, Piaget finds it difficult to understand why anyone would bother to train them. Third, and most important, Piaget, like Rousseau, fears that by tampering with the natural development of concepts we may unknowingly interfere with ongoing spontaneous process to the detriment of cognitive growth as a whole. On this point, Piaget favors the following cryptic illustration: "Is it good to accelerate the learning of these concepts? Acceleration is certainly possible, but first we must find out whether it is desirable or harmful. Take the concept of object permanency. . . . A kitten develops this concept at four months, a human baby at nine months; but the kitten stops right there while the baby goes on to learn more advanced concepts [p. 31].

The message is transparently Rousseauian. If we do not take care to preserve the natural order of things, we may, through our well-meaning interference, make children less like human beings and more like animals. To minimize the risk of damage, we should look to the laws of spontaneous cognitive development for our training procedures. This, as we already have seen, is the core of the Genevan approach to learning. But this approach carries with it a devastating implication that all but trivializes learning research. If we use only treatment variables which embody established laws of cognitive development, we cannot reasonably expect to uncover new acquisition processes. At best, training research serves as a replication ground for findings from cross-sectional and longitudinal studies. Thus, in their recent book on learning, three of Piaget's collaborators (Inhelder, Sinclair & Bovet, 1974) cite confirmation of existing Piagetian laws, rather than the discovery of new ones, as the chief rationale for the experiments reported in the book. For my part, I find it difficult to become enthusiastic about experiments whose horizons are so limited. I think this may also explain why so little learning research has been conducted in Geneva.

Whatever may be the other merits of the thesis that training procedures should or must incorporate the laws of spontaneous cognitive development, self-evidence is not among them. We shall see that the available evidence from learning experiments is either equivocal or nonsupportive. For now, let us be clear about just this much. There is no immutable law—or at least none that anyone has ever been able to discover—that says that spontaneous cognitive development is the best cognitive development. To maintain, as Piaget does, that spontaneous cognitive development *is* the best cognitive development is to betray Rousseauian biases; it is not to state a law of nature. There is no law that says either that major laboratory deviations from spontaneous acquisition processes are likely to be harmful or, more important, that we cannot improve on mother nature by using innovative procedures in the laboratory. The use of procedures that are constrained by what we know (or think we know) about development is a matter of preference and nothing more. To maintain otherwise is to place considerably more faith in the wisdom of mother nature than her past performance indicates that she merits.

Not only is the essential wisdom of mother nature in doubt, two specific findings about the acquisition of Piagetian concepts suggest that she is a good deal less omnipotent than Piaget supposes. The first finding concerns cross-cultural differences in the acquisition of such concepts. Consistent with his emphasis on spontaneous development, Piaget expects only trivial cross-cultural differences. In particular, he predicts that apart from temporal deviations, the concepts associated with his global stages of cognitive development are culturally universal up to and including the concrete-operational stage. A substantial amount of research has been devoted to this problem in recent years (e.g., Bruner, Olver, & Greenfield, 1966; Cole & Scribner, 1974; Scribner & Cole, 1973). There is now reason to believe that familiar concrete-operational concepts such as conservation are not culturally universal. It seems that mother nature has been shamefully neglecting the spontaneous development of primitive peoples. A second finding concerns what learning research has had to say about the particular training procedure, self-discovery learning, that is supposed to embody the laws of spontaneous development. It will be recalled that training methods that fail to provide for self-discovery are not supposed to work very well. Therefore, we should find, at the very least, that there are clear differences between the amounts of learning observed for tutorial methods and those for self-discovery training and that these differences favor the latter. But we shall see that the learning literature provides no support for this prediction.

To summarize, there is no reason to suppose, in advance of the data, that the best procedures for training Piagetian concepts are those which imitate processes operating in everyday life. Although Piaget and his collaborators make this assumption, it can be argued that their reasons for doing so are primarily philosophical. Moreover, a little analysis reveals that the distinction on which the assumption is predicated—the distinction between behavioral changes induced in the laboratory and "spontaneous (that is, outside the laboratory) acquisition"—is not very profound. In fact, it is vacuous. The credibility of the distinction turns on an implicit faith that (a) there is some independently validated continuum of learning methods running from those that are "natural" to those that are "artificial" and "contrived"; and that (b) procedures of the latter sort are to be found in laboratories. But there is no such continuum of learning methods. Even if there were, it would not follow that the most natural procedures (i.e., those best attuned to the state of the organism) are those based on everyday life. The environments inside and outside the laboratory, though somewhat different, are both environments in which learning occurs. There is not the slightest reason to suppose that factors responsible for learning outside the walls of laboratories are, somehow, better attuned to the state of the organism than factors responsible for learning inside the walls of laboratories. The criteria for judging how "natural" a learning procedure is have nothing to do with where we happen to find it. They are concerned with, first, whether a procedure works and, second, how well it works. If an organism derives considerable benefit from a given procedure, then that procedure apparently is attuned to the state of the organism and, consequently, is "natural" for that organism.

THE EFFECTIVENESS OF SELF-DISCOVERY AND TUTORIAL TRAINING

Armed with the working hypothesis that the most natural procedures for learning Piagetian concepts are the ones that are the most effective, we now examine some selected findings on various procedures. We shall be especially concerned to determine whether tutorial procedures are effective methods of training Piagetian concepts and whether active self-discovery training produces learning that is superior to that produced by tutorial training. Concerning tutorial procedures, I noted earlier that the only empirical grounds for rejecting such methods cited by Piaget and his collaborators are the early experiments by Smedslund and Wohlwill. Apart from the obvious logical error involved in inferring the truth of a null hypothesis, this fact poses two problems. First, it turns out that there are design flaws in the experiments of both Smedslund and Wohlwill that probably militated against learning. If these flaws are eliminated, it is possible that children would learn the concepts. Second, even if Smedslund and Wohlwill's original procedures never work, they certainly do not exhaust the universe of tutorial procedures.

We begin with the question of whether tutorial procedures produce learning. Smedslund (1961a,c) used three prediction–outcome procedures to train conservation of weight: direct reinforcement of weight judgments, reinforcement of the addition–subtraction rule, and reinforcement of the size–weight rule. His subjects failed to learn weight conservation as a function of any of these procedures. However, Hatano (1971) has argued that the omission of some rather elementary precautions could have produced the negative findings. For example, learning could not take place in any of Smedslund's conditions if the subjects did not understand how a pan balance works. Since knowledge of the workings of pan balances is not common among first grade children (the age level of Smedslund's subjects), two precautions should have been taken to insure understanding. First, the subjects should have received pretraining on the use of pan balances. Second, the experimenter should have verbalized the outcome of each weighing operation during the training trials (e.g., "the balance says these two objects weigh the same" or "the balance says that this object weighs more"). Neither precaution was taken. An even simpler way to avoid the problem would be to eliminate the balance and allow the subjects to determine relative weight by lifting the objects.

In addition to Hatano's criticisms, there are other problems with Smedslund's three procedures. Concerning his direct reinforcement procedure, it will be recalled that "same" is always the correct response to the classic weight conservation test (Piaget & Inhelder, 1941)—that is, the two objects are always the same weight no matter what they look like. However, on half the direct reinforcement training trials, the two objects were of unequal weight at the outset. Hence, the response that was reinforced following perceptual deformation was the reverse of the response that the subject would be required to make on weight conservation tests administered after training. Concerning addition–subtraction rule training, the effects of adding or subtracting on weight were not unambiguous. On each trial, a piece of clay was added to or subtracted from one of two clay balls. But the subjects were not allowed to weigh the two balls *before* the pieces of clay were added and subtracted. Hence, they did not know whether the objects were equal or unequal to begin with. Concerning size–weight rule training, there is very little reason to believe a priori that this rule is closely connected with the concept of conservation of weight. In fact, just the reverse is true. Normative data indicate that most first grade children understand that weight is not strictly dependent on size. Yet very few of these same children conserve weight. This suggests that if we wish to train weight conservation, the size–weight rule probably is not a very good place to begin.

In view of what has just been said, it is possible that direct reinforcement and addition–subtraction training are more effective than Smedslund's experiments indicate. Studies by Gelman (1969) and

Hatano and Suga (1969) confirm this suggestion. Gelman used direct reinforcement to induce number and length conservation. The training trials consisted of three-term oddity discriminations—that is, three stimuli were present of which two had the same number of elements or were the same length. On the number trials, the subjects were asked, alternatively, to select the two stimuli with the same number or to select the stimulus with a different number. On the length trials, the subjects were asked, alternatively, to select the two stimuli of the same length or select the stimulus of different length. On all trials, the subjects received a token if their choice was correct. Impressive improvements in both number and length conservation were observed. The subjects' explanations of their number and length judgments, which were not reinforced during training, also improved markedly. Training generalized to an untrained conservation concept (quantity), and the effects of training were still evident two to three weeks later. Hatano and Suga (1969) used addition–subtraction training to induce number conservation. Their procedure differed from Smedslund's only in that pan balances were not used and the subject's attention was drawn to addition and subtraction operations by verbalizing the outcomes. Roughly 60% of the subjects acquired number conservation as a function of such training. The learning effect generalized to new materials and was evident on a delayed posttest.

Turning to Wohlwill's experiments (Wohlwill, 1959; Wohlwill & Lowe, 1962), Wohlwill used three tutorial procedures to train number conservation: perceptual set training; rule training; reinforcement of number judgments. None of these methods produced improvements surpassing those of control subjects. However, a complicated apparatus was used that, like Smedslund's pan balance, children may not have understood. In subsequent experiments without this apparatus, all three procedures have produced learning effects (for a review, see Brainerd, 1973a).

Smedslund and Wohlwill's procedures are not the only tutorial methods that have been devised for training Piagetian concepts. There are four others on which reasonably extensive evidence is now available, namely, *simple correction, rule learning, observational learning,* and *conformity training.* Simple correction resembles Smedslund and Wohlwill's direct reinforcement techniques. Subjects who fail a pretest for some concept are given several more administrations of the same test during training. Each of these subsequent administrations is accompanied by verbal feedback from the experimenter (e.g., "you're right" or "you're wrong"), and the subject may also receive a tangible reward (e.g., candy or a token) following correct responses. To date, correction training has been successfully employed in experiments designed to train several types of conservation (Brainerd, 1972a,b, 1974b, 1976b, 1977b; Brainerd & Allen, 1971b; Bucher & Schneider, 1973; Figurelli & Keller, 1972; Overbeck & Schwartz, 1970; Siegler & Liebert, 1972), transitivity (Brainerd, 1974b), and class inclusion (Ahr & Youniss, 1970; Brainerd, 1974b; Youniss, 1971). Moreover, the observed learning effects meet all of the Genevan criteria discussed earlier. The subjects' explanations of their judgments have improved (e.g., Brainerd 1972a; Siegler & Liebert, 1972); the learning effects have transferred to un- trained stimuli (e.g., Overbeck & Schwartz, 1970); the learning effects have transferred to new concepts (e.g., Brainerd, 1974b, 1977b; Brainerd & Allen, 1971b); and the learning effects have been retained across intervals of days or weeks (e.g., Brainerd, 1974b, 1977b; Siegler & Liebert, 1972).

Rule learning consists of teaching subjects some specific rule (or rules) which may subsequently be used to generate correct responses on a concept test. Smedslund's addition–subtraction procedure and Wohlwill's reversibility procedure are special cases of rule learning. Although Genevan investigators have rejected rule learning as a train- ing procedure (cf. Inhelder & Sinclair, 1969; Sinclair, 1973), it has been extensively used outside Geneva to train conservation concepts. In most of these experiments, subjects have been taught an *inversion* rule (the effects of a conservation transformation can be negated by an opposite transformation). However, a *compensation* rule (the effects of a con- servation transformation on a given parameter are compensated by equal and opposite changes in some other parameter) and an *identity* rule (conservation transformations do not affect the quantitative rela- tionship between two stimuli) have also been used. These rules have been taught by demonstrating them and by stating them verbally. Beilin (1965) introduced the latter procedure, which has the advantage of being able to expose children to several rules simultaneously. With the demonstration method, on the other hand, only one rule can be taught at a time. Training single or multiple rules via demonstration and/or verbal presentation has proved to be an effective procedure. Improvements in conservation have resulted from training the inversion rule alone (e.g., Brison, 1966; Schnall, Alter, Swanlund, & Schweitzer, 1972; Wallach & Sprott, 1964), training the compensation rule alone (e.g., Goldschmid, 1968, 1971; Halford & Fullerton, 1970), and train- ing the identity rule alone (Hamel & Riksen, 1973). Improvements in conservation have also resulted from concurrent verbal instruction on more than one rule (e.g., Beilin, 1965; Siegler, 1973; Siegler & Liebert, 1972). As was the case for simple correction, the improvements in conservation as a function of rule instruction satisfy the Genevan criteria of generality and durability.

Observational learning methods have been used in several recent experiments (for a review, see Zimmerman & Rosenthal, 1974a). The basic procedure, which has been employed with considerable success (e.g., Brison & Bereiter, 1967; Charbonneau, Robert, Bourassa & Gladu-Bissonette, 1976; Murray, 1974; Rosenthal & Zimmerman, 1972; Sullivan, 1967; Waghorn & Sullivan, 1970; Zimmerman & Rosenthal, 1974b), consists of having children who fail pretests for some concept observe a model taking the same tests. In certain experiments, the subjects observe a live model, while in others they observe a filmed model. Like observational learning experiments, conformity experiments are inspired by social-learning theory. The training procedure, which was introduced by Murray (1972), is a modification of the Asch-type conformity paradigm. Children who fail pretests for a concept are grouped with one or more children who passed the same tests. During training, several administrations of the pretests are given, and the children are told that they may not give individual responses on these tests. They are instructed to discuss each test question and to formulate a consensual answer. After training, the children who originally failed the pretests are posttested to determine whether or not their performance has improved. Botvin and Murray (1975), Cloutier (1973), Murray (1972), and Silverman and Geiringer (1973) all have reported improvements in conservation following conformity training. In Murray's original research, for example, six conservation concepts (number, mass, space, liquid quantity, discontinuous quantity, weight) were subjected to conformity training in two experiments. Roughly 79% of the pretest nonconservers learned all five concepts. Roughly 81% of the pretest nonconservers showed transfer to two untrained conservation concepts (length and area). Both the judgment and explanation responses of Murray's subjects improved, and all improvements were stable across a 1-week interval.

Generally speaking, therefore, existing neo-Piagetian learning experiments in which tutorial training procedures were used raise serious doubts about the truth of the conjecture (Sinclair, 1973) that "empirical methods, whereby the subject has to accept a link between events because this link is imposed upon him, do not result in progress [p. 57]." The four tutorial methods on which adequate evidence is available have produced improvements in the trained concepts that satisfy all the usual Genevan learning criteria. This brings me to the question of the relative effectiveness of tutorial and self-discovery procedures. If it could be shown that the latter procedures routinely produce more learning than the former, Piaget's view of learning would receive at least partial support. Unfortunately, there exists only one experiment (Botvin & Murray, 1975) that resembles a direct factorial comparison of tutorial and self-discovery training. Botvin and Murray administered pretests of mass, weight, quantity, and number conservation to first- and second-graders. Using the conformity paradigm as their basic procedure, they assigned nonconservers to two training conditions that varied the degree of subjects' active involvement in training. In the "active" condition, nonconservers debated verbally with conservers. In the "passive" condition, nonconservers merely observed subjects in the "active" condition from a distance of about 10 feet. Consistent with Piagetian theory, Botvin and Murray predicted more learning in the first condition. But the amounts of learning observed for the two conditions were not significantly different. In fact, the amount of pretest–posttest improvement was slightly greater in the "passive" condition.

In view of the absence of direct factorial comparisons of tutorial and self-discovery learning, we are left with the rather more hazardous option of comparing the results of purely tutorial experiments with the results of Genevan self-discovery experiments. Such a comparison obviously presupposes that sufficient data are available in both corners so that we may be confident that the key findings are stable and replicable. Although, as we have seen, extensive evidence on tutorial learning is available, the self-discovery data are meager. Genevan investigators have reported only six such experiments—five on conservation (Inhelder et al., 1974, Chapters 1, 2, 3, 6, and 8) and one on class inclusion (Inhelder, Sinclair, & Bovet, 1974, Chapter 7).[4] Moreover, these experiments involve very small numbers of subjects and suffer from the design anomalies discussed earlier. This means that we cannot be very confident about the stability and replicability of learning effects observed in these experiments—at least not at present. Hence, definitive conclusions about the relative effectiveness of tutorial and self-discovery learning must await both the accumulation of a more satisfactory data base on the latter and direct factorial comparisons of the two methods. However, if we are willing to assume the replicability of Genevan findings, it is possible to draw some tentative conclusions. In view of the substantive importance of the relative effectiveness question, I shall make this assumption in what follows.

On the whole, the pretest–posttest improvements observed in

---

[4] It should be noted that self-discovery experiments discussed in earlier papers by these authors (e.g., Inhelder & Sinclair, 1969; Sinclair, 1973) are the same experiments reported in the book by Inhelder et al. (1974).

Genevan self-discovery experiments are not nearly as impressive as those that have been observed with the four tutorial procedures. Five conservation experiments—four concerned with quantity conservation (Inhelder *et al.*, 1974, Chapters 1, 2, 3, and 8) and one concerned with length conservation (Inhelder *et al.*, 1974, Chapter 6)—and one class inclusion experiment (Inhelder *et al.*, 1974, Chapter 7) have been conducted. Rather than report exact quantitative figures for pretest–posttest improvement, Inhelder, Sinclair, and Bovet reported the numbers of trained subjects who evidenced each of three response patterns: *no progress* (posttest performance was more or less the same as pretest performance); *partial progress* (posttest performance was better than pretest performance but was not perfect); *complete progress* (posttest performance was perfect). In the six experiments just mentioned, the percentages of subjects in these categories were roughly as shown in Table 4.1.

A crucial fact about these data is that subjects who showed some evidence of learning on the posttest (partial or complete progress) always had partial knowledge of the trained concept. In four of the five conservation experiments (Inhelder *et al.*, 1974, Chapters 2, 3, 6, and 8), all of the trained subjects had already passed a pretest for conservation of number. In the remaining conservation experiment (Chapter 1), only 15 of the 33 subjects failed all of the conservation pretests. Following training, only 2 of these 15 subjects (13%) showed any evidence of learning, and these subjects made only partial progress. In the class inclusion experiment, 16 of the 19 subjects failed all of the pretests for class inclusion. On the posttests, only 9 of these subjects showed clear improvement. Overall, therefore, the data presented by Inhelder *et al.* (1974) suggest that their self-discovery procedures are moderately successful techniques for teaching subjects who already possess sufficient

TABLE 4.1

Percentages of Subjects Showing No Progress, Partial Progress, and Complete Progress in Genevan Experiments

	No progress	Partial progress	Complete progress
Quantity A (Chapter 1)	46%	33%	21%
Quantity B (Chapter 2)	46%	31%	23%
Quantity C (Chapter 3)	14%	43%	43%
Quantity D (Chapter 8)	21%	53%	26%
Length (Chapter 6)	38%	31%	31%
Class inclusion (Chapter 7)	26%	37%	37%

knowledge of the to-be-trained concept to generalize their knowledge to new situations. However, the effectiveness of self-discovery procedures with subjects who have no prior knowledge of the to-be-trained concept appears minimal. In the only conservation experiment in which nonconservers were studied, self-discovery training produced no evidence of learning in such subjects.

I believe it is fair to say that tutorial experiments, especially those published between 1969 and the present, have produced learning effects that are far more substantial than those reported by Inhelder *et al.* (1974). The Murray (1972) data discussed earlier are illustrative. Moreover, unlike self-discovery procedures, tutorial procedures have produced large learning effects in subjects with no prior grasp of the to-be-trained concept (for reviews, see Brainerd, 1973a, 1977a). Rather than present lengthy supporting documentation for these claims, I think two concrete examples might be more instructive. First, I shall compare the results of Inhelder, Sinclair, and Bovet's initial quantity conservation experiment (1974, Chapter 1) with a very similar tutorial experiment published by Sheppard (1974). Second, I shall compare the results of Inhelder, Sinclair, and Bovet's class inclusion experiment (1974, Chapter 7) with another experiment conducted by Sheppard (1973).

The self-discovery procedure for training quantity conservation, which makes use of the apparatus shown in Figure 4.1, focuses on the compensation rule (changes in the height of a quantity of liquid are compensated by equal and opposite changes in width) and was summarized earlier. Sheppard's (1974) procedure focuses on the same rule and makes use of the apparatus shown in Figure 4.2. The notable differences between Sheppard's procedure and Inhelder, Sinclair, and Bovet's procedure were that Sheppard's subjects were passive observers rather than active participants and that Sheppard's subjects were told whether or not their responses were correct. The training trials began with the experimenter drawing the subject's attention to the height and width differences between the containers in the matrix shown in Figure 4.2. Each trial began with the experimenter filling one of the 16 containers with water and asking the subject to predict what the level of the water would be if it were poured into one of the remaining 15 containers. To provide feedback, the experimenter then poured the water into the previously indicated container and gave the subject a verbal statement of the results. Several trials of this sort were administered, all on the same day. (By comparison, Inhelder, Sinclair, and Bovet's subjects received training trials on two different days.) Of importance is that *none* of the subjects included in Sheppard's experiment showed any evidence of conservation—they failed all the pretests. After train-

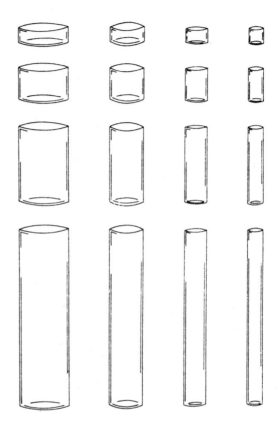

FIGURE 4.2 An apparatus used by Sheppard (1974) to train liquid quantity conservation. [From Shepard, J. L. Compensation and combinatorial systems in the acquisition and generalization of conservation. *Child Development*, 1974, *45*, 717–730. Reprinted by permission.]

ing, Sheppard readministered the pretests. He reported that depending on the particular test, between 30% and 40% of the subjects progressed to perfect performance. Virtually all of the remaining subjects showed partial progress. The observed learning effects generalized to four untrained conservation concepts (number, mass, length, weight), were accompanied by logical explanations, and were stable across a 2-month interval following training. By way of comparison, the corresponding figures for Inhelder, Sinclair, and Bovet's experiment are 21% perfect performance, 33% partial progress, 46% no progress. Moreover, all of the subjects in the first two groups (except two) passed some of the quantity conservation pretests, whereas Sheppard's subjects failed all of the pretests. In short, Sheppard was able to produce better learning in subjects who knew far less about conservation to begin with.

Turning to class inclusion, the Genevan procedure (Inhelder *et al.*, 1974, Chapter 7) consisted of having children add and subtract elements from various concrete classes. Specific addition and subtraction operations were hinted at by the experimenter. However, as is the custom with self-discovery training, the experimenter did not require the performance of given operations and provided no feedback about the correctness of any of the operations actually executed by the subject. The subjects were given a total of six training sessions, each lasting approximately 30 minutes. Sheppard, on the other hand, employed a rule-training procedure. His subjects were trained on an addition rule (the numerical relation between a given class and any other class changes when elements are added to the given class) and an identity rule (the numerical relation between a given class and any other class remains constant as long as no elements are added to or subtracted from the given class). By comparison with the Genevan procedure, Sheppard's method was very brief (10 trials administered during a single session). On posttests administered 1 to 2 weeks after training and 3 to 4 months after training, 40% of the subjects had progressed to perfect class inclusion performance and 20% had made partial progress. As noted earlier, the corresponding figures for self-discovery training were 37% and 37%, respectively. All of Sheppard's subjects failed all of the pretests, whereas some of the Genevan subjects passed some of the pretests.

The What of Learning

Précis of Piaget's Views

Learning is reduced to development in Piagetian theory (cf. Piaget, 1967, Chapter 5, 1970a, pp. 713–715). In other words, learning, in the usual sense of the word, is viewed as a special case of development: "Learning is no more than a sector of cognitive development which is facilitated by experience [Piaget, 1970a, p. 714]." We have just reviewed some of the implications of this hypothesis for the training regimens used in neo-Piagetian learning experiments. We now examine some of the consequences of this hypothesis for the dependent variables measured in these same experiments.

The primacy of development is said to impose definite limits on what children can be taught in a learning experiment. To begin with, they are supposed to be unable to learn any stage-related concept that has not already spontaneously evolved to a measurable degree: "As for teaching children concepts that they have not attained in their spontaneous development, it is completely useless [Piaget, 1970b, p. 30]." It is presumed to be possible to teach children to apply a naturally acquired concept to new materials and situations, but it is not considered possible to teach the concept in the first place. We now briefly examine the underlying rationale for this surprising prediction.

In Piaget's theory, cognitive development is a stagelike process in which learning is always "subject to the general constraints of the current developmental stage" (Piaget, 1970a, p. 713) and, consequently, is believed to "vary very significantly as a function of the initial cognitive levels of the children [p. 715]." Each stage is characterized by its own unique set of mental structures. When they are in a given stage, children generate the concepts associated with that stage from their mental structures in roughly the same manner that a mathematician generates theorems from previously given rules of inference. Teaching children to acquire such a concept is described as teaching them how to apply their mental structures to new content. Unless the structures appropriate to a given concept are already present, learning cannot operate to induce the concept. If a child's current stage is several steps below the one at which a given concept spontaneously emerges, then training the concept is "completely useless" because the relevant structures are absent. But if a child is at, or only slightly below, the correct stage, the relevant structures will be present and learning may take place.

Since most neo-Piagetian learning experiments have dealt with concrete-operational concepts, the practical implication of the above is that it should not be possible to teach concepts such as conservation, transitivity, or class inclusion to children who possess preoperational mental structures. For example, Inhelder and Sinclair (1969) claim that "operativity is malleable only within certain limits . . . children at the preoperational level do not acquire truly operational structures [p. 19]." Logic suggests that this prediction should be examined by attempting to train various concrete-operational concepts in children who have been independently shown not to possess concrete-operational mental structures. Unfortunately, research of this sort poses an insuperable logical difficulty. The structures that define Piaget's stages—the socalled groupings in the case of the concrete-operational stage—are circular constructs. No methods exist for measuring these structures other than the stage-related concepts whose existence the structures are supposed to explain (cf. Brainerd, 1976a, 1977a; Siegel, this volume).[5] This fact does not seem to bother Piaget, who acknowledges circularity as though it were inescapable: "Without the grouping there could be no conservation of complexes or wholes, whereas the appearance of a grouping is attested by the appearance of a principle of conservation [Piaget, 1950, p. 42]." For our purposes, the important point that follows from the circularity of Piagetian mental structures is that, in learning experiments, we are relegated to examining the acquisition of specific concrete-operational concepts. Fortunately, there are some clear predictions for us to consider. But I wish to emphasize that since none of these predictions is directly concerned with the hypothesized structures that define the concrete-operational stage, data consistent with them may not be construed as providing support for the theory. But data *inconsistent* with them may be construed as providing evidence against the theory. This situation is undesirable, but it is scarcely avoidable.

In Genevan analyses of learning, two principal lines of evidence are interpreted as supporting the hypothesis that development constrains the amount that can be learned in the laboratory. First, there is a presumed interaction between pretest performance and trainability. In Genevan learning experiments, as we have just seen, subjects who show no evidence of the to-be-trained concept on the pretests make little or no progress as a result of training, while subjects who pass some of the pretests make moderate-to-good progress. Subjects of the former sort are called frankly preoperational (Inhelder & Sinclair, 1969, p. 11). The precise behavioral meaning of this label is obscure, but it seems to imply at least two things. First, if we are training some concrete-operational concept (say, conservation) in some specific content area (say, weight), then the frankly preoperational child fails all the pretest items in that area. Second, he also fails conservation pretest items in at least one other content area (say, length). In Genevan experiments, children who satisfy these criteria have not shown any evidence of learning. Subjects who show clear evidence of learning violate one or both criteria.

On the basis of such findings, two claims are made about the pretest performance–trainability interaction, namely, children who fail to meet either or both of the preceding criteria will be easier to train than

---

[5] Hooper, Brainerd, and Sipple (1975) and Weinreb and Brainerd (1975) have reported batteries of tests for the grouping structures. These tests, which are characterized by both high reliability and high construct validity, have not yet been employed as predictor variables in learning research.

children who meet both criteria, and children who meet both criteria will be virtually impossible to train. There are two further predictions that follow from these claims, although neither is explicitly discussed in Genevan writings. First, preschoolers should be almost completely untrainable. Although conservation is known to be acquired at different times in different content areas, even the earliest version of the concept (number conservation) is not usually observed before age 6. Therefore, a sample of, say, 3- and 4-year-olds will ordinarily satisfy both the aforementioned criteria. Since 3- to 4-year-olds fall within the first half of the nominal age range for the preoperational stage, it should be safe to assume that concrete-operational mental structures are not present. Second, the earliest conservation concepts should be far more difficult to train than the later ones. Number conservation, in particular, should be virtually impossible to train. Since normative data show that number conservation is the first conservation concept, a group of children who show no evidence of number conservation is also a group of children that satisfies the aforementioned criteria.

The second line of evidence that is believed to show that development constrains learning is that certain things can only be learned in certain orders. More explicitly, the natural order in which concepts are acquired during spontaneous development cannot be altered in the laboratory. As Sinclair (1973) puts it, "environment can accelerate or retard development, but only rarely can it change its course [p. 58]." This particular variation on the old readiness theme refers to concept development sequences that the theory calls *vertical décalages*. Given any two Piagetian stages, A and B, children are supposed to acquire all of the concepts that characterize A before they acquire any of the concepts that characterize B. Any sequence a–b between some specific concept a from A and some specific concept b from B is a vertical décalage. One is not supposed to be able to reverse a sequence of this sort via training.

Although definitive data have not yet been reported on this prediction, it is rather easy to envision a relevant experiment. The conceptual continuities between successive Piagetian stages seem to provide the most appropriate testing ground. Conservation is the classic illustration. Conservation, of course, is characteristic of the concrete-operational stage. However, the sensorimotor object concept (Piaget, 1954) and the preoperational identity concept (Piaget, 1968) have been interpreted as precursors of conservation. Consider the identity concept and the conservation concept. Suppose that we have a sample of children who possess neither concept. Suppose that we divide our sample into two groups, and that we administer identity training and conservation training to both groups. One group is trained on identity first and conservation second, while the other group is trained on conservation first and identity second. If development constrains learning, the first group should make more progress with conservation than the second group. If development does not constrain learning, the groups should make equal progress with conservation—or at least so Genevan investigators would have us believe. A second experiment that examines more or less the same prediction but more strongly resembles recent Genevan experiments runs as follows. We begin with two groups of subjects. The subjects in one group have passed pretests for identity and failed pretests for conservation. The subjects in the other group have failed pretests for both concepts. The same conservation training treatment is administered to both groups. The second group should make virtually no progress. Depending on the nature of the training treatment, the first group may make moderate-to-good progress.

Analysis of Piaget's Views

There are some logical objections to using either of the preceding lines of evidence as grounds for concluding that development constrains what can be learned in the laboratory. Neither, it turns out, involves findings that are either unique to Piagetian theory or foreign to learning theory. Consequently, neither can tell us anything of significance about the relation between cognitive development and children's concept learning. Both lines of evidence appear, at bottom, to be non sequiturs. In addition to the logical problems, there are experimental data that appear to contradict one of the lines of evidence.

First, let us reconsider the presumed interaction between pretest performance and learning. I noted above that two general claims about this interaction are made in Genevan writings on learning: (a) subjects who pass some pretest items for the to-be-trained concept in the to-be-trained area or who pass all the pretest items for the to-be-trained concept in some not-to-be-trained area are easier to train than subjects who fail all items of both kinds; (b) subjects who fail all items of both kinds are virtually impossible to train. From the standpoint of the learning–development relation, prediction a seems to be a non sequitur. All this prediction says is, first, that it is easier to produce evidence of learning in children who partially grasp a concept than in children who do not grasp it at all and, second, that it is easier to teach children to *transfer* a concept they already grasp to new content than it is to teach them the concept in the first place. The available data on these predictions has been reviewed elsewhere (Brainerd, 1977a), and there does not yet appear to be any direct support for them. But whether or not these predictions are ultimately confirmed by the data, they cannot possibly tell us anything about the presumed relationship between learning and development because neither serves to distinguish Piagetian theory from learning theory. Barring ceiling and floor effects, most learning theories would say that subjects who partially grasp a concept (say, conservation) will be easier to train than subjects who do not. To argue otherwise, as is repeatedly done in Genevan writings on learning, is to suggest a thorough lack of acquaintance with the laws of learning.

Prediction *b* is contradicted by empirical fact. Children who uniformly fail pretests for Piagetian concepts have not proved to be untrainable—far from it. Many investigators using tutorial procedures have reported clear learning effects with subjects who showed no evidence of the trained concept on the pretests. More detailed discussions of these experiments may be found in recent reviews (e.g., Brainerd, 1973a, 1977a). In these experiments, the subjects failed pretests for the trained concept in the to-be-trained area and failed pretests for the trained concept in one or more not-to-be trained areas. For example, Murray (1972) and Rosenthal and Zimmerman (1972) reported impressive learning effects with subjects who failed conservation pretests in six areas. Some of these experiments are subject to the caveat that they did not include pretests for number conservation. Since number is the first area in which conservation usually appears, we cannot be completely certain about the second criterion in prediction *a* above unless subjects are pretested for number conservation. Fortunately, number conservation pretests have been included in several highly successful experiments (e.g., Botvin & Murray, 1975; Gelman, 1969; Murray, 1972; Rosenthal & Zimmerman, 1972; Zimmerman & Rosenthal, 1974b).

There is extensive evidence that subjects who fail all the pretest items in the to-be-trained area and who do not possess conservation in any other area (including number) are trainable. In Gelman's experiment, for example, pronounced learning effects were produced in both trained and untrained areas using children who failed pretests for number, length, mass, and liquid quantity. Gelman's subjects performed perfectly on posttests in the two trained areas (length and number). They gave correct responses about 60% of the time on posttests in the two untrained areas. Similarly, Murray (1972) produced clear evidence of learning in subjects who failed pretests for number, space, mass, liquid quantity, weight, and discontinuous quantity. As mentioned earlier, roughly 79% of the subjects who failed all the pretests learned conservation in the six pretested areas, and 81% showed transfer to untrained areas. Impressive learning effects were also reported by Botvin and Murray (1975), Rosenthal and Zimmerman (1972), and Zimmerman and Rosenthal (1974b).

The training of number conservation per se is also relevant to prediction *b* above. Since number is the first area in which conservation appears, it should be especially difficult to train. Subjects who fail number conservation pretests across the board should show little or no evidence of learning. There is considerable evidence to the contrary. Many successful number conservation learning experiments have been reported. [See Brainerd (1977a) for a more detailed review of number training experiments.] In most of them, some of which have already been discussed, large learning effects were observed with subjects who failed pretests for number conservation across the board. Many of these subjects (e.g., more than 75% in Murray's experiment) performed *perfectly* on the posttests. Thus, the available data on training number conservation does not suggest that this concept is either impossible or even especially difficult for children to learn.

Finally, learning research with preschool children is relevant to prediction *b*. Since preschoolers are far below the nominal age at which concrete-operational thinking structures are supposed to emerge, it should not be possible for such children to learn concrete-operational concepts. Unfortunately, neo-Piagetian learning experiments with preschoolers have been rare. Kindergarten and first grade children are almost always studied. Recently, however, six comprehensive studies have been reported by Brainerd (1974b), Bucher and Schneider (1973), Rosenthal and Zimmerman (1972, Experiment IV), Emrick (1968), and Denney, Zeytinoglu, and Selzer (1977, Experiments 1 & 2). In the Brainerd experiment, separate groups of preschoolers were trained on conservation, transitivity, and class inclusion via the correction procedure described earlier. Improvements of 57%, 87%, and 41% were noted for conservation, transitivity, and class inclusion, respectively, in the trained area (length). All three learning effects transferred to an untrained area (weight) and were stable across a 1-week interval following training. In Bucher and Schneider's experiment, number, mass, and liquid quantity conservation were taught to preschoolers via a graded correction procedure. The procedure produced generalizable and temporally stable conservation in slightly more than half the subjects. Finally, Rosenthal and Zimmerman used a modified version of the observational learning procedure described earlier to teach preschoolers to conserve number, space, mass, weight, liquid quantity, and discontinuous quantity. On the posttests, the subjects passed roughly

35% of the items for the six trained areas. They also passed roughly 30% of the items for untrained areas.

Emrick (1968) trained 4-year-olds on number and length conservation via a learning set procedure and an operant technique. Subjects were posttested for number, length, mass, and liquid quantity conservation two or three weeks after training. On the number and length tests, the subjects passed roughly 73% of the items. There was also clear evidence of transfer. The same subjects passed roughly 41% of the items on the mass and liquid quantity posttests. Denney, Zeytinoglu, and Selzer (1977) reported two experiments. In the first one, they trained 4-year-olds on number and length conservation. The subjects' performance was virtually perfect on number and length tests administered 1 week after training, but no transfer to mass conservation posttests was observed. In the second experiment, they trained 4-year-olds on length and substance conservation. The subjects passed 72% of the items on length and substance posttests administered 1 week after training. This time, transfer was also observed. On posttests for number and weight conservation, the subjects passed 61% and 51% of the items, respectively.

In brief, although a good deal more research is needed with preschool subjects, the available data provide no grounds for supposing that preschoolers cannot be taught concrete-operational concepts. Assuming that there is regularity in nature and these experiments can be replicated, there is every reason to believe that preschoolers are, in fact, trainable.

Now, let us turn to the order in which Piagetian concepts are learned. It will be recalled that the theory states that vertical décalages cannot be reversed in the laboratory. The basic problem with this prediction is that, like prediction a above, it is apparently a non sequitur. It fails to take account of the fact that the vertical décalages between concepts belonging to different Piagetian stages are, for the most part, logically guaranteed. Other writers have commented on this fact (e.g., Flavell, 1972; Flavell & Wohlwill, 1969). Given any two global Piagetian stages, a given concept from a later stage almost always presupposes one or more concepts from the earlier stage. Simply put, concepts associated with the later stage consist of concepts from the earlier stage "plus some other things." This fact entails that any test for concepts from the later stage will also be a test for one or more concepts from the earlier stage and, hence, the later concepts are necessary to pass the test. The previous example of conservation (concrete-operational stage) and identity (preoperational stage) provides an excellent case in point.

Consider the classic number conservation paradigm. We begin with two rows of objects, A and B, whose numerical equivalence is obvious from the fact that the two rows are perceptually identical. Row B is then shortened to yield B'. Behaviorally, conservation concepts consist of asserting that A and B' are numerically equivalent though perceptually nonidentical. Brainerd and Hooper (1975) have observed that this response may be viewed as a conditional statement of the form "If $A = B$, then $A = B'$." What is it that makes this statement true? The question can be answered by reformulating the conservation problem as a syllogism of the form

1. $A = B$ (given by their perceptual identity);
2. $B = B'$ (given by the identity concept);
3. therefore $A = B'$ (conservation response).

Note that Premise 2, which is not given at the outset, is essential to the eventual conclusion. If Premise 2 is not true, then neither is the inference $A = B'$. If Premise 2 is true (and if $A = B$ also), then so is the inference $A = B'$. Now, Premise 2 is the identity concept. It consists of understanding that qualitative and quantitative properties of *single stimuli* are not affected by irrelevant perceptual transformations. Conservation, on the other hand, consists of understanding that the quantitative equivalence of *pairs* of perceptually identical stimuli is not affected when perceptual identity is destroyed. As the syllogism makes clear, it is logically inconceivable that conservation could be understood before identity. This means that although it is possible to construct a test of identity that does not measure subjects' understanding of conservation, it is impossible to construct a valid test of conservation that does not also measure subjects' understanding of identity, albeit indirectly.

I believe the significance of examples such as this is made clearer by leaving the realm of Piagetian theory and considering arithmetic and algebra instead. Standardized mathematics achievement tests administered to millions of school children during this century show, among other things, that children invariably understand arithmetic before they understand algebra. Suppose, just for the sake of argument, that we borrow Piaget's stage metaphor and posit that "mathematical development" is characterized by two global stages which we shall somewhat unimaginatively call the arithmetic stage and the algebra stage. We have a long list of concepts that by virtue of the fact that they are arithmetical may be said to belong to the arithmetic stage. The list includes concepts such as integer, fraction, addition, subtraction, multiplication, division, and so on. We have another list of concepts

101

that by virtue of the fact that they are algebraic may be said to belong to the algebra stage. Concepts such as real number, complex number, power, root, factor, logarithm, and so on appear on the second list. We know that every concept on the second list is a special case of one or more concepts on the first list. Hence, although it is possible to measure all the concepts on the first list without measuring any of the concepts on the second list, it is impossible to devise a valid measure of any of the concepts on the second list that does not also measure some of the concepts on the first list. For example, since the concept of real number is a generalization of the concept of fraction, any test that validly measures the former must also measure the latter. Similarly, since raising a number to a power and converting to logarithms are special cases of multiplication, a valid test of these concepts must also be a test of multiplication. The consequences of these facts are straightforward. First, assuming that we have a group of subjects who fail both arithmetic and algebra pretests, it is obvious that they will learn more about algebra if we teach them arithmetic first than if we do the reverse. Second, if we simply teach them algebra, it is obvious that they will not learn very much because they do not grasp the necessary prerequisite concepts. (Imagine trying to teach a subject who knows no division to take a cube root!) Third, if we teach algebra exclusively, it is likely that we shall only be successful with pupils who already know arithmetic. Note that none of these thoroughly uninteresting outcomes tells us anything about the relationship between learning and development. To borrow Piaget's metaphor again, note in particular that these findings do not show that learning mathematical concepts is somehow constrained by one's stage of mathematical development. Both findings are guaranteed by the nature of our measurement procedures and have nothing whatsoever to do with development.

The implication of these remarks for learning research is this. Since concepts belonging to later Piagetian stages always presuppose concepts belonging to earlier Piagetian stages, training research on vertical décalages tells us nothing of significance about the putative relationship between cognitive development and children's concept learning. When it is claimed that we should be able to reverse such sequences if learning is not constrained by development, we must at least be able to conceive of an alternative sequence. With Piagetian concepts this normally is not possible (cf. Flavell & Wohlwill, 1969). Therein lies the problem. Confirmation of such sequences in training experiments is a completely trivial finding. Even if we found contradictory data, we could not believe them. Our only reasonable conclusion about such data would be that gross measurement or sampling errors had been committed (Brainerd, 1977c; Brainerd & Hooper, 1975).

Conclusions

Piaget has proposed that a new approach to children's concept learning is needed: "we have to redefine learning. We have to think of it differently . . . development is not the sum total of what the individual has learned [quoted from Evans, 1973, p. 67]." This proposal, with its emphasis on the primacy of development and its implicit invocation of the redoubtable readiness principle, strikes a responsive chord in most developmental psychologists. Its intrinsic appeal to developmental audiences notwithstanding, a compelling case has yet to be made for it. The specific claims about conditions under which concept learning occurs and about what concepts can be taught in the laboratory that follow from the proposal suffer from logical problems and from lack of empirical confirmation.

Concerning the conditions under which learning is presumed to occur, the distinction between training procedures that embody laws of spontaneous cognitive growth and artificial laboratory-based procedures is stressed by Piaget and his collaborators. Although much is made of this distinction, it appears to be vapid. It is based on a philosophical bias rather than a law of nature. Further, the appropriate criterion for judging whether a procedure is natural (i.e., attuned to the state of the organism) is how well it works, not whether it is found in children's everyday environments. When this criterion is used, the available data fail to show either that concept learning occurs only with procedures embodying the Piagetian construction principle or that the learning produced by such procedures is superior to that produced by other procedures. On the contrary, the learning effects which have been observed with tutorial procedures are generally more substantial than those that have been observed with active self-discovery. In six experiments reported by Inhelder *et al.* (1974), self-discovery training repeatedly failed to produce evidence of learning in subjects with no prior knowledge of the concepts being trained. In contrast, tutorial procedures have produced large learning effects in such subjects. The doubts expressed by Genevan investigators about the effectiveness of tutorial procedures may reflect lack of acquaintance with the recent literature.

In retrospect, it hardly seems surprising that self-discovery training does not work very well in children with no knowledge of the target concept. When a child possesses no prior knowledge of a concept, common sense suggests that he probably will not suddenly "discover" it during a brief unstructured training session. It should be obvious that experimenters will have to *work* to get such children to learn. Training trials will have to be carefully arranged in a sequence of progressive approximations to the target concept. It may also be necessary to shape up some prerequisite skills before training begins on the target concept. If such procedures work (and we have seen that they do), then it would seem reasonable to conclude that self-discovery is neither the best nor the most natural approach to inducing Piagetian concepts. This statement assumes that the claims about self-discovery learning reviewed earlier in this paper are hypotheses that can be confirmed or disconfirmed by data. Unfortunately, there is a definite aura of untestability associated with these claims. In Genevan learning writings, highly structured procedures that do not involve self-discovery (feedback, learning set, etc.) are characterized as "coercion" (Inhelder *et al.*, 1974, p. 25) and as running "counter to the idea that for true learning to occur the child must be intellectually active [p. 26]." Even if researchers obtain sizeable training effects using non-self-discovery methods, they are still liable to criticism that these effects are not "true learning." But what is true learning? Since, as we have seen, the same learning indexes are employed in Genevan and non-Genevan experiments, this phrase has no discernible empirical meaning. Apparently, it is simply a means of dismissing contradictory findings.

While we are on the subject of untestability, another issue merits brief mention. Suppose, for the sake of argument, we stipulate that the training effects observed in tutorial experiments are instances of "true learning." Genevan investigators can even explain this finding: "Being cognitively active does not mean that the child merely manipulates a given type of material; *he can be mentally active without physical manipulation, just as he can be mentally passive while actually manipulating objects* [Inhelder *et al.*, 1974, p. 25; italics added]." This statement is capable of explaining all possible outcomes and, therefore, is tautologous. If experimentation shows that active self-discovery treatments work better than tutorial treatments, then, fine—the theory is correct. But if experimentation shows that tutorial treatments work as well as, or better than, self-discovery, the theory is not necessarily wrong because tutorial trainees may have been "mentally active" or self-discovery trainees may have been "mentally passive" or both.

To summarize, in the earlier review of what learning research has to say about self-discovery versus tutorial training, it was implicitly assumed that Genevan statements about the former were hypotheses to be submitted to empirical test. Under this assumption, the hypotheses received no support. But the suggestion of untestability is so strong in the Genevan writings that I think we must also consider the possibility that tautologies rather than hypotheses are being advanced.

Turning to the question of what children can be taught, Piaget emphasizes the distinction between learning and development. He argues that development imposes constraints on learning and that children cannot learn concepts that exceed their current stage of cognitive development. Three predictions were discussed in conjunction with this argument: learning interacts with children's prior knowledge of to-be-trained concepts; frankly preoperational children cannot learn concrete-operational concepts; concepts belonging to different stages must be learned in a certain order. The first prediction, which has not yet been confirmed (cf. Brainerd, 1977a), may be trivial. All it says is that it is easier to generalize something that is already learned than it is to learn it in the first place. There are few learning theories that would fail to make this prediction. The second prediction does not square with empirical fact. Concrete-operational concepts have been learned by children who showed no evidence of them prior to training. Moreover, preschool subjects, whose ages fall within the first half of the nominal age range for the preoperational stage, have been taught concrete-operational concepts. The third prediction also is trivial. When two concepts are logically connected such that a test of one is always a test for the other but not conversely, the order in which these concepts are learned tells us nothing about development or the constraints development may impose on learning. Instead, it tells us something about the nature of our measurement operations. The third prediction may not be worth researching because we could not permit ourselves to believe contradictory findings.

To conclude, it may very well be true, as Piaget maintains, that a new approach to children's concept learning is needed that stresses the idea of readiness to learn. Certainly, there is no denying the existence of readiness effects in other areas of children's learning. Classic illustrations include learning voluntary bladder control (McGraw, 1940) and learning fine motor coordinations (Gesell & Thompson, 1929). But although we may need a readiness perspective on concept learning, Piaget's approach does not seem to be it.

REFERENCES

Ahr, P. R., & Youniss, J. Reasons for failure on the class inclusion problem. *Child Development*, 1970, *41*, 131–143.

Beilin, H. Learning and operational convergence in logical thought development. *Journal of Experimental Child Psychology*, 1965, *2*, 317–339.

Beilin, H. The training and acquisition of logical operations. In M. F. Rosskopf, L. P. Steffe, & S. Taback (Eds.), *Piagetian cognitive-developmental research and mathematical education.* Washington: National Council of Teachers of Mathematics, 1971.

Botvin, G. J., & Murray, F. B. The efficacy of peer modeling and social conflict in the acquisition of conservation. *Child Development*, 1975, *46*, 796–799.

Braine, M. D. S. Piaget on reasoning: A methodological critique and alternative proposals. In W. Kessen & C. Kuhlman (Eds.), Thought in the young child. *Monographs of the Society for Research in Child Development*, 1962, *27*, 2 (Whole No. 83).

Brainerd, C. J. Reinforcement and reversibility in quantity conservation. *Psychonomic Science*, 1972, *27*, 114–116. (a)

Brainerd, C. J. The age–stage issue in conservation acquisition. *Psychonomic Science*, 1972, *29*, 115–117. (b)

Brainerd, C. J. Neo-Piagetian training experiments revisited: Is there any support for the cognitive-developmental stage hypothesis? *Cognition*, 1973, *2*, 349–370. (a)

Brainerd, C. J. Judgments and explanations as criteria for the presence of cognitive structures. *Psychological Bulletin*, 1973, *79*, 172–179. (b)

Brainerd, C. J. Postmortem on judgments, explanations, and Piagetian cognitive structures. *Psychological Bulletin*, 1974, *80*, 70–71. (a)

Brainerd, C. J. Training and transfer of transitivity, conservation, and class inclusion of length. *Child Development*, 1974, *45*, 324-334. (b)

Brainerd, C. J. Rejoinder to Bingham–Newman and Hooper. *American Educational Research Journal*, 1975, *11*, 389–394.

Brainerd, C. J. "Stage," "structure," and developmental theory. In G. Steiner (Ed.), *The psychology of the twentieth century*. Munich: Kindler, 1976. (a)

Brainerd, C. J. Does prior knowledge of the compensation rule increase susceptability to conservation training? *Developmental Psychology*, 1976, *12*, 1–5. (b)

Brainerd, C. J. Cognitive development and concept learning: An interpretative review. *Psychological Bulletin*, 1977, in press. (a)

Brainerd, C. J. Feedback, rule knowledge, and conservation learning. *Child Development*, 1977, in press. (b)

Brainerd, C. J. Response criteria in concept development research. *Child Development*, 1977, in press. (c)

Brainerd, C. J., & Allen, T. W. Training and transfer of density conservation: Effects of feedback and consecutive similar stimuli. *Child Development*, 1971, *42*, 693–704. (a)

Brainerd, C. J., & Allen, T. W. Experimental inductions of the conservation of "first-order" quantitative invariants. *Psychological Bulletin*, 1971, *75*, 128–144. (b)

Brainerd, C. J., & Hooper, F. H. A methodological analysis of developmental studies of identity conservation and equivalence conservation. *Psychological Bulletin*, 1975, *82*, 725–737.

Brison, D. W. Acceleration of conservation of substance. *Journal of Genetic Psychology*, 1966, *109*, 311–322.

Brison, D. W., & Bereiter, C. Acquisition of conservation of substance in normal, retarded, and gifted children. In D. W. Brison & E. V. Sullivan (Eds.), *Recent research on the acquisition of conservation of substance*. Toronto: Ontario Institute for Studies in Education, 1967.

Bruner, J. S., Olver, R. R., & Greenfield, P. M. *Studies in cognitive growth*. New York: Wiley, 1966.

Bucher, B., & Schneider, R. E. Acquisition and generalization of conservation by preschoolers using operant training. *Journal of Experimental Child Psychology*, 1973, *16*, 187–204.

Charbonneau, C., Robert, M., Bourassa, G., & Gladu-Bissonette, S. Observational learning of quantity conservation and Piagetian generalization tasks. *Developmental Psychology*, 1976, *12*, 211–217.

Cloutier, R. The role of training and personal variables in formal reasoning. Unpublished doctoral dissertation. McGill University, 1973.

Cole, M., & Scribner, S. *Culture and thought.* New York: Wiley, 1974.

Denney, N. W., Zeytinoglu, S., & Selzer, S. C. Conservation training in four-year-olds. *Journal of Experimental Child Psychology*, 1977, in press.

Emrick, J. A. The acquisition and transfer of conservation skills by four-year-old children. Unpublished doctoral dissertation, University of California at Los Angeles, 1968.

Evans, R. I. *Jean Piaget: The man and his ideas.* New York: Dutton, 1973.

Figurelli, J. C., & Keller, H. R. The effects of training and socio-economic class upon the acquisition of conservation concepts. *Child Development*, 1972, *43*, 293–298.

Flavell, J. H. *The developmental psychology of Jean Piaget.* Princeton, N.J.: Van Nostrand, 1963.

Flavell, J. H. An analysis of cognitive-developmental sequences. *Genetic Psychology Monographs*, 1972, *86*, 279–350.

Flavell, J. H., & Wohlwill, J. F. Formal and functional aspects of cognitive development. In D. Elkind & J. H. Flavell (Eds.), *Studies in cognitive development.* New York: Oxford University Press, 1969.

Gelman, R. Conservation acquisition: A problem of learning to attend to relevant attributes. *Journal of Experimental Child Psychology*, 1969, *7*, 167–187.

Gesell, A., & Thompson, H. Learning and growth in identical infant twins: An experimental study by the method of co-twin control. *Genetic Psychology Monographs*, 1929, *6*, 1–124.

Glaser, R., & Resnick, L. B. Instructional psychology. In P. H. Mussen & M. Rosenzweig (Eds.), *Annual review of psychology,* Palo Alto, CA: Annual Review, 1972.

Goldschmid, M. L. The role of experience in the acquisition of conservation. *Proceedings of the American Psychological Association*, 1968, *76*, 361–362.

Goldschmid, M. L. Role of experience in the rate and sequence of cognitive development. In D. R. Green, M. P. Ford, & G. B. Flamer (Eds.), *Measurement and Piaget.* New York: McGraw-Hill, 1971.

Gruen, G. E. Note on conservation: Methodological and definitional considerations. *Child Development*, 1966, *37*, 977–983.

Halford, G. S., & Fullerton, T. J. A discrimination task which induces conservation of number. *Child Development*, 1970, *41*, 205–213.

Hamel, B. R., & Riksen, B. O. M. Identity, reversibility, rule instruction, and conservation. *Developmental Psychology*, 1973, *9*, 66–72.

Hatano, G. A developmental approach to concept formation: A review of neo-Piagetian learning experiments. *Dokkyo University Bulletin of Liberal Arts and Education*, 1971, *5*, 59–76.

Hatano, G. A., & Suga, Y. Equilibration and external reinforcement in the acquisition of number conservation. *Japanese Psychological Research*, 1969, *11*, 17–31.

Hooper, F. H., Brainerd, C. J., & Sipple, T. S. *A representative series of Piagetian concrete operations tasks.* Madison Wisconsin Research and Development Center for Cognitive Learning, 1975.

Hooper, F. H., Goldman, J. A., Storck, P. A., & Burke, A. M. Stage sequence and correspondence in Piagetian theory: A review of the middle-childhood period. In *Research relating to children,* Bulletin 28. Washington, D.C.: U.S. Printing Office, 1971.

Inhelder, B. Apprentissage et développement chez l'enfant. *Accademia nazionale dei lincei*, 1968, *365*, 283–291.

Inhelder, B. Information processing tendencies in recent experiments in cognitive learning: Empirical studies. In S. Farnham-Diggory (Ed.), *Information processing in children*. New York: Academic Press, 1972.

Inhelder, B., Bovet, M., Sinclair, H., & Smock, C. D. On cognitive development. *American Psychologist*, 1966, *21*, 160–164.

Inhelder, B., & Sinclair, H. Learning cognitive structures. In P. H. Mussen, J. Langer, & M. Covington (Eds.), *Trends and issues in developmental psychology*. New York: Holt, Rinehart, & Winston, 1969.

Inhelder, B., Sinclair, H., & Bovet, M. *Learning and the development of cognition*. Cambridge, MA: Harvard University Press, 1974.

McGraw, M. B. Neural maturation as exemplified in achievement of bladder control, *Journal of Pediatrics*, 1940, *16*, 580–589.

Murray, F. B. Acquisition of conservation through social interaction. *Developmental Psychology*, 1972, *6*, 1–6.

Murray, J. P. Social learning and cognitive development: Modelling effects on children's understanding of · conservation. *British Journal of Psychology*, 1974, *65*, 151–160.

Overbeck, C., & Schwartz, M. Training in conservation of weight. *Journal of Experimental Child Psychology*, 1970, *9*, 253–264.

Piaget, J. *The psychology of intelligence*. New York: International Universities Press, 1950.

Piaget, J. Jean Piaget. In E. G. Boring et al. (Eds.), *A history of psychology in autobiography* (Vol. 4). Worcester, MA: Clark University Press, 1952.

Piaget, J. *The construction of reality in the child*. New York: Basic Books, 1954.

Piaget, J. *Biologie et connaissance*. Paris: Gallimard, 1967.

Piaget, J. *On the development of memory and identity*. Worcester, MA: Clark University Press, 1968.

Piaget, J. Piaget's theory. In P. H. Mussen (Ed.), *Carmichael's manual of child psychology*. New York: Wiley, 1970. (a)

Piaget, J. A conversation with Jean Piaget. *Psychology Today*, 1970, *3* (12), 25–32. (b)

Piaget, J., & Inhelder, B. *Le développement des quantités chez l'enfant*. Neuchatel: Delachaux et Niestle, 1941.

Reese, H. W., & Schack, M. L. Comment on Brainerd's criteria for cognitive structures. *Psychological Bulletin*, 1974, *81*, 67–69.

Rosenthal, T. L., & Zimmerman, B. J. Modeling by exemplification and instruction in training conservation. *Developmental Psychology*, 1972, *6*, 392–401.

Russell, B. *A history of western philosophy*. New York: Simon & Schuster, 1945.

Schnall, M., Alter, E., Swanlund, T., & Schweitzer, T. A sensory motor context affecting performance in a conservation task: A closer analogue of reversibility than empirical return. *Child Development*, 1972, *43*, 1012–1023.

Scribner, S., & Cole, M. Cognitive consequences of formal and informal education. *Science*, 1973, *182*, 553–559.

Sheppard, J. L. Conservation of part and whole in the acquisition of class inclusion. *Child Development*, 1973, *44*, 380–383.

Sheppard, J. L., Compensation and combinatorial systems in the acquisition and generalization of conservation. *Child Development*, 1974, *45*, 717–730.

Siegler, R. S. Inducing a general conservation of liquid quantity concept in young children: Use of a basic rule and feedback. *Perceptual and Motor Skills*, 1973, *37*, 443–452.

Siegler, R. S., & Liebert, R. M. Effects of presenting relevant rules and complete feedback on the conservation of liquid quantity. *Developmental Psychology,* 1972. *7,* 133–138.

Silverman, I. W., & Geiringer, E. Dyadic interaction and conservation induction: A test of Piaget's equilibration model. *Child Development,* 1973, *44,* 815–820.

Sinclair, H. Recent Piagetian research in learning studies. In M. Schwebel & J. Raph (Eds.), *Piaget in the classroom.* New York: Basic Books, 1973.

Smedslund, J. Apprentissage des notions de la conservation et de la transitivité du poids. *Etudes d'épistémologie Génétiques,* 1959, *9,* 3–13.

Smedslund, J. The acquisition of conservation of substance and weight in children. II. External reinforcement of conservation of weight and the operations of addition and subtraction. *Scandinavian Journal of Psychology,* 1961, *2,* 71–84. (a)

Smedslund, J. The acquisition of conservation of substance and weight in children. III. Extinction of conservation of weight acquired "normally" and by means of empirical controls on a balance scale. *Scandinavian Journal of Psychology,* 1961, *2,* 85–87. (b)

Smedslund, J. The acquisition of conservation of substance and weight in children. IV. An attempt at extinction of the visual components of the weight concept. *Scandinavian Journal of Psychology,* 1961, *2,* 153–155. (c)

Strauss, S. Inducing cognitive development and learning: A review of short-term training experiments. I. The organismic developmental approach. *Cognition,* 1972, *1,* 329–357.

Sullivan, E. V. Acquisition of conservation of substance through film modeling techniques. In D. W. Brison, & E. V. Sullivan (Eds.), *Recent research in the acquisition of conservation of substance.* Toronto: Ontario Institute for Studies in Education, 1967.

Waghorn, L., & Sullivan, E. V. The exploration of transition rules in conservation of quantity (substance) using film mediated modeling. *Acta Psychologica,* 1970, *32,* 65–80.

Wallach, L., & Sprott, R. L. Inducing number conservation in children. *Child Development,* 1964, *35,* 1057–1071.

Weinreb, N., & Brainerd, C. J. A developmental study of Piaget's groupement model of the emergence of speed and time concepts. *Child Development,* 1975, *46,* 476–485.

Werner, H. *Comparative psychology of mental development.* New York: International Universities Press, 1948.

White, S. H. The learning theory tradition and child psychology. In P. H. Mussen (Ed.), *Carmichael's manual of child psychology.* New York: Wiley, 1970.

Wilson, K. Romanticism, science and the humanistic tradition. Paper presented at the conference on Conceptual Foundations of Humanistic Psychology, Center for Advanced Study in Theoretical Psychology, University of Alberta, October, 1975.

Wohlwill, J. F. Un essai d'apprentissage dans le domaine de la conservation du nombre. *Etudes d'Epistémologie Génétique,* 1959, *9,* 125–135.

Wohlwill, J. F., & Lowe, R. C. An experimental analysis of the conservation of number. *Child Development,* 1962, *33,* 153–167.

Youniss, J. Classificatory schemes in relation to class inclusion before and after training. *Human Development,* 1971, *14,* 171–183.

Zimmerman, B. J., & Rosenthal, T. L. Observational learning of rule-governed behavior by children. *Psychological Bulletin,* 1974, *81,* 29–42. (a)

Zimmerman, B. J., & Rosenthal, T. L. Conserving and retaining equalities and inequalities through observation and correction. *Developmental Psychology,* 1974, *10,* 269–268. (b)

5

A Perceptual-Salience Account of Décalage Relations and Developmental Change

RICHARD D. ODOM

Vanderbilt University

Introduction

Over 30 years ago Jean Piaget introduced developmental psychology to the term *décalage*. He used it to refer to the performance of children who had been given various types of conservation problems (see, e.g., Piaget & Inhelder, 1941). Since that time the conservation décalage has come to serve as the prototype for all décalages. A clear example of the conservation décalage is provided by Elkind's (1961) frequently cited replication of Piaget's work. In that study, three types of conservation were assessed in children from 5 to 11 years of age. These subjects were given the task of determining whether the mass, weight, or volume of two pieces of clay remained the same following an irrelevant change in the shape of one of the pieces. The results indicated that the majority of children 7 years of age and older could solve the mass problem; by 9 years of age and older a majority could also solve the weight problem; and not until after the age of 11 years could the volume problem be solved.

Although the reliability of the conservation décalage has been demonstrated, it has never been clear from Piaget's theory why it should ever occur. Because conservation is presented as a unitary construct comprised of logical operations that characterize the concrete-operational stage, the failure of mass, weight, and volume conservation to appear simultaneously seems counter to what would be expected from the theory. It appears that this issue has been skirted by invoking the term *décalage* as an apparent account of content-specific conservation.

It should be emphasized, however, that décalage is not a theoretical construct and in no way provides an explanation or account of any aspect of psychological development. It is a descriptive term that summarizes the relation between (*a*) differences in the performance of various age groups and (*b*) differences in information contained in problem-solving tasks that have the same solution requirements. In the conservation décalage described above, for example, the solution requirements of each of the three tasks were the same; only the verbally presented information that specified type of quantity (i.e., mass, weight, and volume) was varied.

Cognitive-Change Position

Since the time that Piaget first used the term *décalage,* a substantial amount of developmental research has been stimulated by the adoption of cognitive- or conceptual-change positions that focus on the emergence and development of processes and operations that evaluate task- or environment-based information. These evaluation processes have been described in various ways, for example, as attitudes, concepts, rule and transformational structures, and decision strategies. Although Piaget's theory has been the most widely adopted of the cognitive-change positions, the décalage relation is not found exclusively in Piagetian research. It also exists in research designed to assess the development of cognitive processes that have been proposed in other cognitive-change positions. It is striking, therefore, that little effort has been directed toward understanding the décalage and its implications for cognitive-change positions.

Cognitive-change research is concerned with the general area of human problem solving. In studies exploring the development of processes associated with problem solving, the subject is typically given a task with alternative response choices. These consist of one alternative that is relevant to solving the problem and one or more alternatives that are irrelevant to solution. The solution-relevant alternative is predetermined by an adult experimenter who considers its increasingly reliable choice to be a reflection of problem-solving processes. In this research, it is common to find differences in the performance of subjects at different age levels. These differences often favor older subjects, who usually solve problems more accurately and more rapidly than younger subjects. The accounts of such differences are typically in terms of qualitative and/or quantitative changes in cognition, and the cognitive constructs that have been introduced may be characterized generally as operations that evaluate task information. Two such constructs that are commonly proposed to account for performance change with development are (a) structures of logical thought (e.g., Piaget & Inhelder, 1969) and (b) attentional and verbal mediators (e.g., Hagen & Hale, 1973; Kendler & Kendler, 1962). For the Piagetians, development is assumed to proceed with the emergence of qualitatively different and more adult-like structures that are described by models of logic. For the mediationalists, the assumed cause of age-related differences in problem solving is the development of cognitive, mediational processes. These processes determine evaluation and selection of information relevant to problem solution by either attending to relevant information and ignoring that which is irrelevant (e.g., Hagen & Hale, 1973) or transforming and organizing information into dimensions or concepts (e.g., Kendler & Kendler, 1962).

Assumptions about Perception

Because cognitive-change positions contain no clear or distinct theoretical role for perceptual development and its consequent effects on the perceptual characteristics of task information, there appears to be an implicit assumption that all information in a problem-solving task is perceived identically at all developmental levels. Consequently, age-related performance differences are considered to result from different cognitive structures that evaluate the same information. It can be argued, however, that décalage relations that have been reported in the extant literature or that may be found in future research challenge such an assumption as well as the appropriateness of cognitive-change interpretations.

It is obvious that information contained in a problem-solving task must be perceived before it can be cognitively evaluated. However, what happens to the relation between perception and cognition in the course of development is not clear in cognitive-change positions.

113

One commonly expressed view is that younger children are more perceptually oriented than older children and therefore more likely to evaluate certain irrelevant information that is perceptually misleading in a problem. Such a view, however, does not address itself to the question of why older children are not also perceptually misled by the same available information. Furthermore, it is unreasonable to consider the older child less perceptually oriented than the younger child when the former's successful solution to a problem indicates that perception of at least the relevant information has occurred. Understanding the nature of the perceptual system and the characteristics of the information it detects may therefore be necessary to understanding the nature of cognitive evaluation. The present chapter is designed to demonstrate the importance of the role of perceptual factors and to propose a perceptual-change position as an account for décalage relations.

Problems with Cognitive-Change Accounts

In the case of the décalage associated with, for example, mass, weight, and volume conservation, each problem has the same basic solution requirements and, from a cognitive-change perspective, should involve use of the same cognitive structures and operations. But what of the different information in each task that specifies the type of quantity to be conserved? If such differences in task information were assumed to be unimportant because the perception of information across development is considered invariant, then the particular task used to assess the presence of structures relevant to conservation should not matter. However, it can be seen from the conservation décalage that ignoring differences in task information can result in age-related performance differences that are difficult to explain using a cognitive-change position. For example, if 8-year-olds were given a task involving mass and 10-year-olds were given one involving volume, the conclusions drawn from the results would be that younger children, who were able to conserve mass, demonstrated greater cognitive competence than the older children, who were unable to conserve volume.

Due to a preference for cognitive-change positions, a large number of developmental psychologists would find such a conclusion difficult to accept, even though it is consistent with the rationale and approach from which conclusions about the advanced cognitive development of older children are drawn. (Note that when older children solve problems more rapidly and accurately than younger children, there is little hesitation in drawing conclusions about which age group is more cognitively advanced or mature.) Nevertheless, as a part of the data associated with conservation and other décalages, results showing that the problem-solving performance of younger subjects either equals or exceeds that of older subjects needs to be explained. Such data would seem to highlight the importance of considering the role played by perceptual characteristics of information in tasks that are used to assess the development of cognitive processes.

Component Relations of the Décalage

From these considerations of the décalage, two component relations that have implications for accounts of developmental change can be identified. The first is between the information characteristics in tasks with the same solution requirements and the performance accuracy of subjects within the same age or developmental level. The second relation is between the performance accuracy of subjects of one age or developmental level and that of subjects of other developmental levels in tasks that have the same solution requirements but that may or may not differ in information characteristics. As in the case of the décalage involving quantity conservation, both component relations are often present when both age and task information are varied.

The first component relation is illustrated in the performance of 7-year-olds who solve problems involving mass conservation but fail problems involving weight or volume conservation. Among the numerous examples of this relation in the literature are those found in Piagetian studies designed to explore the development of transitive inference operations. In these studies, the performance accuracy of subjects within the same age level is found to vary as a function of task information that differs across problems with the same solution requirements (Braine, 1959; Coon & Odom, 1968; Halpern, 1965; Odom & Coon, 1967; Smedslund, 1963; Youniss & Furth, 1966). The sources and characteristics of task information in these studies of transitivity have varied considerably in terms of the type of information, the amount of information presented verbally, and the amount of irrelevant information. In contrast, studies designed to explore mediational constructs of attention and internalized verbalization have used task information that has differed on fewer characteristics. Furthermore, certain characteristics (e.g., salience) of the task information are more clearly specified. In this research, the performance accuracy of subjects within the same age level has been shown to vary as a function of information characteristics in tasks with solution requirements involving concept identification (Mitler & Harris, 1969; Odom & Mumbauer, 1971; Suchman & Trabasso, 1966), location recall (Odom, 1972), and transfer shift (Caron, 1969; Mumbauer & Odom, 1967; Smiley & Weir, 1966).

The second component relation contained in the décalage has implications for the issues being raised when no difference exists between the performance of younger and older subjects or when the younger subjects' performance is more accurate than that of the older subjects. An example of the latter is when the response accuracy of 8-year-olds in a conservation problem involving mass is greater than that of 10-year-olds in one involving volume. Because of the widespread acceptance of cognitive-change positions, the second component relation is rarely expected, and when it occurs, it is likely to be viewed as anomalous or unimportant. Each of the studies reviewed in the subsequent sections of this chapter contains instances of the second relation of the décalage.

Perceptual-Change Position

These component relations contained in décalages have not been clearly recognized or considered in cognitive-change positions. In contrast, they are of central importance in the perceptual-change position presented here and elsewhere (e.g., Odom & Guzman, 1972). In this position, such relations are assumed to provide information about developmental changes in the perceptual system and how that system determines what information is processed by cognitive structures. It is also assumed that understanding the function and role of the perceptual system is necessary before strong and persuasive conclusions can be made about developmental changes in cognitive structures of evaluation. In this alternative position, certain of Gibson's (1969) ideas about perception have been adopted. These are (a) that relations (dimensions of difference, invariants of events) serve as basic information for the perceptual system; (b) that they are present in the external environment and are not mediated products of cognitive structures, images, stored associations, or inferences; and (c) that they are discovered in increasing numbers by the perceptual system as development proceeds.

Perceptual Sensitivity

We have extended these ideas by proposing that the perceptual system becomes differentially sensitive to information once that information has been detected. Changes in sensitivity are assumed to be primarily a function of perceptual experience per se (e.g., Caron, 1969) and/or particular environmental contexts and events (for examples of these, see Trabasso & Bower, 1968, pp. 146–147). As perceptual experience increases with development, perceptual sensitivity to certain relations and categories would therefore be expected to increase. Furthermore, it is proposed that the degree of sensitivity to relations or categories determines how they are perceptually organized and the order in which they are cognitively evaluated for problem solution. That is, the greater the perceptual sensitivity to given information, the higher the probability of its being cognitively evaluated, regardless of the information's appropriateness for problem solution. It would therefore be expected that with increasing development, an increasing amount of both relevant and irrelevant information would be cognitively evaluated and either accepted or rejected for problem solution.

Salience Measures of Perceptual Sensitivity

With this point of view, we have been assessing, and have found, age-related differences in the relative sensitivity of the perceptual system to common relations, categories, and dimensions. This assessment has involved traditional salience tasks in which subjects match items that are most alike in values representing particular categories. In these tasks there is no problem to solve, and therefore no solution-relevant choices. Several choice alternatives are provided, and no evaluative feedback is given by the experimenter. (For details on the construction of salience tasks, see Odom & Guzman, 1972.) A rank-ordered hierarchy of salience scores associated with the assessed categories is obtained for each child, and groups from different development levels are then assigned to problem-solving tasks in which the solution requirements are held constant while the salience of solution-relevant and -irrelevant information is varied. From this approach, salience is viewed as a perceptual characteristic of information, and the salience hierarchy is seen as a product of the perceptual system's detection of, experience with, and organization of information.

Perceptual Salience and the Development of Problem Solving

In the following sections, several studies are described that offer support for a perceptual-change account of décalage relations. In these

117

studies, the salience of information in different kinds of problem-solving tasks was varied. The problem-solving tasks used in the last two studies had solution requirements like certain tasks used by investigators in the mediationalist tradition. Those used in the following two studies had solution requirements that were similar to those used in Piagetian research.

Studies from the Piagetian Tradition

According to Piagetian theory, what is required for solving any conservation task (as well as other concrete-operational tasks) is the use of cognitive operations that coordinate information from at least two different sources. Inhelder and Piaget (1964) have claimed that the most direct way of assessing the development of such competence is through the use of the matrix task. In a recent study (Odom, Astor, & Cunningham, 1975), we manipulated salience to assess the potential effects of perceptual characteristics on performance in matrix problems.

A series of matrices composed of three values from each of two categories was presented to 4- and 6-year-old children. Approximately 3 weeks prior to presenting the matrix tasks, the salience of form, color, and position was assessed, and an ABC hierarchy, with A the most salient and C the least salient dimension, was obtained for each child. Half the children from each age group were assigned to an AB condition and received nine different matrix problems composed of values from their A and B dimensions. The remaining half were assigned to an AC condition and received identically structured matrices composed of values from their A and C dimensions.

The goal in each problem was to select that compound stimulus from a set of four alternatives that appropriately filled an empty cell in the 3 × 3 matrix. A sample matrix with its four choice cards is shown in Figure 5.1. The correct card contained both of the dimensional values appropriate to the empty cell in the matrix. Two of the other cards contained one dimensional value appropriate to the empty cell and one value that was inappropriate. The appropriate value on one of these cards was from the more salient dimension, and the appropriate value on the other card was from the less salient dimension. The inappropriate value on each of these two cards appeared in one of the filled matrix cells. Both values of the fourth card were inappropriate and did not appear in the matrix.

The results showed that the salience of the relevant dimensions affected matrix solution. More accurate performance was associated with the AB than the AC matrices for both age groups. The younger children

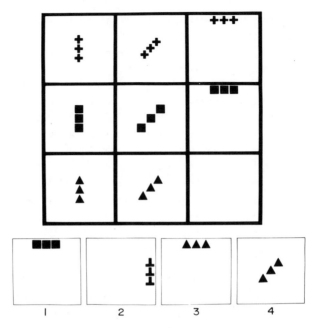

FIGURE 5.1.
A sample matrix and choice cards.

failed to solve an average of 4.20 and 5.10 matrices in the AB and AC conditions, respectively, while the older children failed an average of 1.55 and 3.50 matrices in the two respective conditions. These findings represent a case of the first component relation contained in the décalage and can be accounted for in terms of the salience characteristics of the relevant information. Although both the AB and AC tasks had the same solution requirements, the performance of each age group was affected by the absolute salience of the less salient dimension (B or C) in each task.

Even though each matrix problem required a different choice card for solution, the relevant dimensions were the same for all nine problems. Therefore, the effects of an increase in the perceptual sensitivity to, and subsequent evaluation of, the relevant dimensions may be reflected in the decreasing number of errors made on successive problems by the age groups in both conditions. On the last three problems of the nine-problem series, the performance of the 4-year-olds in the AB condition and the 6-year-olds in the AC condition was comparable (mean errors = .8 and .9, respectively). This finding is an instance of the second component relation contained in the décalage. It indicates that given certain task information, the 4-year-old children were able

119

to solve the matrix problems as successfully as the older children. There are no compelling reasons to assume that the younger children used cognitive processes different from those used by the older children to accomplish this.

The results of this study provide clear evidence for coordination structures in 4- as well as 6-year-old children. In an earlier study, Odom and Corbin (1973) also demonstrated that young children can solve problems by coordinating information from multidimensional sources. Salience was varied, and the solution requirements of the problem involved reconstructing arrays of compound stimuli from memory. The age-related differences in performance found in both of these studies seem better explained by a perceptual-change account in which cognitive operations are given an important function than by a cognitive-change account in which the theoretical role of the perceptual system is minor and unclearly specified. The greater overall accuracy of the older subjects may reflect more mature evaluation processes, but how that greater cognitive maturity should be characterized is not clear. From a perceptual-change account it could be reasoned that the older subjects' greater accuracy was due not to greater cognitive maturity but to both of the relevant categories in each problem being more absolutely salient than they were for the younger subjects. Although there was no preassessment measure of absolute salience, its effects were demonstrated in the performance of both age groups. The greater accuracy on AB than on AC matrices indicates that the B dimension was absolutely more salient than the C dimension, even though both were relatively less salient than A in each of the problems.

The matrix study demonstrates that when problems are constructed so that the solution-relevant information is highly salient for young children, their performance can reflect a level of cognitive processing that is often attributed only to older children and adults. Conversely, when they are given problems in which the solution-irrelevant information is high in salience, their performance accuracy is low relative to that of older subjects (e.g., Odom & Mumbauer, 1971).

Tasks used in research involving different age groups are designed by adults with the hope that the youngest subjects will find them engaging enough to at least try to solve them. Consequently, the quantity of information is usually kept low. If the absolute salience of information does increase with age, then more of the information in most of these tasks is likely to be more absolutely salient for older than for younger subjects. Thus, more information is likely to be evaluated and more problems solved, overall, by older than by younger subjects. (Older subjects realize yet another potential advantage over younger subjects in most developmental research: The fact that adults design such problems indicates that they are solvable, at least under certain conditions, by adult subjects and older subjects approaching the adults' developmental level. The only evidence of the ability of very young subjects to solve problems designed by the adult must come from their task performance.)

One way to assess the adequacy of the perceptual-change position is to construct problems in which the quantity or type of information is such that the older subject is likely to evaluate and accept highly salient, but solution-irrelevant, information. With this approach, the accuracy of the older subject's performance might well reflect the effects of perceptual characteristics in the way they are reflected in the inaccurate performance of younger subjects. It is also possible that the solution-irrelevant information in such tasks would not be highly salient for the younger subjects, and evaluation and acceptance of relevant information could result in their performing more accurately than older subjects. This would be a case of the second component relation of the décalage.

In a quest for such problem-solving tasks, we discovered in informal pilot work that many adults failed to solve the following problem.

> Imagine that I have two cans. One has red beads in it, and it is called the red-bead can. The other has blue beads in it and is called the blue-bead can. There are the same number of red beads in the red-bead can as there are blue beads in the blue-bead can. Let me repeat that. There are the same number of red beads in the red-bead can as there are blue beads in the blue-bead can. Now imagine that I dip a cup into the red-bead can and take out five beads. I pour them into the blue-bead can. Then I mix up all of the beads in the blue-bead can. I then dip the cup into the blue-bead can and take out five beads and pour them into the red-bead can. Will the number of red beads in the red-bead can and the number of blue beads in the blue-bead can be the same or different?

This is a type of conservation problem, and even though the information is of a different type, the solution requirements are much the same as those of traditional conservation problems that are given to young children. The correct answer to the question at the end of the problem is "same." An appropriate justification for this answer would involve either adding and subtracting operations with specific numbers of colored beads or something general like "the number of red beads left in the blue-bead can equals the number of blue beads taken to the red-bead can." Task solution therefore requires that perceptually given information about the the number and color of beads be evaluated through cognitive operations involving adding and subtracting.

We speculated that failure to give a "same" response to this problem was due to the cognitive evaluation of information about the mixing of beads. Such evaluation might result in probability estimates of, for example, returning fewer red beads to the red-bead can than were originally taken from it because the sample would contain blue as well as red beads. However, a correct solution to the problem could be achieved by assuming that five beads of the same color were returned to the red-bead can whether mixing did or did not occur. The mixing information, therefore, was irrelevant and unnecessary to solving the problem.

Although the tasks in most research on salience have contained a predominant amount of information that was visual in nature, all of the information in the bead problem was presented verbally. Even though an empirical basis for salience effects in linguistic contexts may be limited, it seems reasonable to assume that the perceptual system is differentially sensitive to the content and structural relations in auditory contexts in much the same way that it is to relations in visual and tactual contexts.

We used the bead problem in a study that included other task conditions designed to assess the effects of certain factors that are not discussed here (Odom, Cunningham, & Astor, 1975). The problem was verbally presented to college adults and third grade children (mean CA = 8:4). All subjects were probed for explanations or operations to justify their judgments.

Because of their past experience, the adults were expected to be sensitive to the mixing information; that is, it would be high in salience and therefore likely to be cognitively evaluated. The mixing information was expected to be low in salience for the children because they had had no formal training in probability and sampling concepts and had had fewer years and opportunities than the adults to experience instances of them in informal situations. Therefore, the children were expected to be less likely than the adults to make judgment errors as a result of cognitively evaluating the mixing information.

As expected, only a small number of the adults (15%) gave correct "same" judgments, whereas all but one of the children (95%) correctly responded with "same." None of the adults who gave "same" judgments gave a satisfactory explanation. Of the adults incorrectly responding with "different," only one corrected his judgment and gave a satisfactory explanation. In their explanations, 70% of the adults gave probability accounts involving the mixing information. In 78%

of these accounts there was recognition that it was possible, but not probable, that all red beads could be drawn from the blue-bead can and that this outcome would require a "same" judgment. Because only one of the two possible judgments could be correct, it would seem that recognizing that if one possible outcome would result in a judgment of "same," then a reasonable conclusion would be that all outcomes would result in a judgment of "same." However, this did not occur.

The children who gave a correct judgment also demonstrated the adding and subtracting operations necessary for a satisfactory explanation when the experimenter had them produce specific numbers as they went back through the steps of the problem. To the experimenter's initial questions concerning why subjects had judged as they had, all but two children answered with something like "five beads were taken and five were returned." The one child who gave an incorrect judgment changed it and gave a satisfactory explanation. Some of the children (65%) were probed for a probability concept, and 85% of those probed indicated that in a hypothetical situation where repeated samples of five beads each were drawn from the blue-bead can following mixing, there would be more cups containing both red and blue beads than cups with beads of a single color. Prior to the probe for a probability concept, 40% of the total sample of children spontaneously indicated that the returning cup would have both red and blue beads in it. These data provide more than suggestive evidence that the mixing information was sufficiently salient to be perceived and that the effects of mixing were cognitively understood. However, the mixing information was apparently not salient enough to be evaluated for problem solution, and none of the children mentioned it in their explanations.

In an attempt to make the irrelevant mixing information salient for subjects at this developmental level, another group of third-graders was given a slightly modified version of the bead problem. This version contained additional phrases emphasizing the mixing operations and noting the presence of both red and blue beads in the returning cup. In contrast to the accurate performance of children given the original problem, only 10% of these subjects gave a correct judgment of "same." When the irrelevant information was made highly salient, and therefore likely to be evaluated for solution, 90% of the children gave an incorrect judgment of "different" just as 85% of the adults had done. There was no clear evidence to suggest that the age groups' performance was determined by different cognitive processes.

Both component relations of the décalage were present in this study. The first component can be seen in the performance differences between the two groups of children given a problem with the same solution requirements but with different salience characteristics of the irrelevant information. The second component can be seen in the equally inaccurate performance of the adults and the second group of children as well as in the first group's performance, which was at a strikingly higher level of accuracy relative to that of the adults. The décalage containing these components can be explained by a perceptual-change position. The performance of the two age groups was primarily determined by differences and similarities in the perceptual characteristics of the task information and by the type of information that was evaluated, rather than by differences in the processes that evaluated the information.

Studies from the Mediationalist Tradition

In the remaining studies to be described, we explored the role of perceptual salience in tasks designed to assess selective-attentional processes. In recent years, considerable developmental research on attention has been performed using incidental recall tasks. In an initial problem, subjects are typically required to recall the locations of values from a relevant category or dimension. After completion of this task, a recall measure is taken to assess the amount of incidental or irrelevant information acquired while solving the initial problem. The recall accuracy of both relevant and irrelevant information is assumed to reflect the level of selective attention. Hagen and Hale (1973) have reviewed several incidental recall studies involving subjects from 7 to 13 years of age. The results indicated that although the recall of older subjects was more accurate than that of younger subjects on the initial problem-solving task, a similar amount of incidental recall was usually found for all age groups. That older and younger subjects recalled different amounts of relevant, but not incidental, information led Hagen and Hale (1973) to conclude that older children are better able than younger children to attend selectively to central or relevant information and to ignore that which is incidental to solving a problem. However, the perceptual characteristics of the task information in these studies was not assessed. Consequently, characteristics such as salience may have played a major role in determining the subjects' performance.

In contrast to the results of these studies, our research has shown that more incidental as well as relevant information is recalled with increasing age (Odom, 1972; Odom, Cunningham, & Astor-Stetson, 1977). In this research the salience of the task information was manipulated, and instances of the décalage were obtained. The results were in accord with a perceptual-change position in that the recall of both relevant and irrelevant information was determined by the salience of the information. Such findings do not support a cognitive-change position that posits a developmental change in attentional processes that determine the selection of only solution-relevant information.

In the first of these studies (Odom, 1972), the task was comprised of a horizontal array of six cards, each of which contained a compound stimulus consisting of a different value from each of the four dimensions of form, color, number, and position. For example, the far left array card might contain two red squares positioned across its upper horizontal edge. Kindergarten, third grade, and sixth grade children were given repeated presentations of the array in a problem requiring the recall of the location of each value representing only one of the four dimensions; the values of the other three dimensions were incidental to solving the task. For a given subject, form might be the relevant dimension. Following each exposure of the array, a probe card containing one of the six forms would be presented, and the subject would be asked to point to the place over the covered array that corresponded to the location of that particular form value. While the solution requirements for each problem were the same for all subjects, the salience value of the relevant dimension was varied. The salience of the four dimensions was assessed 2 to 3 months prior to presenting the recall task.

The results indicated that fewer recall errors were made by each age group when the relevant dimension was high in salience than when it was low. This is an instance of the first component relation of the décalage. Recall was found to increase with increasing age; however, the youngest group made no more errors when their relevant dimension was high in salience than the two oldest groups made when their relevant dimension was low in salience. This is an instance of the second component relation of the décalage.

After the initial problem-solving task, the array was never exposed, and subjects were probed on the recall of the array locations of values from the three incidental dimensions. Recall of these values was positively related to both age and the salience of the incidental dimensions that they represented.

Results that show more incidental learning in older than younger subjects are not easily explained by the selective-attention position. In the research reviewed by Hagen and Hale (1973), the values of the relevant and incidental dimensions were usually separated spatially (e.g., an animal paired with a household object), whereas in the study by Odom (1972) the relevant and incidental stimulus components were presented as compound stimuli (e.g., two red squares positioned along the top of the card). Focusing on this difference between compound and component stimuli, Hagen and Hale (1973) proposed that when component values of relevant and incidental dimensions are presented in a compound stimulus, it is more efficient for older subjects to process both types of values because considerable effort may need to be expended in distinguishing the components (p. 126). Before this interpretation can be seriously entertained, however, it will be necessary to resolve the problem of what kind of performance measure one should use to assess the development of attentional processes. The problem is not resolved by claiming more mature selection processes for older than younger subjects when the older subjects show *less* incidental recall and then claiming greater efficiency for older subjects when they show *more* incidental recall than the younger subjects. If a decrease in incidental recall with age is used as an indication of a developmental increase in selective attention, it logically follows that an increase in incidental recall with age would indicate a developmental decrease in that ability. The finding that older subjects had a relatively higher level of incidental recall might therefore indicate that, in some sense, they had greater difficulty ignoring the incidental information than did the younger subjects.

We have attributed such age-related differences in recall to differences in the salience of the information. The selection and evaluation of both relevant and incidental information is assumed to be determined by the perceptual system's differential sensitivity to that information. Because there was no assessment of the salience characteristics of the categories represented by the component values used in the research reviewed by Hagen and Hale, we assessed and manipulated salience in a recent study using component values to represent the solution-relevant and -irrelevant categories (Odom, Cunningham, & Astor-Stetson, 1977). In this study, kindergarten and sixth grade children were given a recall problem that was similar in general procedure to the one used by Odom (1972). Approximately 3 weeks prior to being given the problem-solving task, the salience of form, color, and position was assessed; and an ABC hierarchy, with A the most salient and C the least salient dimension, was obtained for each subject. Half of the subjects from each grade level were assigned to Condition AC, in which their A dimension was relevant to solving the initial problem; the values of their C dimension were incidental and irrelevant to solution. The remaining subjects were assigned to Condition CA and given a problem in which their C dimension was relevant and their A dimension irrelevant to solution. In both conditions, recall of the locations of the incidental values was assessed after the initial problem was completed.

In this task a horizontal array of cards was presented in a tray with six compartments. In each compartment were two cards: one containing a value from the relevant dimension (e.g., a centered, black square representing the form dimension), the other containing a value from the irrelevant or incidental dimension (e.g., a blue, asymmetrical shape representing the color dimension). The card pairs were spatially separated in a vertical relation to one another, and the above–below location of the six values from each dimension was alternated randomly across the six compartments of the tray.

The array was repeatedly exposed for brief intervals by raising a lid. Following each of 24 exposures, a card containing a relevant dimensional value identical to one in the array was held up, and the subject was asked to indicate the array location of that value on the top of the closed lid. In a second task, the array was never exposed, and subjects were probed on the location recall of values from the incidental dimension.

A décalage was manifested in the results of this study and can be explained by the effects of perceptual salience. In the AC and CA conditions of the initial problem, the kindergarten children made, respectively, 11.75 and 15.45 errors, while the sixth-graders made 8.19 and 10.44 errors in the two conditions. Both age groups made fewer errors in the recall problem when the more salient dimension (A) was relevant. This is an instance of the first component relation of the décalage. It can also be seen in these data that the total recall accuracy of the younger group in the AC condition approached that of the older group in the CA condition, and during the last six probes of the task, the younger AC group had mean errors of 1.81 whereas the older CA group had mean errors of 2.31. This is an instance of the second component relation of the décalage.

Salience affected the recall of incidental information in that fewer errors were made when the incidental dimension was high in salience ($M = 3.47$) than when it was low in salience ($M = 4.72$). Furthermore, the sixth-graders made fewer errors ($M = 3.78$) recalling incidental information than did kindergarteners ($M = 4.41$). To determine whether incidental recall occurred at a better than chance level (M errors $= 5.00$), t tests were performed on the data. Only the recall of kindergarteners in the AC condition was found to be at chance level (M errors $= 5.13$), indicating that they recalled no incidental information. Such results are counter to what would be expected from a cognitive-change position. Interpreting the incidental recall data from that position would lead one to conclude that the older subjects were less successful than the younger subjects in ignoring solution-irrelevant information. The incidental recall data and the décalage associated with the initial problem, however, are both compatible with a perceptual-change position. Selection and evaluation of both incidental and relevant information was determined by age-related differences in the salience characteristics of that information.

Conclusions

In each of the four studies described above, instances of the décalage and its component relations have been identified. Although the problem-solving tasks used in this research are associated with particular theoretical traditions and were designed to assess different aspects of psychological development, the obtained décalages have implications for any theory concerned with the development of processes associated with problem solving. Other studies in the problem-solving literature also contain décalage relations. In some of these studies, décalage relations are given little or no recognition; in others, they are given incomplete and unclear interpretations. One approach toward satisfactory interpretations is the development of a theoretical basis for determining characteristics of task information that are associated with age-related performance. In the research reviewed here, the characteristic of perceptual salience was identified as a significant determinant of the obtained décalages. In research where salience has not been manipulated but where décalage components are found, it is reasonable to assume that salience or some other perceptual characteristic of the task information played an important role in producing those components.

With further research on the role of salience and other characteristics of information in problem solving, a perceptual-change position may prove to be a desirable alternative to positions that focus on cognitive change. That is, we may become persuaded that the basic and significant changes that occur in psychological development are primarily or exclusively based on the perceptual system's changing sensitivity to relations in the environment rather than on changes in cognitive processes that evaluate those relations. Although at present it cannot be said with any certainty which alternative account will prove more adequate, existing research clearly indicates that a perceptual-change account should at least be viewed as an important extension of a general cognitive-change position. It is also clear that if we are to understand the development of the structure and function of cognitive processes that evaluate and transform information, we must also understand the perceptual nature of that information and how it changes with development.

A number of years has passed since Piaget first used the term *décalage* to refer to what has become a frequently occurring relation associated with age-related performance in tasks varying in type and characteristics of information. It is time that we direct a more concerted effort toward understanding the potential problems and implications that the décalage relation has for accounts of what is and is not changing in the course of psychological development.

REFERENCES

Braine, M. S. The ontogeny of certain logical operations. Piaget's formulation examined by nonverbal methods. *Psychological Monographs*, 1959, *73*, (5, Whole No. 475).

Caron, A. J. Discrimination shifts in three-year-olds as a function of dimension salience. *Developmental Psychology*, 1969, *1*, 333–337.

Coon, R. C., & Odom, R. D. Transitivity and length judgments as a function of age and social influence. *Child Development*, 1968, *39*, 1133–1144.

Elkind, D. The development of quantitative thinking: A systematic replication of Piaget's studies. *Journal of Genetic Psychology*, 1961, *98*, 37–46.

Gibson, E. J. *Principles of perceptual learning and development.* New York: Appleton-Century-Crofts, 1969.

Hagen, J. W., & Hale G. A. The development of attention in children. In A. D. Pick (Ed.), *Minnesota symposia on child psychology* (Vol. 7). Minneapolis: University of Minnesota Press, 1973.

Halpern, E. The effects of incompatibility between perception and logic in Piaget's stage of concrete operations. *Child Development*, 1965, *36*, 491–497.

Inhelder, B., & Piaget, J. *The early growth of logic in the child.* New York: Norton, 1964.

Kendler, H. H., & Kendler, T. S. Vertical and horizontal processes in problem solving. *Psychological Review*, 1962, *69*, 1-16.

Mitler, M. M., & Harris, L. Dimension preference and performance on a series of concept identification tasks in kindergarten, first- and third-grade children. *Journal of Experimental Child Psychology*, 1969, *7*, 374–384.

Mumbauer, C. C., & Odom, R. D. Variables affecting the performance of preschool children in intradimensional and extradimensional shifts. *Journal of Experimental Psychology*, 1967, *75*, 180–187.

Odom, R. D. Effects of perceptual salience on the recall of relevant and incidental dimensional values: A developmental study. *Journal of Experimental Psychology*, 1972, *92*, 285–291.

Odom, R. D., Astor, E. C., & Cunningham, J. G. Effects of perceptual salience on the matrix task performance of four- and six-year-old children. *Child Development*, 1975, *46*, 758–762.

Odom, R. D., & Coon, R. C. A questionnaire approach to transitivity in children. *Psychonomic Science*, 1967, *9*, 305–306.

Odom, R. D., & Corbin, D. W. Perceptual salience and children's multi-dimensional problem solving. *Child Development*, 1973, *44*, 425–432.

Odom, R. D., Cunningham, J. G., & Astor, E. C. Adults thinking the way we think children think, but children don't always think that way: A study of perceptual salience and problem solving. *Bulletin of the Psychonomic Society*, 1975, *6*, 545–548.

Odom, R. D., Cunningham, J. G., & Astor-Stetson, E. C. The role of perceptual salience and type of instruction in children's recall of relevant and incidental dimensional values. *Bulletin of the Psychonomic Society*, 1977, *9*, 77–80.

Odom, R. D., & Guzman, R. D. Development of hierarchies of dimensional salience. *Developmental Psychology*, 1972, *6*, 271–287.

Odom, R. D., & Mumbauer, C. C. Dimensional salience and identification of the relevant dimension in problem solving: A developmental study. *Developmental Psychology*, 1971, *4*, 135–140.

Piaget, J., & Inhelder, B. *Le Developement des Quantites chez l'enfant*. Neuchatel et Paris: Delachaus et Niestle, 1941.

Piaget, J., & Inhelder, B. *The psychology of the child*. New York: Basic Books, 1969.

Smedslund, J. The development of concrete transitivity of length in children. *Child Development*, 1963, *34*, 389–405.

Smiley, S. S., & Weir, M. W. Role of dimensional dominance in reversal and non-reversal shift behavior. *Journal of Experimental Child Psychology*, 1966, *4*, 296–307

Suchman, R. G., & Trabasso, T. R. Stimulus preference and cue function in young children's concept attainment. *Journal of Experimental Child Psychology*, 1966, *3*, 188–198.

Trabasso, T. R., & Bower, G. H. *Attention in learning: Theory and research*. New York: Wiley, 1968.

Youniss, J., & Furth, H. Prediction of causal events as a function of transitivity and perceptual congruency in hearing and deaf children. *Child Development*, 1966, *37*, 73–81.

6

Language and Thought
in Piagetian Theory

TIMOTHY E. MOORE
ADRIENNE E. HARRIS
York University, Toronto, Canada

The relationship of language and thought has provoked a long and extensive debate in linguistics, philosophy, and psychology. Watson (1924) viewed language and thought as one and the same thing. While the Russian view differs from the peripheralist approach of American behaviorism, in which thought was treated as unvocalized speech, they nonetheless assume a tight interdependence of thinking and speaking (Sokolov, 1969). Vygotsky (1962) maintains the interdependence of language and thought, but argues for independent genetic roots for both activities. The Whorfian hypothesis (1940), in its strong form, asserts that language is a determining vehicle or constraint for thought.

Today, controversy continues, although the nature of the claims

The data reported here are part of a larger study investigating class inclusion, conservation, comprehension and production of passives, and semantic and syntactic categories. Only the data on conservation and passivizations are included in this discussion. We are grateful to E. Hopkins of the Bayview Glen Daycare Centre for use of subjects and facilities. Portions of this study were reported at the annual meeting of the Canadian Psychological Association, Quebec City, 1975.

131

has changed. In psychology two major competing explanations regarding the relationship of language and thought can be identified. Chomsky has suggested that the capacity to learn a first language is determined in large part by the presence of language-specific principles of organization which are innate properties of the human mind. The early appearance of systematic rule-bound grammatical structures in the productions of young children has led a number of researchers to conclude that linguistic knowledge (often of a surprisingly specific nature) is an innate property of the species (McNeill, 1970). The Piagetian position, on the other hand, purports to examine language activity in the context of the developing intellectual capacities of the child. Logical development is seen as providing the foundation for language. Language skills are regarded as a reflection of a more general underlying cognitive competence that manifests itself in various activities, including language behavior. Piaget often stresses that language *reflects* rather than *determines* cognitive development.

> Linguistic progress is not responsible for logical or operational progress. It is rather the other way around. The logical or operational level is likely to be responsible for a more sophisticated language level [Piaget, 1972, p. 14].

Such a position is very different from—if not incompatible with—Chomsky's claim that

> the child acquires his language . . . at a time when he is not capable of complex intellectual achievements in many other domains. This achievement is relatively independent of intelligence or the particular course of experience [Chomsky, 1968, p. 66].

How might these apparently discordant positions be resolved? First, one could attempt a formal comparison of the two theoretical systems. Can current views about language acquisition be accommodated within the general framework of Piagetian theory? Can the field of developmental psycholinguistics be characterized by some explicit and minimally necessary theoretical statements or principles—which could then be examined for their compatibility (or lack of it) with principles of Piagetian theory? This is an ambitious task and a particularly difficult one because there is no "theory" of language acquisition, as such. Considerable disagreement exists regarding the mental operations or competence that ought to be attributed to children on the basis of what they say (Moore, 1973). In the absence of any consensus on what constitutes language competence, it is perhaps premature to engage in a general theoretical analysis of its means of acquisition.

Another approach would be to attempt empirical tests of the Piagetian claim that linguistic competence necessarily implies and requires some prior or concomitant level of cognitive achievement in nonverbal activity. This chapter will describe one such attempt. In light of its prevalence, Piaget has relatively little to say about language. There are very few empirical studies that directly address language development within the context of Piagetian cognitive development. Given this dearth of empirical support (not to mention the theoretical uncertainty in psycholinguistics), it is noteworthy that some of the Piagetian claims are as strong as they are. The relevant experiments (most of which will be reviewed in what follows) are usually interpreted as demonstrating that (a) cognitive development determines language development, or that (b) language development does *not* determine cognitive development. The possibility of interdependence is largely ignored; thus, when (b) is purportedly demonstrated, it is implied that (a) must be the case.[1]

For example, Sinclair (1967) demonstrated a difference in the use of comparative terms (*bigger, smaller*) between conservers and nonconservers. Conservers were more likely than nonconservers to use somewhat more complex descriptive terms. This gross correlation is interpreted by Sinclair (1969) as indicating that correct use of *more, less*, etc. is "closely linked to operational progress [p. 324]." The same data are interpreted by Piaget (1970a) as showing "a relationship between operational level and linguistic level [p. 49]." During the same study, Sinclair tried to teach the nonconservers the sorts of comparative expressions that they had not produced previously. This attempt met with moderate success, but was ineffective in bringing about the acquisition of the conservation skills that these children had lacked before the verbal training. Nonconservers who received some training in the use of certain comparative terms did not, subsequent to this training, become conservers. On this basis, Sinclair (1969) concluded that "language is not the source of logic, but is on the contrary structured by logic [p. 325]." Similarly, Piaget (1972) concludes that "operational level is likely to be responsible for a more sophisticated language level [p 14]"; and Furth (1970) elaborates at length on the "dependency of linguistic use on operational level [p. 256]." These conclusions are all unwarranted, as Fodor, Bever, and Garrett (1974) point out. Few, if any, contemporary investigators of language acquisition would ad-

---

[1] We do not mean to imply that either of these two unidirectional dependencies (or independence) exhaust the possible interpretive frameworks. A practicable *juste milieu* will be proposed in the conclusion section.

here to a strong Whorfian position; thus defenses against such a conception seem rather gratuitous.

More specific criticisms of the Sinclair study are also in order. First, while it is true that conservers were more likely than nonconservers to use the more complex comparatives, conservers were also, on the average, several months older than nonconservers. Sinclair does not provide enough data to permit a definitive analysis, but it is quite possible that the overall positive correlation that she observes is mediated by age, and thus would not constitute evidence of a unidirectional dependency. A demonstration that both language skills and operative functioning improve with age is uninteresting.

Second, conservation performance depends, at least partly, on the comprehension and use of certain verbal expressions. The child's competent use of comparative and dimensional terms is already being measured, to some extent, on conservation tasks—and then is measured again in a nonconservation setting. The study thus correlates two activities both of which require the same linguistic competence.

Lastly, Sinclair found that teaching children "operator-like words" (*more, less, as much as*) was only marginally and temporarily successful in inducing conservation. The words were correctly "understood" in simple situations, but not used precisely or reliably in the absence of some demonstrated operational skills. Sinclair refers to these "operator" terms as "syntactical structures," and concludes that their correct use is closely tied to operative functions. This is a rather idiosyncratic use of the term *syntax*. The structure of the child's speech is not analyzed. Instead, the manipulation of particular lexical items is the subject of training and of experimental analysis. It is the child's referencing skill—his accurate use of specific adjectival terms—that seems more closely linked to the operative level. Given the nature of the terms and the measures of operativity, an overall correspondence is not at all surprising. This study does not really concern itself with the structural properties of language (specifically syntax), and typifies the Piagetian view of language as a medium for the expression of cognitive operations.

Furth (1970) interprets another of Sinclair's studies (1968) in a distressingly tautological fashion. Sinclair required children of various ages (3:6 to 7:6) to comprehend, produce, and repeat various passive constructions. In the repetition condition, the children were asked to repeat passive statements and then to demonstrate the appropriate action through the use of toys. (*Montre-moi ce qui se passe.*) There were few correct repetitions accompanied by incorrect actions. When this did occur (among the 4- and 5-year-olds), imitation was very good—with correct phrasing and intonation, but without apparent comprehension. Furth views the solicitation of repetitions as "training."

> The dependency of linguistic use on operational level—and not vice versa—became apparent when preoperational children were trained to use the more mature linguistic sentences. They learned the words but there were only minimal improvements in general operational performances. . . . The speaker's developed capacity to transform active into passive sentences was primarily a function of having attained reversible operations. [p. 256].

The major problem with this study, which makes Furth's interpretations particularly unpersuasive, is that there were no independent measures of operativity. One cannot use comprehension of the passive construction as evidence of concrete-operational thought and then turn around and argue that comprehension of the passive *depends upon* the presence of concrete operations, as measured by correct comprehension of passives.

An analogy between the competence implied by an understanding of the active–passive structure and the cognitive implications of "operativity" has been extensively described by Sinclair and Ferreiro (1970). On a conservation task, for example, the child must ignore an irrelevant perceptual transformation; whereas when comprehending a passive, the child must accommodate a reversal of subject–object order and a change in verb form, at the same time recognizing no change in meaning. Sinclair and Ferreiro describe a number of stages in the development of the passive. One of their experimental tasks required children to express an observed action sequence, and to begin their statement by designating the figure or element that had been the object of the observed action. First there is a stage of incomplete production—fragments of an utterance are produced (subject–verb, verb–object). Next is a stage of simple production in the *active* form. Third, a stage of subject–object reversibility with *no* corresponding compensation in the verb. This renders an incorrect description. Finally, there is a stage of subject–object reversal combined with a change in verb form and the use of a preposition. Thus the development of the ability to generate a passive construction is described in terms compatible with a Piagetian analysis of the development of conservation—where successful performance requires the coordination of reversibility and compensation as the surface dimensions of stimuli change. Unfortunately, Sinclair and Ferreiro did not test any of their subjects on Piagetian tasks; the relationship is implied but not empirically demonstrated.

A study which *did* include independent measures of operativity was performed by Beilin (1975). He classified 86 children on a reversibility dimension—low, medium, and high. Performances on sensorimotor reversibility, conservation of continuous and discontinuous quantity, seriation, and classification tasks were used to assign subjects to one of the three levels of reversibility. The same children were also tested on a variety of language tasks, all of which were designed to demonstrate an understanding of the active–passive construction. Performance on both sets of measures improved with age. In general, comprehension and production of passives were related to the reversibility level of subjects. However, we do not agree with Beilin (1975) that this not-unexpected overall correspondence constitutes evidence of a "postulated relationship between reversibility level and linguistic performance [p. 52]"; nor can we agree with the more general conclusion "that language development occurs *as a consequence of* and in association with the development of cognitive structures and functions [p. 83; italics added]." When passives were solicited from the children as descriptions of the experimenter's enactment of "Mark pushing Susan," 23% of the productions of subjects showing low-level reversibility were complete descriptions in a passive form. Turning to synonymy judgments, 15 out of 39 low-reversibility subjects were able to state at an above-chance level that the active and passive forms of an utterance read by the experimenter were equivalent in meaning. In a different task subject and object were reversed in pairs of active and passive descriptions. The children were required to recognize non-synonymy by choosing the appropriate pictorial representation of the utterance and its reversal form, *and* by judging whether or not the two sentences as read by the experimenter were the same in meaning. Here, 19 of the 39 low-reversibility subjects performed at an above-chance level. In summarizing his findings, Beilin qualifies his position somewhat by acknowledging that "the evidence does not point to a perfect one-to-one cognitive–linguistic mapping, because being at a low reversibility level did not necessarily preclude a subject from demonstrating adequate linguistic performance [p. 364]." In a more recent article, Beilin (1976) elaborates upon possible interdependencies between linguistic and cognitive development.

Only one other study that we know of has attempted to test directly a relationship between general cognitive skill and linguistic facility. Scholnick and Adams (1973) tested reversibility by means of a matrix-permutation test, and then tested the subjects' comprehension of passives by requiring them to correctly identify the pictorial version of a passive utterance. "There was little evidence of a strong relationship between passive and reversal skills" [p. 744].

Reversibility

The concept of reversibility is extremely ubiquitous. It is sometimes treated as something that can be experienced—thus children may receive "reversibility training" (Wallach, Wall, & Anderson, 1967), although this use of the term "does not clearly encompass these processes as defined by Piaget [Sigel & Hooper, 1968, p. 261]." "The preoperational child's thought lacks reversibility," according to Ginsburg and Opper (1969) although they do attribute to the preoperational child the ability to "predict an empirical reversibility [p. 167]." According to Piaget and Inhelder (1969), however, reversibility is "already functioning at the sensorimotor level [p. 20]" and "grows until it reaches the form in which it is most familiar to us: that of the most general characteristics of operations as a whole [Inhelder & Piaget, 1964, p. 291]." Reversibility, then, in its various forms, is found at all developmental stages—from the relatively simple circular reactions of the sensorimotor period to the more complex processes of conservation during the later stages of concrete operations. Given its extreme pervasiveness, it is perhaps disputable whether or not reversibility can be construed as a specific unitary cognitive operation (Brainerd, 1970). Assuming, for the sake of argument, that it can be so construed, how can we best characterize reversibility in meaningful psychological terms? Taylor (1971) has provided as clear a statement as we could find:

> Thought is "reversible" when it can operate [upon] transformations and still recover its point of departure. Now, properly to understand something is to be able to follow the changes it undergoes, or could undergo, and to grasp well enough what is involved in these changes so that one can say what would be required to return the object to its initial state; and this either by simple reversal, or by compensating operations of some kind whose relations to the original one understands. . . . The growth . . . towards reversibility . . . can be seen as a growth in objectivity [and] to see the world objectively is to see it as a coherent set of transformations, as something which would ideally be manipulable in a coherent way [p. 410].

Since reversibility is assumed to underly a wide variety of cognitive tasks, which differ greatly in difficulty and age of acquisition, it is not surprising to find it involved in the case of children's facility with passives.[2]

---

[2] We do not wish to defend the use of the concept of reversibility—or its implementation in the case of passives. Such implementation is already a fait accompli (Sinclair, 1968, 1971; Sinclair & Ferreiro, 1970; Beilin, 1975; Scholnick & Adams, 1973). Some criticisms of the concept are provided by Brainerd (1970). Macnamara

Timothy E. Moore and Adrienne E. Harris

The initial formalization of a passive transformation looked like this:

If S_1 is a grammatical sentence of the form

$$NP_1 - Aux - V - NP_2$$

then the corresponding string of the form

$$NP_2 - Aux + be + en - V - by + NP_1$$

is also a grammatical sentence [Chomsky, 1957].

Not only is the second string grammatical, but it is equivalent in meaning to the first string. A child who behaves as if *John hit the ball* and *the ball was hit by John* mean the same thing is assumed to be in possession of a grammatical rule that embodies this identity—not just for John, balls, and hitting, but for *all* utterances of the form S_1.[3]

(1976a) has recently questioned the applicability of reversibility to the passive construction. He asks "of what significance is it to psychology whether or not children's mastery of the passive keeps pace with their . . . reversibility [p. 650]?" The significance, as we see it, is this: It is one of the few instances where Piagetians have been explicit enough about some alleged relation between language and thought to allow any sort of empirical test of their claims. We are, therefore, attempting an empirical test of a hypothesis that Macnamara dismisses out of hand as being ill-conceived.

[3] This point merits some discussion since it is central to much previous work and is also relevant to the present study. Essentially, the claim is that structural differences between passives and actives involve shifts in surface dimensions that can be decoded to yield an underlying semantic equivalence. Anisfeld and Klenbort (1973) note that the shift from active to pasive voice is basically one of "structural paraphrase which maintains essential content and lexical composition." This notion is consistent with Chomsky's later views (1965) that the passive is signaled by an obligatory transformation on a kernel string which has the optional tag "manner adverbial." Passive and active forms are thus assumed to have identical base structure. Equivalence, therefore (as in the Piagetian conservation tasks), is at an abstract, structural level—whether termed syntactic or logicosemantic.

A number of investigators have empirically tested the degree and nature of equivalence in structural paraphrases of active–passive shifts. Clark (1965) for example had subjects generate sentences from incomplete sentence frames. The pattern of uncertainty in subject, verb, and object differed between actives and passives, as did the use of animate nouns as subject and object. Passives were not treated simply as transformed actives. Other investigators have used the semantic differential to examine the connotative and evaluative meaning of lexical items occurring in either voice, and in subject or object position (Gumenik & Dolinsky, 1969; Howe, 1970; Johnson, 1967). For the most part, active–passive sentence pairs are understood to be equivalent in meaning—with some differences in connotative meaning as a function of voice and/or grammatical position. Stylistic variation

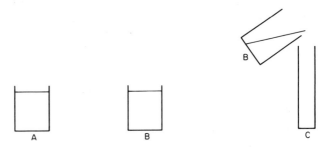

FIGURE 6.1

A conventional conservation task would require the child to judge that the volumes of liquid in A and C are equivalent, having first judged the volumes in A and B to be equivalent. Failure to recognize the equivalence of volumes, following a change in shape of one of the containers, is attributed to the child's lacking the mental operation of reversibility.

Considering the passive in Piagetian terms, we might say that the semantic content of an utterance is being "conserved," although its form of expression is changed—just as a successful conserver realizes that the volume of water in the tall narrow beaker (C) is equivalent to that in (A), even though the shape of the container has been altered (see Figure 6.1). In each case, a form of reversibility as articulated by Taylor (1971) seems clearly implicated. We examined children's performances on a wide range of conservation tasks in order to further investigate alleged dependencies between cognitive and linguistic operations.

Method

Subjects

The subjects were 72 upper middle class children attending a private day care center. They ranged in age from 3 years, 5 months to 8 years, 11 months.

(Gregory, 1967), presupposition (Tannenbaum and Williams, 1968), focus (Hornby, 1971) and intonation (Hornby & Hass, 1970) may all exert some subtle differences on interpretation of actives and passives, but these variables are often inoperative for subjects asked to judge or rate equivalence. It is thus possible to admit many of the current arguments and analyses which surround topic–comment distinction and presupposition, while maintaining the claim of functional equivalence across structural paraphrase.

Procedures

CONSERVATION TESTS

Twelve different conservation tests, presented in counterbalanced orders, assessed the children's ability to conserve number, substance, two-dimensional space, continuous quantity, discontinuous quantity, and weight. This battery has been developed by Goldschmid and Bentler (1968) to provide the "psychometrically best assessment of conservation [p. 795]." The 12 tasks consisted of:

1. *Unprovoked correspondence:* The subject is presented with a row of poker chips and is asked to pick from a larger pile of chips the same number of chips as are in the row.

2. *Provoked correspondence:* Six toy bottles are laid out in a row. The subject is asked to match each bottle with a glass. The bottles are then moved closer together, and the subject is asked if there is still the same number of bottles as glasses.

3. *Conservation of substance (a):* The subject is presented with two balls of clay and is asked to make them the same size (A = A'). Then the experimenter rolls A' out into a sausage shape, and the subject is asked if the two shapes represent the same amounts of clay.

4. *Conservation of substance (b):* The above task is repeated, with the difference that instead of being rolled into a sausage shape, A' is broken into three separate pieces. The subject is asked whether the three pieces contain the same amount as A.

5. *Conservation of two-dimensional space (a):* The subject is shown two identical squares (A and A'), each composed of two equal-sized triangles, the bases of which form the diagonal of each square. The subject is asked if the two squares are equal. The two triangles from A' are then realigned to form a pyramid. The subject is asked if the square and the pyramid cover the same area.

6. *Conservation of two-dimensional space (b):* Eight matchsticks are arranged to form two squares of four matches each. The subject is asked if the two squares are the same size. The matches from one of the squares are then arranged to form a straight line. The subject is asked if it is as far around the square as it is along the line.

7. *Conservation of continuous quantity (a):* Two beakers (A and A') of the same size and containing equal amounts of water are placed in front of the subject. The subject is asked if they

contain equal amounts. If the subject answers yes, testing proceeds; if not, the subject is asked to adjust the contents until each beaker contains the same amount as the other. The experimenter then pours the contents of A into two smaller beakers (B and B'). The subject is asked if B and B' (combined) then contain the same amount as A'. The contents of B are then poured into two still smaller beakers C and C', and, likewise, the contents of B' are poured into D and D'. The subject is asked to compare the amount of liquid in A with that in C, C', D, and D'.

8. *Conservation of continuous quantity* (*b*): The initial part of the above procedure is repeated. Contents of A are poured into a short fat beaker. The subject is asked to compare the contents of A with that of the different-shaped beaker.

9. *Conservation of discontinuous quantity* (*a*): The same procedure as in 7 is followed, using beads rather than water. Experimenter and subject place one bead at a time into each of A and A' in order to establish the initial correspondence.

10. *Conservation of discontinuous quantity* (*b*): The same procedure as in 8 is followed, with the modification noted in 9.

11. *Conservation of weight* (*a*): A ball of clay is placed on each side of a balance scale. The subject adjusts the balls until a balance is attained. The experimenter then changes the shape of one of the balls, and the subject is asked if the two pieces still weigh the same.

12. *Conservation of weight* (*b*): Similar to 11, except that one of the balls, after balance is attained, is broken into three pieces.

Correct explanations as well as correct judgments were necessary in order for the subject to be scored as "correct" on any of the tasks. For the most part, correct judgments *were* accompanied by correct explanations. Pains were taken in an attempt to ensure that the subject understood what was being asked of him or her. Colloquial expressions were often used; the experimenter frequently repeated tasks and/or instructions. It is certainly possible that failure on any of these tasks could be attributed to a lack of facility with the relevant terminology, rather than a lack of the cognitive operation in question (see Siegel's discussion, Chapter 3). However, these tasks are modeled after the procedures described by Piaget (1950) and have a long history of use in the Piagetian tradition. It was our intent to measure as fairly and as faithfully as possible the extent of conservation skills, as they are tapped by these conventional methods. Each subject received a score of from 0 to 12 on the conservation battery. Subjects were tested until there were 18 children with scores of 0, 18 with scores of 12, and 36 with scores ranging from 1 to 11.

LANGUAGE TASKS

A week to 10 days after the conservation tasks were administered, all subjects were tested again by a different experimenter on six different tasks, of which the comprehension and production of passives were a part. The experimenter was unaware of the subjects' previous performances on the conservation battery. Both the comprehension and production tasks utilized five toys: a boy doll, a girl doll, a horse, a cow, and a car.

· *Comprehension test:* Each child's comprehension of actives and passives was measured through his ability to correctly demonstrate with the toys the appropriate action of an utterance read to the subject by the experimenter in the active or passive voice. For example, the experimenter might say "The car is bumped by the horse." In order to be scored correct, the subject was required to strike the car with the horse. An ambiguous action involving the subject's moving the recipient of the action in addition to the actor was scored incorrect. Ten sentences were read to each subject in predetermined random orders. Five actives and five passives were used—all of which, with one exception, expressed a different event (i.e., one event was expressed in both active and passive form).[4] Each child received a score of 0 to 5 on the com-

---

[4] It could be argued that in order to demonstrate reversibility in the linguistic domain, one would have to solicit synonymy judgments of active–passive pairs (Beilin, 1975); or show that the subject understands (or can produce) both forms of the same sentence; or correctly judge the truth value of pictures relative to their verbal description in the active or passive voice (Olson & Filby, 1972; Clark & Chase, 1972). We believe that such dependent measures may introduce more problems than they solve. Verification measures require explanations of how perceptual events might be encoded, as well as how such encodings might be compared to their appropriate verbal descriptions. Much of the focus in such studies is on the process by which subjects compare sentence representations against (relatively) independent perceptual representations. With adults it is assumed from the outset that actives and passives are part of the subject's repertoire. We made no assumptions, but sought a straightforward means of demonstrating the presence or absence of the passive structure. If the subject can reliably follow directions phrased in the passive voice, or produce correct descriptions in the passive voice, then he has the passive in his repertoire. A conscious reflection upon the "transformational rule" (which may or may not be involved) is a criterion that untutored adults and not-so-naive linguists might have difficulty meeting—not to mention children.

While children (or adults) may behave as if actives and passives are function-

prehension test. (All subjects could comprehend and produce actives.)

Production test: Production was tested by having each subject describe an action performed by the experimenter with the toys. Ten actions were performed. For half of them, passives were solicited by asking the child to begin his sentence with the word X, where X was the logical object or recipient of the action. All sentences, in both comprehension and production tests, were reversible. Colloquial forms of the passive (The boy got runned over by the car) were scored as correct. For half the subjects, the production test preceded the comprehension test, and for the other half, the order was reversed. Moreover, at least one other task intervened between comprehension and production tests.

Results and Discussion

No sex differences were observed on any of the measures taken. Of particular interest was the performance of poor conservers on the language tasks. If correct use of the passive structure is dependent upon the prior presence of reversibility operations, as measured by conservation tasks, then children with poor conservation performances should show correspondingly poor performance on the language tests. Specifically, there should be no evidence of facility with passives, in the absence of conservation skills.

Table 6.1 provides the mean scores for comprehension and production of passives, as a function of subjects' scores on the conservation battery. Performance on all tasks improved with age. Those subjects with perfect conservation scores received almost perfect scores on the language tests, although one subject produced no passives. Production scores dropped off appreciably as conservation scores dropped. Five subjects with almost perfect conservation scores produced no passives. Of those subjects who could not conserve at all, six received a score of 3 or more on the comprehension test, and only 3 subjects received scores of 0 on the comprehension tests. Table 6.2 provides a breakdown

---

ally equivalent, it does not necessarily follow that the linguistic transformation which formally expresses the equivalence has some isomorphic correspondence in the child's "mental" grammar. A rule that may be simple, elegant, general, and economical on linguistic criteria may be inelegant and unmanageable for the language processing system. It is conceivable that actives and passives have separate and independent psychological representations (see Bever, 1970b; Watt, 1970). However, so long as actives and passives can be demonstrated to exist, then some form of reversibility is implicated by their functional equivalence.

TABLE 6.1

Mean Scores on the Language Tests as a Function of Conservation Score

Conservation score (max. = 12)	Age (months)	N	Passive comprehension (max. = 5)	Passive productions (max. = 5)
12	91.4	18	4.8	4.3
	(68–107)		3–5	(0–5)
7.2	79.3	36	4.3	2.7
(2–11)	(62–102)		(1–5)	(0–5)
0	47.1	18	2.1	.8
	(41–66)		(0–4)	(0–4)

Note: Ranges are in parentheses.

of the comprehension and production scores of the nonconservers.

These data constitute evidence for the appearance of logical operations in language *prior to* their emergence in cognitive nonverbal activity (at least as these latter are measured by conservation tasks). Children who cannot conserve demonstrate some facility with the passive construction. If the same mental operation (i.e., reversibility) is at work in each task, then Piaget's claim that operational progress will give rise to more sophisticated language skills is not substantiated by these data. It is possible that the logical operations implied by conservation skills could become manifest *first* in the domain of language—perhaps because children typically have more practice and experience manipulating and using word strings than they do with beakers of water, balls of plasticene, or rows of matchsticks.

Analyses of language by the Genevan school often entail a distinction between figurative and operative knowing (Piaget, 1970b; Furth,

TABLE 6.2

Scores of Nonconservers on Passive Comprehension and Production Tests

Score (maximum = 5)	Comprehension	Production
4	(4)	(1)
3	(2)	(1)
2	(6)	(2)
1	(3)	(3)
0	(3)	(11)

Note: Numbers in parentheses indicate the number of subjects obtaining that score.

1970). Figurative knowing implicates a range of mental activities—perceptions, imitations, some forms of imagery. In general, these involve mental representations of objects, events, or states that are static and nontransforming. Furth (1970) has suggested that figurative knowing is relatively closely tied to sensory input, in contrast to operative knowing, which involves some restructuring and transforming of mental schemata. It is through operative knowing that form is extracted from content and becomes part of the existing mental schemata of the knower. Applied to language use, operative knowing actually defines or elaborates the meaning of linguistic material. The semantic interpretation of any lexical item is tied to the existing level of operative functioning. Furth seems to imply, however, that the initial acquisition of lexical items (i.e., "the medium of a symbol") involves figurative functioning. Notwithstanding his caution against reifying the figurative–operative distinction, it is an unusual proposal that words are first learned in some figurative manner, with meaning being subsequently attached or extracted through operative functioning (see Clark, 1973).

What is often confusing in the Piagetian treatment of language is the insistence that language, as one aspect of semiotic functioning, is partially figurative and partially operative. Additional confusion is generated by the tendency, in practice, to concentrate on the figurative aspects of language despite the claims for operativity.[5] These confusions can be somewhat ameliorated if one remembers that Piagetians are making distinctions about semiotics that originate in the work of Pierce

---

[5] Another source of difficulty surrounding the figurative–operative distinction concerns the roles of *assimilation* and *accommodation*. These two processes are defined by Furth in a manner that does not appear consistent with more standard treatments. Thus Furth (1970, p. 245) states that the figurative aspect of knowing is given in the accommodation to the particular, static configuration of the [object]; the operative aspect refers to the assimilation of sensory input to operative structures through which the beholder understands . . . the construction and functioning of the [object]." Ginsberg and Opper (1969, p. 18) however, suggest that "the process of accommodation describes the individual's tendency to change in response to environmental demands. . . . Assimilation is the complementary process by which the individual deals with an environmental event in terms of his current structure. . . . Thus the individual not only modifies his structure in reaction to external demands (accommodation) he also uses his structure to incorporate elements of the external world (assimilation)." For Furth, accommodation seems more closely linked to sensory input, whereas Ginsberg and Opper imply that mental structures are transformed through the accommodation of current structure to environmental demands. Regardless of which of these interpretations is the most appropriate, there is skepticism in some quarters regarding the explanatory adequacy of these constructs (Macnamara, 1976b).

(1955). *Symbols*, which can have some iconic or enactive remnant of the significant to which they refer, can be *internalized* but this representation is primarily figurative. *Signs* which are both arbitrary and social are *interiorized* as a result of the transforming activity of operative knowing. Language thus has both symbolic and signifying potential.

In theory we might expect discussions of operative knowing to bear both on the cognitive activity of children (the familiar Piagetian terrain) and on the novel and specialized constructions that have been noted in the extended sentence strings of very young children. In practice, the Piagetian school has tended to treat language primarily as a symbolic medium, an optic through which to observe the emergence and manipulation of preexisting logical structures. The origin and nature of this medium qua medium receive scant attention. Furth tends to reduce many of the most dynamic and structurally sophisticated aspects of language use to an exclusively figurative level.

In much of the psycholinguistic work of the Genevan school, it is the referencing aspect of discrete signs that receives the most attention. When language is regarded as no more than a discrete set of signifiers, distinct from, but available to, operative schemata, it is not clear how to account for the use of extended and structurally rich strings of symbols with organizational constraints (i.e., syntax). Somewhat surprisingly, given the counsel about viewing figurative and operative knowing as bound in an interdependent dialectic, Furth's (1970) discussion of syntax suggests that grammatical knowledge represents a relatively primitive rule system, apprehensible within the context of figurative knowing:

> An implicit knowing of syntactic rules is by no means identical with operational knowing in the strict sense. Much of ordinary rule learning—e.g., implicit mastery of rules in perceptual, social and play behavior—focuses primarily on figurative rather than operative functioning. The particular circumstance that the child who has mastered language manipulates symbolic elements does not automatically raise this knowing to high-level operative understanding [Furth, 1970, p. 254].

In asserting the primacy of logical over linguistic structures, Furth insists that no medium is the primary source of intellectual growth. This may or may not be true, but it behooves any theory of intellectual development to explain the origins and nature of a medium that is as complex as human language, and that is acquired as early as it is. Much of the thrust of modern psycholinguistics has been to suggest that syntactic knowledge is captured in a set of rules that are both abstract and not explicitly rendered in surface production. Since the linguistic patterns in question appear in creative productions, and with novel content, it is most unlikely that they could be learned through imitation, as Furth implies. A learning process that could incorporate the properties of figurative knowing without trivializing the language phenomena at issue might be some sort of associationist model like contextual generalization. Furth seems headed in that direction when he asserts that "there is the acquisition of sequential patterns of what comes before and after [p. 249]." However, contextual generalization has been shown to be deficient on both linguistic and psychological grounds, and one of its primary advocates, Braine (1963), has long abandoned the position.

Conclusions

The Piagetian position on language asquisition seems vulnerable on at least two counts. First, the concentration on discrete reference and preoccupation with exclusively figurative aspects of language have given rise to a distinctly nonstructural analysis of language. An unnecessarily reified version of figurative thinking has lead to misunderstanding or underestimation of the nature of syntactic structure and its acquisition. Second, there are some curious and unsupported generative implications in the Piagetian treatment of language learning whereby meaning evolves first through figurative, and then through operative, knowing.

The relationship of logical structures and linguistic structures is bound to be a complex one whether the problem is treated dyachronically or synchronically, as Piaget (1970c) himself has acknowledged. While genetic epistemology and transformational grammar have resulted in interesting contradictory claims, one of which has been tested in the study reported here, there are features of both theories that seem compatible. The genetic and structural features of Chomsky's linguistics ought to have suggested interesting prospects for integration in a structural account of cognition. Evidence of mentalism has been noted in the implicit assumptions of both Piaget (Bever, 1970a) and Chomsky (Weimar, 1973). Perhaps a clue to the orthodoxy in Piagetian interpretations of language activity and the resultant rejection of much of Chomsky's work lies in some negative references to Chomsky's antiempiricism and insistence on an innate grammar—at least in its kernel form (Piaget, 1970c; Furth, 1970). The explicit nativism espoused by Chomsky may well have rendered the potentially useful insights arising from an application of transformational grammar to childrens' language quite un-palatable to the Genevan school.

An examination of the most recent writing on the topic by Piaget himself shows a subtle but potentially important theoretical shift. The initial accounts of the relationship between language and thought held that preexisting logical structures predict language functioning. This view appears in Piaget's writing as late as 1970. However, in the preface to Ferreiro's (1971) work on the expression of temporal relations in language activity, there seems to be an interesting departure from orthodoxy. In proposing a relationship between language and thought, Piaget suggests *two* options. On the one hand, it is possible to see cognitive operations as the motor of language: "Les operations consti-tueraint le moteur des progres du language mais un moteur en quelque sorte externe [in Ferreiro, 1971, p. xii]." Linguistic transformations ex-press underlying logical structure. Cognitive development arises in partic-ular areas of experience (des domaines effectivement délimités) and is ex-tended into the area of language activity. Alternatively, one might see *parallel* development in the linguistic and cognitive domain, with dif-ferent levels of operativity accountable through décalage. Decoding linguistic structure and solving various cognitive tasks are parallel prob-lems to which the child brings epistemological strategies. In 1971 this second position is, for Piaget, the preferable and more probable in-terpretation. Predictions about dependency and primacy seem to be giving way to statements about correlation. Beilin (1976) has also noted this apparent change in theoretical perspective.

The present study does not support the contention that language skills necessarily follow operative achievements in nonverbal activity. Regardless of their theoretical linguistic perspective, many investigators of children's language consistently attribute to children language struc-tures or skills that appear to be more complex and abstract than the cognitive apparatus assigned by Piagetian theory to a child of that age. One may conceive of the early appearance of language structures with-out postulating that language per se necessarily contributes to, or is responsible for, intellectual growth. Nor need one postulate the presence of elaborate, innate language-specific formations to account for the ob-served skills (McNeill, 1970). Language learning—or any other sort of learning—entails the induction of general principles from specific in-stances, but there is no reason to suppose that some single inductive strategy will account for all types of learning.

Some of Sinclair's more recent work is relevant in this regard. For example, Sinclair and Bronckart (1972) present evidence consistent with Bever's (1970) hypothesis that children decode language on the basis of perceptual strategies. According to Bever, a rule that (for the child) interprets a noun–verb–noun sequence as actor–action–object would account for the misinterpretation of passives on the part of younger children. Since the active form is probably the one most commonly encountered by children, it is reasonable to suppose that such perceptual strategies are learned—at least partly—as a result of "inductions over his experience, as opposed to being due to internal cognitive developments independent of specific experience [Bever, 1970b, p. 311]." In the Sinclair and Bronckart (1972) study, children from 3 to 6 years were asked to interpret (i.e., act out) word string combinations of either two nouns and one verb or two verbs and a noun in all possible permutations. Both transitive and intransitive verbs were used. The authors observed a developmental hierarchy of strategies for forming interpretations of these strings. After initial, primitive strategies in which the utterance is treated as having only two components, children tended to impose an agent–action–patient gloss on linguistic strings that they encountered. At first, they appear to use proximity to the verb as a clue for establishing either agent–action or action–patient relationships between lexical items. Later, a word order strategy is established in which noun–verb–noun (indeed any string with initial noun) is treated as agent–action–patient. The progressive modification of these decoding strategies is ascribed to the subjects' imposing "whatever structural linguistic knowledge they possessed [p. 347]" onto the deviant strings—such strategies becoming successively more sophisticated over time, as the amount of structural knowledge on which they are based is increased. Little reference is made to any concomitant unfolding of more general cognitive structures. However, the same data are discussed elsewhere (Sinclair, de-Zwart, 1973) within a broader theoretical context. Here Sinclair prefers to attribute the appearance of such strategies to the growth of more general cognitive processes—that is, to "some universal psychological factor [p. 15]"—rather than to some language-specific induction principle, or to some innately acquired universal linguistic "base." Again, however, as with some of the earlier mentioned Piagetian research, there is no independent demonstration of the existence of any substantive, generic, cognitive operations from which these strategies might emerge—beyond the very general observation that between the ages of 2 and 7, children come to differentiate between themselves and objects or actions in their environment. Just how these growing distinctions between self, agent, object, action, and so on "give rise to the first grammatical functions of subject–predicate and object–action [p. 23]" remains to be explicated.

In summary, a perusal of Piagetian literature on language acquisition, in conjunction with the data reported here, provides scant evidence for the contention that language skills are a reflection of more general cognitive operations. Constant exposure to linguistic data affords children the opportunity to begin language learning early. They accomplish the task relatively quickly—by means of various inductive procedures and perceptual strategies, the nature of which is the focus of much ongoing research. If the origins of these learning skills exist within more general cognitive operations, it remains for Piagetian theory to stipulate what these universal operations are, and how they are invoked in the particular case of language learning. At a minimum, they must be as complex and as general as the strategies implicated in early language learning. Rather than defining language phenomena in such a way that extant theory can accommodate them, it is reasonable to expect that the theory be adapted to account for the data. In its present form, Piagetian theory looks like an unlikely candidate for the elucidation of language learning procedures.

REFERENCES

Anisfeld, M., & Klenbort, I. On the function of structural paraphrase: The view from the passive voice. *Psychological Bulletin*, 1973; *79*, 117–126.

Beilin, H. *Studies in the cognitive basis of language development.* NY: Academic Press, 1975.

Beilin, H. Constructing cognitive operations linguistically. In H. Reese & Lipsitt (Eds.), *Advances in child development and behavior.* NY: Academic Press, 1976.

Bever, T. G. 'Discussion' of H. Sinclair's Sensorimotor action patterns as a condition for the acquisition of syntax. In R. Huxley & E. Ingram (Eds.), *Language acquisition: Models and methods.* NY: Academic Press, 1970. (a)

Bever, T. G. The cognitive basis for linguistic structure. In J. R. Hayes (Ed.), *Cognition and the development of language.* NY: Wiley, 1970. (b)

Braine, M. S. On learning the grammatical order of words. *Psychological Review*, 1963, *70*, 323–48.

Brainerd, C. J. Continuity and discontinuity hypotheses in conservation. *Developmental Psychology*, 1970, *3*, 225–28.

Chomsky, N. *Syntactic structures.* The Hague: Mouton, 1957.

Chomsky, N. *Aspects of the theory of syntax.* Cambridge: Massachusetts Institute of Technology Press, 1965

Chomsky, N. Language and the mind. *Psychology Today*, February, 1968.

Clark, E. What's in a word? On the child's acquisition of semantics in his first language. In Timothy E. Moore (Ed.), *Cognitive development and the acquisition of language.* NY: Academic Press, 1973.

Clark, H. Some structural properties of simple active and passive sentences. *Journal of Verbal Learning and Verbal Behavior*, 1965, *4*, 365–370.

Clark, H., & Chase, W. On the process of comparing sentences against pictures. *Cognitive Psychology*, 1972, *3*, 472–517.

Ferreiro, E. *Les relations temporelles dans le langage de l'enfant.* Geneva: Librarie Droz, 1971.

Fodor, J., Bever, T. G., & Garrett, M. *The psychology of language.* NY: McGraw-Hill, 1974.

Furth, H. On language and knowing in Piaget's developmental theory. *Human development,* 1970, *13,* 241–57.

Ginsburg, H., & Opper, S. *Piaget's theory of intellectual development.* Englewood Cliffs, NJ: Prentice-Hall, 1969.

Goldschmid, M., & Bentler, P. The dimensions and measurement of conservation. *Child development,* 1968, *39,* 787–802.

Gregory, M. Aspects of varieties differentiation. *Journal of Linguistics,* 1967, *3,* 177–198.

Gumenik, W. E., & Dolinsky, R. Connotative meaning of sentence subjects as a function of verb and object meaning under different grammatical transformations. *Journal of Verbal Learning and Verbal Behavior,* 1969, *8,* 653–57.

Hornby, P. A. Surface structure and topic-comment distinction: A developmental study. *Child Development,* 1971, *42,* 1975–88.

Hornby, P. A., & Hass, W. A. Use of contrastive stress by preschool children. *Journal of Speech and Hearing Research,* 1970, *3,* 395–399.

Howe, E. S. Passive transformation, cognitive imbalance, and evaluative meaning. *Journal of Verbal Learning and Verbal Behavior,* 1970, *9,* 171–175.

Inhelder, B., & Piaget, J. *The early growth of logic in the child.* NY: Norton, 1964.

Johnson, M. G. Syntactic position and rated meaning. *Journal of Verbal Learning and Verbal Behavior,* 1967, *6,* 240–46.

McNeill, D. *The acquisition of language: The study of developmental psycholinguistics.* NY: Harper & Row, 1970.

Macnamara, J. A general theory of cognitive and linguistic development. *Contemporary Psychology,* 1976, *21,* 649–50. (a)

Macnamara, J. Stomachs assimilate and accommodate, don't they? *Canadian Psychological Review,* 17, 3, 1976. (b)

Moore, T. E. (Ed.), *Cognitive development and the acquisition of language.* NY: Academic Press, 1973.

Olson, D., & Filby, N. On the comprehension of active and pasive sentences. *Cognitive Psychology,* 1972, *3,* 361–381.

Piaget, J. *The psychology of intelligence.* NY: Harcourt, 1950.

Piaget, J. *Genetic epistemology.* NY: Columbia University Press, 1970. (a)

Piaget, J. Piaget's theory. In P. Mussen (Ed.), *Carmichael's manual of Child psychology* (Vol. 1). NY: Wiley, 1970. (b)

Piaget, J. *Structuralism.* NY: Basic Books, 1970. (c)

Piaget, J. Problems of equilibration. In C. Nodine, J. Gallagher, & R. Humphrey (Eds.), *Piaget and Inhelder on equilibration.* Philadelphia: Jean Piaget Society, 1972.

Piaget, J., & Inhelder, B. *The psychology of the child.* NY: Basic Books, 1969.

Pierce, C. S. *The philosophical writings of Pierce.* NY: Dover, 1955.

Scholnick, E., & Adams, M. Relationships between language and cognitive skills: Passive voice comprehension, backward repetition, and matrix permutation. *Child Development,* 1973, *44,* 741–46.

Sigel, I., & Hooper, F. (Eds.), *Logical thinking in children.* NY: Holt, Rinehart and Winston, 1968.

Sinclair, H. *Acquisition du language et dévelopment de la pensée.* Paris: Dunod, 1967.

Sinclair, H. L'acquisition des structures syntaxiques. *Psychologie Française,* 1968, *13,* 167–74.

Sinclair, H. Developmental psycholinguistics. In D. Elkind & J. Flavell (Eds.), *Studies in cognitive development.* NY: Oxford, 1969.

Sinclair, H. Piaget's theory and language acquisition. In M. Rosskopf, L. Steffe, & S. Taback (Eds.), *Piagetian cognitive-development research and mathematical education.* Washington: National Council of Teachers of Mathematics, 1971.

Sinclair, H., & Bronckart, J. S–V–O: A linguistic universal? A study in developmental psycholinguistics. *Journal of Experimental Child Psychology,* 1972, *14,* 329–48.

Sinclair, H., & Ferreiro, E. Étude génétique de la compréhension, production et répétition des phrases au mode passif. *Archives de psychologie,* January, 1970.

Sinclair-de-Zwart, H. Language acquisition and cognitive development. In T. E. Moore (Ed.), *Cognitive development and the acquisition of language.* NY: Academic Press, 1973.

Sokolov, A. N. Studies of the speech mechanisms of thinking. In M. Cole & I. Maltzman (Eds.), *A handbook of contemporary Soviet psychology.* NY: Basic Books, 1969.

Tannenbaum, P., & Williams, F. Generation of active and passive sentences as a function of subject or object focus. *Journal of Verbal Learning and Verbal Behavior,* 1968, *7,* 246–50.

Taylor, C. What is involved in a genetic psychology? In T. Mischel (Ed.), *Cognitive psychology and epistemology.* NY: Academic Press, 1971.

Vygotsky, L. S. *Thought and language.* Cambridge: Massachusetts Institute of Technology 1934/1962.

Wallach, L., Wall, A., & Anderson, L. Number conservation: The roles of reversibility, addition–subtraction, and misleading perceptual cues. *Child Development,* 1967, *38,* 425–42.

Watson, J. B. *Behaviourism.* NY: Norton, 1924.

Watt, W. On two hypotheses concerning psycholinguistics. In J. R. Hayes (Ed.) *Cognition and the development of language.* New York, Wiley, 1970.

Weimar, W. B. Psycholinguistics and Plato's paradoxes of the *Meno. American Psychologist,* 1973, *28,* 15–33.

Whorf, B. J. Science and linguistics. *The Technology Review,* 1940, *42,* 229–31.

7

The Necessity of Logical
Necessity in Piaget's Theory

VERNON C. HALL
DANIEL B. KAYE
Syracuse University

Several years ago Jan Smedslund introduced into the field of cognitive psychology a procedure that he labeled "experimental extinction." This label was probably unfortunate because it differed in important ways from a much-investigated process already in the area of learning psychology and also called experimental extinction. In the latter case *extinction* has been defined as a cessation of a formerly reinforced response as a result of the removal of the reinforcement. Smedslund (1961), on the other hand, used the term for a situation in which a subject was forced to account for an empirical event that was contrary to the subject's prediction. If the subject's explanation of the event did not remain consistent with the logic that the subject had originally used, he was said to have *extinguished*. In later research, if the subject changed his prediction on subsequent trials to be consistent with his new logic, he was also said to have extinguished.

The purposes of this chapter are (*a*) to review the brief history of this procedure, including what the present authors believe to be the important findings to date; and (*b*) to critically evaluate the findings as they relate to Piaget's specific concept of logical necessity and to his theory in general.

153

In the original study, Smedslund used the extinction procedure to compare natural weight conservers (subjects who came into the experiment as weight conservers) with subjects whom he had trained through reinforcement procedures to conserve to the degree to which they believed in the "logical necessity" of conservation of weight.[1] In actual practice subjects were initially shown two balls of clay that were equal in weight. Smedslund then changed the shape of one of the pieces of clay and at the same time secretly removed a small piece. The subject was then shown that the two pieces of clay were not the same weight. Finally, Smedslund used a probing technique to determine how the subject accounted for this inequality. If the subject was unable to arrive at an explanation that allowed him to be consistent with his original belief that changing shape did not change weight (e.g., some clay must have dropped on the floor), he was said to have extinguished. The fact that all trained subjects ($N = 11$) were unable to produce such an explanation whereas 6 of the 13 natural conserving subjects were able to was used as evidence that natural conservers were more apt to believe in the "logical necessity" of conservation of weight than trained subjects. This study gained wide acceptance in Piagetian circles as evidence for the difference between subjects trained and those acquiring conservation "naturally." The implication is that the quality of the response of the trained subject is much different from that of the natural conserver (Baldwin, 1967; Beilin, 1970).

It has been in this area of conservation-training studies that the major controversy between Piagetians and American learning psychologists has centered. It is one thing to report normative data showing that children do not give conserving responses until a specific age or stage has been reached; it is another to suggest that they do not have

---

[1] The weight conservation task has been operationalized in a number of ways. Basically, the experimenter shows the subject two objects (generally balls of clay) and it is determined that they weigh the same amount (through some sort of mutual agreement on the part of the experimenter and subject or by actually weighing the objects on a balance scale). Next, the shape of the one of the objects is changed, and the child is asked whether or not the two objects still weigh the same amount (the actual questions asked have been shown to influence answers given by nonconservers). Conservers say the weights are the same whereas nonconservers indicate that the objects now weigh different amounts. Generally, at least three such tasks are used. Those conserving on all three tasks are labeled conservers. Those conserving on one or two tasks are often labeled as partial conservers, whereas those not conserving on any of the tasks are labeled nonconservers. Other types of conservation (e.g., length) are measured in a similar manner.

the capacity to learn to give such responses. From a Piagetian stand-point, however, giving the conserving response is not enough. Evidence must be provided to show that trained conservers really believe in the logical necessity of conservation. The reaction of Piagetians to initial training studies where only a conserving response was required was to set up additional criteria that must be met in order for researchers to maintain that their trained subjects were indeed equivalent to natural conservers. For instance, Inhelder and Sinclair (1969) maintained that successfully trained conservers must include in their conservation re-sponses: (a) appropriate explanations; (b) persistence of conservation over time; (c) generalization to nontrained material; and (d) resistance to countersuggestion.

In an attempt to meet such criteria, a measurement procedure for a conservation training study was designed (Kingsley & Hall, 1967). In this case *countersuggestion* was defined as a situation in which the experimenter did not give the subject the appropriate option when he asked the child the conservation question. (The child was asked "Which piece of clay will be heavier?" when in fact the correct answer was "They will be the same.") To provide added evidence that training was successful, the subjects were also presented at the end of the posttest with an extinction of weight trial. In addition, the experimenters post-tested a number of so-called natural conservers as an added comparison group. To the dismay of the researchers the subjects in this group an-swered all of the conservation questions correctly (length, weight, and mass conservation questions were included), gave logical explanations for conservation, resisted countersuggestion, and yet extinguished (failed to give a logical explanation for the difference in weight of two initially equal clay balls when a piece of clay had been removed from one). This was in contrast to the fact that 3 of 17 trained conservers resisted extinction by stating, "You must have taken some clay away."

Subsequently, there have been a number of training studies in which extinction trials were included. There have also been several studies designed to measure the process of extinction itself. As Table 7.1 indicates, these studies employed a variety of techniques and tasks. Important procedures that have been added since early studies include (a) the practice of presenting several extinction trials and using subse-quent predictions as criteria for extinction; (b) the use of probing in an attempt to give the subjects every opportunity to resist extinction; (c) the use of posttests after some time has elapsed; (d) inclusion of a group of nonconservers or partial conservers (subjects who either predict that changing shape always changes weight or that it sometimes

TABLE 7.1

Summary of Major Extinction Studies

Study	Subjects		Criteria for extinction	Type of task	Results (percentage extinguishing)	
Smedslund (1961)	Trained conservers	$N = 11$	Neither accuse the experimenter of removing clay nor claim the scale is incorrect	Weight conservation	Trained	100
	Natural conservers	$N = 13$			Natural conservers	54
	Age 5–7					

Substance conservation

	Both Questions	1st only	2nd only
Trained	0	8.3	16.7
Natural conservers	16.7	25	0

Study	Subjects		Criteria for extinction	Type of task	Results (percentage extinguishing)	
Brison (1966)	Trained conservers (correct responses on some items)	$N = 12$	Specifically, if it is stated that the glass with the thick bottom contained more substance than the other glass	Substance conservation		
	Conservers	$N = 12$				
Kingsley and Hall (1967)	Trained conservers (Age 5–6)	$N = 23$	Same as Smedslund (1961)	Weight conservation	Trained	82
	Natural conservers (Age 6–12)	$N = 15$			Natural conservers	100
Hall and Simpson (1968)	Study 1 Natural conservers (Second-graders)		Same as Smedslund (1961)	Weight conservation	Child experimenter	85
	Child experimenter	$N = 20$			Adult experimenter	75
	Adult experimenter	$N = 20$				
	Study 2 Natural conservers	$N = 20$	Same as Smedslund (1961) and subject giving at least one prediction different from original prediction	Weight conservation	Natural conservers	95
	Nonconservers	$N = 20$			Nonconservers	95
	Partial conservers given conserving feedback	$N = 20$				
	Partial conservers given nonconserving feedback	$N = 20$				
Hall and Kingsley (1968)	Study 1 (Study 2 in the article) Natural conservers Age 5–12	$N = 17$	Smedslund (1961) Definition	Weight conservation	Natural conservers	100

Smedslund (1961) — Study 2 (Study 4 in the article)

Subjects	N	Task	Results
College undergraduates	N = 17	Weight conservation	Undergraduates 76
College graduate students	N = 47		Graduate students 68

Smith (1968) — Criterion: Smedslund (1961)

Subjects: Natural conservers (N = 10); Nonconservers (N = 60); Transitional conservers, Grades 1–2 (N = 60) — Task: Weight conservation

	Counter-suggestion trials	Delayed posttest
Trained (A.S. group) (R.P.)	56	40
(V.R.I.)	40	55
	25	55
Informal conservers	44	18

Miller (1973) — Criterion: Failure to deny validity of nonconservation outcome and changing predictions

Subjects: Young conservers (Grades 2–3) (N = 23); Old conservers (Grade 5) (N = 18) — Task: Weight conservation

	Changed prediction	Perceptual responses
Young conservers	69	66 (45 for nonconservation responses)
Old conservers	64	64

Miller and Lipps (1973) — Criterion: Failure to deny nonconservation and changing prediction

Subjects: Conservers, Grades 3–4 (N = 17); Grade 6 (N = 17) — Task: Weight conservation

Trials of nonconservation answers

	Immediate test		Delayed posttest	
	Changed prediction	Changed + perceptual prediction explanation	Changed prediction	Changed + perceptual prediction explanation
Young conservers	66	40	79	47
Old conservers	81	66	57	40
Young transitive	42	26	23	9
Old transitive	18	5	2	0

Miller, Schwartz, and Stewart (1973) — Criterion: Failure to deny nonconservation

Subjects: College undergraduates (N = 36) — Task: Weight (conservation and transitivity)

Failed to give at least one denial	16.7
Failed to give all denials	61
Nonconserving judgment + perceptual explanation	3

changes weight) who are given conserving experience, and (e) addition of a measure of surprise as an additional criterion for extinction resistance.

We believe that these studies have done much to increase our knowledge concerning this paradigm and that there are several major findings. One finding that we consider important is often ignored: When nonconservers and partial conservers are given extinction trials, a large percentage give consistent conserving responses. In addition, it has been found that a substantial number of these subjects retain these responses and also give what Piagetians would be forced to classify as adequate explanations. Miller (1973) reports that "nonconservers who changed to conservation were able to provide a logical justification for 89% of their answers. Over all, nonconservers gave conservation judgments plus logical explanations on 48% of the trials following the first feedback [p. 58]." A review of data gathered in an earlier study (Hall & Simpson, 1968) using procedures similar to those employed by Miller revealed that 22% of the nonconservers who observed conservation gave logical explanations (the smaller percentage in this study as compared to that of Miller was probably due to the fact that Hall and Simpson did not probe). Thus, it seems that observation of the fact that changing shape does not change weight leads a sizable number of nonconservers spontaneously to become conservers (i.e., they provide explanations without coaching that resemble those given by subjects diagnosed as natural conservers). This should be surprising to Piagetians who have maintained that nonconservers are so resistant to training.

The second, and obviously most quoted, finding is that a relatively large percentage of those subjects classified initially as natural conservers do indeed extinguish. This is found for subjects in grades up to and including the sixth. There is also some evidence that adults under some, but not all, conditions also extinguish (Hall & Kingsley [1967] found that a substantial number of college students extinguished in a group presentation, and Hall regularly replicates this finding in college classes. Miller, Schwartz, and Stewart [1973] gave individual presentations with probing to college undergraduates and failed to obtain evidence for extinction). Even more surprising is the fact that about the same percentage of conservers change their prediction over extinction trials as nonconservers. In addition, a large percentage of the younger natural conservers revert to perceptual explanations resembling nonconservers (e.g., "it looks bigger"). Miller (1973) found that the proportion of "young conservers who switched to nonconservation choices accompanied by perceptual explanations was 45%. Thus, again the two groups (conservers and nonconservers) proved equivalent [p. 57]."

The most damaging findings with regard to the concept of logical necessity are those reported by Miller. While he accepted the possibility that conserving subjects might well fail to arrive at a logical explanation for nonconservation, Miller reasoned that they should at least seem surprised. Therefore, he had experimenters rate the degree of surprise registered by conservers and nonconservers when their predictions were not confirmed. He failed to find support for his hypothesis in that the number of subjects registering surprise was negligible. In a subsequent study, Miller and Lipps (1973) also found that older subjects (sixth-graders) showed significantly less resistance to extinction of weight than did younger subjects. On a posttest given after a 2-week delay, both young and old subjects still exhibited a substantial number of nonconserving responses. For the posttest the younger natural conservers exhibited more nonconserving responses than they did during extinction trials. A final finding that concerned extinction of transitivity of weight will be discussed later. Thus it has been determined in a number of studies that when natural or trained conservers are faced with empirical evidence contrary to their previously stated belief in weight conservation, a large percentage of them change their belief in favor of nonconservation (e.g., they extinguish).

The important question, of course, is will Piagetians extinguish on the concept of logical necessity in the face of contradictory evidence, or will they arrive at an explanation that allows logical necessity to remain within Piagetian theory? As one might have predicted, the tendency has been to resist extinction.

Those associated with Piagetian theory have attempted to respond to these contradictory findings in several ways. Smedslund (1969) has now come full circle and has suggested that the extinction procedure is not a good one to use in diagnosing whether or not a child is a true conserver:

> Although theoretically sound, this method [extinction] has several weaknesses. First, it is often difficult to interpret the subject's behavior when faced with the apparent contradiction, especially if he does not comment on it. Second, the maintenance of the symptom-response need not mean that the subject has a grasp of conservation, but merely that one or a few contradictions or countersuggestions are not enough to upset a learned response bias. Conversely, the contradictions or counter-suggestions may eliminate the symptom-response, even in the presence of genuine conservation, simply because of the child's general dependence on adults. Therefore, the contradiction or extinction technique, although promising, has serious weaknesses [p. 243].

This statement seems to be a rather significant retreat from his initial position. Smedslund now maintains that a learned response bias can be responsible for resistance to extinction (the purpose of his original study was to show that subjects with such response bias would not resist extinction).

It is also significant that Smedslund is willing to place the blame for natural conservers exhibiting extinction on "the child's general dependence on adults." He did this in spite of the fact that in several cases this adult has used extensive probing and predicted that the conserving children would not extinguish. In addition, it ignores the fact that in at least one study (Hall & Simpson, 1968) a child was used as an experimenter. In essence, Smedslund still believes in logical necessity but does not leave any way of behaviorally determining its existence.

Kuhn (1974) is one Piagetian who has evidentally decided to ignore the concept of logical necessity. She has rejected the use of countersuggestion as a criterion for showing that trained subjects have genuine conservation (she refers to the Smedslund extinction article, so presumably she is talking of extinction). She does this on the grounds that some natural conservers in Smedslund's original study also extinguished. This also seems to be a particularly weak argument against extinction because it assumes that the initial classification of conservers without countersuggestion was a correct one. One could contend that part of the definition of a conserver is resistance to countersuggestion and, therefore, Smedslund had only identified a few natural conservers.

Finally, Miller (1973) has made two suggestions about how Piagetians could retain their belief in logical necessity in light of contradictory findings. The first is to adopt the concept of a "stabilization phase" for any concept before it reaches the degree of meaning necessary for subjects to resist extinction. This means that subjects do not reach logical necessity immediately; it takes considerable time. This could be equated with saying that the child who has a greater history of confirming experience will be less likely to extinguish. It also means children do not become true conservers until well after they have passed through the concrete-operational period. As mentioned earlier, research conducted after this suggestion by Miller has led to the finding, contradictory to this stabilization hypothesis, that older conservers offered less resistance to extinction than younger conservers.

A second suggestion by Miller is more plausible. He hypothesizes that Piagetian concepts may vary in the extent to which they are subject to extinction. He provides evidence for this hypothesis (Miller & Lipps, 1973) in finding that when transitivity of weight is used as the task, the results are more congruent with those that would be predicted by Piagetians. Although a large percentage of younger subjects (second-graders) extinguish, most older subjects (sixth-graders) do not. Miller and Lipps justify the use of transitivity rather than conservation in the following way:

> Any concept, however, no matter how logical at base, requires some grounding in physical experience and physical knowledge as well. It can be argued that the role of physical experience is in general greater for conservation than it is for transitivity. For conservation the child must learn to cope with the effects of numerous different transformations, in numerous content domains–transformations, moreover, which have varying effects depending on the domain in question (a particular transformation, e.g., may conserve weight but not length). For transitivity, there are not transformations, and the same abstract rules are directly applicable whatever the properties of the objects. Thus, however equivalent the underlying *logical* systems for the two concepts may be, their *psychological* application may differ. Application of principles of conservation may always be more contingent on and hence more susceptible to disruption by physical knowledge and physical feedback [p. 390].

Miller and Lipps' statement raises an important point. Conservation of object characteristics does not always follow the same rules or represent the same specific abilities. That is, changing shape may change length but not weight. In this situation the realization that the object can be changed back to its original form (exhibiting that the child has the reversibility property) helps with weight but not with length. For length conservation, the experimenter usually uses the moving manipulation. This means that logical necessity, to be of any utility, must be situation- or concept-specific and that knowledge as well as the ability to use the appropriate grouping is also important.[2] In an earlier study, Hall found that most adults do not understand that making small changes in the shape of parallelograms changes the area. In fact, adults often give perceptual reasons for their answers (e.g., "they look the same").

---

[2] Interestingly enough, American psychologists never seem to address themselves to the question of exactly what is being measured in the various conservation tasks. While they generally mention the properties involved, they fail to point out that these same properties can act similarly on different operators and combinations of operators resulting in different groupings. It is also true that across groupings, the properties can assume different forms (e.g., reversibility takes the form of inversion negation and also of reciprocity). The tasks used (e.g., conservation) then represent specific groupings; but the specific properties (e.g., associativity, reversibility) are restricted neither to particular tasks nor to particular groupings.

It should also be pointed out that if one adheres strictly to theory, a change in shape can result in a change of weight if it changes the distance of the object's center of gravity from the earth's center of gravity.

Conservation is merely a task that allows children or adults to show that they have the capacity for using specific groupings, but it does not mean that all objects in nature follow these logical rules. Logical necessity could then only have utility when children have extended experience with a particular task that follows these logical rules.

Having this extended experience does not seem to be of much use, however, unless the child has reached a particular stage of cognitive development. According to Piaget, the child inherits the functions of accommodation and assimilation. Through the use of these functions, he or she interacts with the world and proceeds through an invariant sequence of stages. Experiences that require abilities too far above the child's current level cannot be assimilated, and thus advance does not occur. Thus, with regard to tasks requiring advanced logic, the child is initially unable to perform in the correct manner but eventually acquires the capability to handle these more advanced tasks. The ability is acquired first through trial and error, but then often—and quite suddenly—the correct performance becomes logically necessary.

> In fact, a study of the development of logico-mathematical structures in a child reveals that the necessity for them is imposed on the subject, not from the beginning, but as we have already said, very gradually, often until such time as it crystallizes rather suddenly. . . . For so long as seriation, let us say $A < B < C$ . . . , simply causes the child to make a construction by groping of an empirical kind, the structure cannot be said to be closed, and consequently the transitivity applied to the objects ($A < C$ if $A < B$ and $B < C$) appears to the child to be not necessary but simply possible or probable. As soon as seriation is established operationally by the persistent choosing of the smallest element remaining or available, with the resultant realization that any element E is both bigger than A, B, C, D that precede it and smaller than F and G that follow it, then the structure becomes whole and closed; that is, relations within it are interdependent and can be composed among themselves without recourse to anything outside the system. In that case, transitivity appears "necessary" and this logical "necessity" is recognized not only by some inner feeling, which cannot be proved, but by the intellectual behavior of the subject who uses the newly mastered deductive instrument with confidence and discipline [Piaget, 1971, p. 316].

Piaget's description of how and what happens when mathematical structures become logically necessary is similar in many ways to a Gestaltist description of what happens when insight (or understanding) takes place. The similarities include rapid, permanent improvement in performance as well as the insistence upon an internal organizing process. As Flavell (1963) points out, however, Piaget emphasizes the importance of experience more than the Gestaltists do. Piaget probably has the Gestaltists to thank for the fact that both learning and cognitive theorists now would recognize that, descriptively, behavior arising from sudden crystallization (as described by Piaget) occurs. It is the theoretical interpretation of that behavior (learning theorists rely on transfer) and assumptions about its necessary antecedents that constitute the different positions of the two groups. Unfortunately, psychologists have as yet been unable to specify the exact antecedents necessary for such behavior. We have no way of knowing which experiences natural conservers have had. In the case of extinction the important question is how Piaget would operationally define "confidence and discipline." There is nothing to suggest that such a definition would include denying empirical evidence.

The concept of logical necessity is also discussed by Nagel (1961). He points out that if natural laws are logically necessary, then it would be appropriate to establish the logical necessity of such laws through mathematical proof. In this case, if one were to encounter an empirical contradiction, he would have two options open. He could reject the law he had already established or he could deny the validity of the specific evidence. Nagel does not believe this is a particularly good approach to use. "It is, however, fantastic to suggest that when the truth of an alleged physical law, for example about light, is in doubt, the physicist ought to proceed as a mathematician does [p. 54]."

Mathematical laws can be used to explain large classes of empirical phenomena. However, one can encounter empirical exceptions to these laws. This does not mean that the laws should be rejected in those cases where they hold (which may be the large proportion of cases). It does mean that by using logical necessity, one may be limiting one's options—at least, excluding the option that empirical information is valid. If this last option holds true, as Nagel implies, one must accept the fact that "none of the statements generally labeled as laws in the various positive sciences are in point of fact logically necessary, since their formal denials are demonstrably not self-contradictory [p. 53]." This rejection of the logical necessity of laws in no way detracts from the "roles in science that are assigned to them." For example, Nagel points out that Archimedes' "law" of buoyancy explains and predicts a large class of phenomena, "even though there are excellent reasons for believing that the law is not logically necessary [p. 54]." Thus, the assumption of logical necessity is not dependent on its success at explanation and prediction and "plays no identifiable part in the actual use made of the law [p. 54]." If the human being is to be thought of as a maximally adaptive organism, then it would follow that he would tend to construct laws explaining his universe. A person can demonstrate his understanding by meeting the standard criteria (i.e., prediction, explanation, persistence, generalization). However, when faced with contradictory evidence, he must be able to deny logical necessity and recognize exceptions to laws if they prove valid. At the same time, he should be able to invoke the general laws in those instances where they are applicable.

It is still important to account for the finding that older children are less apt to extinguish on the transitivity of weight concept than younger children. As Miller mentions, transitive relations do generalize across all object characteristics, and thus the child would have far more experience with transitivity. What he fails to mention is that transitive relations do not always hold. For instance, take the popular game in which, at the count of three, children form their hands into rocks, scissors, or paper. As we all know, rocks break scissors, scissors cut paper, and paper wraps rocks. It is interesting that we often have difficulty in accepting such relationships. Gardner (1974) reports in an article on nontransitive relations: "If the nontransitivity is so counterintuitive as to boggle the mind, we have what is called a nontransitive paradox [p. 120]." An example of nontransitivity in a different context is that if A likes B and B likes C, it does not necessarily follow that A likes C. Again we see that the same logic in one situation does not always help in another similar situation. The fact that transitivity may hold in more situations than conservation may account for the increased resistance to extinction. The fact that transitivity does not hold true in all situations illustrates the point that logical necessity, to be of any value, must be situation-specific, and thus knowledge of, or experience in, each situation is required. Again, having the ability to exhibit transitivity only helps when transitivity is appropriate. It could be predicted that if the child has a long backlog of empirical experience in specific situations, he would be more likely to resist extinction. Such resistance should not be limited to Piagetian concepts but should apply to any concepts where the child has had such experience.

Thus, the authors believe that Piagetians may well have ignored a significant fact: If a child or adult automatically applied the properties of a specific logical grouping in the specified manner in all situations where it could be applied and held to his answer (i.e., instituted logical necessity) in the face of contradictory empirical evidence, his behavior would be maladaptive. Both logic and empirical experience are necessary for determining correct descriptions of the world. What extinction studies show is that children, when faced with empirical evidence contrary to predictions that they have made, often attempt to evaluate the validity of the empirical feedback rather than automatically rejecting it. The manner in which they do this depends upon the options they have available (from past experience and the level of their logical sophistication). Thus explanations for extinction given by children vary with the age (experience) of the subject. If the concept of logical necessity rejects empirical evidence in favor of logic, it is appropriate for describing either how a child acts or what would be an adaptive way of adjusting to the world. If logical necessity merely means that the more experience the child has with a specific situation, the less likely he is to accept a discrepant finding, then it is not unique to Piagetian theory.

We believe, however, that the real problem that extinction studies raise for Piaget's theory, may not be how natural conservers react to nonconservation but how nonconservers react to conservation. This latter reaction seems to entail the subject's not only quickly learning the correct answer but also spontaneously giving a correct explanation. Although Miller did not include a group of nontransitive subjects in his study, Trabasso (1974) summarized a series of studies in which 4- and 5-year-old children were able to exhibit transitive answers to five-term problems if they were able to recall the correct pair relationships. Trabasso's position on the development of cognitive abilities is quite clear:

> What does this approach mean developmentally? Cognitive development, under this view, may be seen as continuous and qualitatively similar to the target, adult model. The growth of a child's capacity for immediate, short-term and long-term memory is likely to be gradual and quantitative. If the processing of information occurs within the limits of these systems then the upper limit of this capacity is also continuously rising as one stores more information from a variety of task experiences, learns more and better ways for coding and chunking information, acquires symbol systems such as language, etc. Certainly at some age, a child will be able to perform operations involving class concepts before he is able to perform propositions since the latter involve relations among the former and hence are more complex. The added complexity may approach his then current limit for handling several classes simultaneously [p 4].

This position is, of course, in direct contrast to the structural theory of Piaget, in which growth progresses through qualitatively different stages. It is Trabasso's view that his position also represents a different approach to developmental psychology. If psychologists are interested in describing the normal course of cognitive development, much of Piaget's theory may be of use. If, on the other hand, the theorist is interested in determining the child's ultimate capacity at any given time, he would use the approach exemplified by Trabasso. In this case we may find that the child's abilities are more adult-like than originally predicted. It is this latter strategy and position to which we adhere.

REFERENCES

Baldwin, A. L. *Theories of child development*, New York: Wiley, 1967.

Beilin, H. The training and acquisition of logical operations. Paper prepared for the Conference on Piaget-type Research in Mathematical Education, Columbia University, 1970.

Brison, D. W. Acceleration of conservation of substance. *Journal of Genetic Psychology*, 1966, *109*, 311–322.

Flavell, J. H. *The developmental psychology of Jean Piaget*. Princeton, NJ: Van Nostrand, 1963.

Gardner, M. Mathematical games, on the paradoxical situations that arise from nontransitive relations. *Scientific American*, 1974, *231* (4), 120–125.

Hall, V. C., & Kingsley, R. Conservation and equilibration theory. *Journal of Genetic Psychology*, 1968, *113*, 195–213.

Hall, V. C., & Simpson, G. J. Factors influencing extinction of weight conservation. *Merrill-Palmer Quarterly of Behavior and Development*, 1968, 14, 197–210.

Inhelder, B., & Sinclair, H. Learning cognitive structures. In P. Mussen, J. Langer, & M. Covington (Eds.), *Trends and issues in developmental psychology*. New York: Holt, Rinehart and Winston, 1969.

Kingsley, R., & Hall, V. C. Training conservation of weight and length through learning sets. *Child Development*, 1967, *38*, 1111–1126.

Kuhn, D. Inducing development experimentally: Comments on a research paradigm, *Developmental Psychology*, 1974, *10* (5), 590–600.

Miller, S. A. Extinction of conservation: A methodological and theoretical analysis, *Merrill-Palmer Quarterly of Behavior and Development*, 1971, 17, 319–334.

Miller, S. A. Contradiction, surprise, and cognitive change: The effects of disconfirmation of belief on conservers and nonconservers. *Journal of Experimental Child Psychology*, 1973, *15*, 47–62.

Miller, S. A., & Lipps, L. Extinction of conservation and transitivity of weight. *Journal of Experimental Child Psychology*, 1973, *16*, 388–402.

Miller, S. A., Schwartz, L. C., & Stewart, C. An attempt to extinguish conservation of weight in college students. *Developmental Psychology*, 1973, *8*, 316.

Nagel, E. *The structure of science: Problem in the logic of scientific explanation.* New York: Harcourt, Brace, and World, 1961.

Piaget, J. *Biology and knowledge.* Chicago: University of Chicago Press, 1971.

Smedslund, J. The acquisition of conservation of substance and weight in children III. Extinction of conservation of weight acquired "normally" and by means of empirical controls on a balance scale. *Scandinavian Journal of Psychology*, 1961, 2, 85–87.

Smedslund, J. Psychological diagnostics. *Psychological Bulletin*, 1969, 71 (3), 237–248.

Smith, I. D. The effects of training procedures on the acquisition of conservation of weight. *Child Development*, 39, 515–526.

Trabasso, T. Representation, memory, and reasoning: How do we make transitive inferences? Paper presented at the Minnesota Symposium on Child Psychology, 1974.

8

Piagetian Theory and Early Childhood Education: A Critical Analysis

JOSEPH T. LAWTON
FRANK H. HOOPER
University of Wisconsin

Introduction

There is little question that one of the more current preoccupations among certain developmental psychologists cum early childhood educators is the extrapolation to the classroom of Piagetian developmental theory and associated research. The claim of utilizing the "dynamic" principles of Piaget's theory to innovate educational programming probably approaches the fadism accorded to Dewey's similar views during the 1920s and 1930s (cf. Sullivan, 1967, 1969). General discussions of the putative relevance of the Genevan perspective to education are indeed numerous (e.g., Aebli, 1951; Athey & Rubadeau, 1970; Beard, 1969; Bingham-Newman & Saunders, 1976; Brearly & Hitchfield, 1969; Bruner, 1960; Furth, 1970; Hooper, 1968; Hooper & DeFrain, 1974; Kohlberg, 1968; Schwebel & Raph, 1973; Sigel, 1969; and Wallace, 1965). Moreover, Piaget, himself, has produced a commendable number of articles and texts on educational issues and applications of his dialectical position; (e.g., Piaget, 1928, 1930a,b, 1931, 1934, 1935,

1951, 1964, 1970b, 1973). Unfortunately, while there have been certain explicit attempts to "operationalize" Piaget's concepts and principles in actual educational programming (almost exclusively at the preschool and early elementary school age–grade levels), there have been very few cases of equally explicit *evaluations* of these curriculum development endeavors. Piaget's' views have been rather glibly accepted as demonstrating prima facie validity and relevance for educational application.

The specific objective of this chapter is to describe the elements within Piagetian theory and associated normative–experimental research that purport to be relevant to educational application and innovation. At the same time, possible artificial dichotomies between development and learning in educational practice are discussed. Four representative Piagetian educational programs will be briefly reviewed and their common elements delineated. In this endeavor we openly acknowledge the more conservative and guarded commentary of such writers as Beilin (1971a), Evans (1975), Kaufman (1975), and Sullivan (1967, 1969) in cautioning the aspirant educational planner against a premature total acceptance of the Genevan educational doctrine. We would hope to find a more balanced middle-ground orientation between these views and those promoted by the more Orthodox Genevan writers, prominent among whom are Furth (1970), Kamii & DeVries (1974), and Piaget (1970a, 1973).

To anticipate the discussion to follow, there is much substantive content in the general Piagetian model of cognitive development which seriously questions the role of controlled educational enrichment (at least those programmatic endeavors of a rather highly structured, teacher-initiated type) as a necessary and sufficient determinant of normative logical-concept acquisition. Moreover, the implications of the rather extensive literature dealing with the *experimental* manipulations of Piagetian concept attainments remain conjectural at this time (cf. Beilin, 1971a; Brainerd, 1973; Klausmeier & Hooper, 1974; Strauss, 1972). We are currently engaged in devising instructional programs for the young child that are explicitly accountable in terms of straightforward behavioral objectives and associated requirements and, at the same time, designed in the spirit of Piaget's stated long-range goals for educational programs. In terms of the latter essential consideration, we are in agreement with Piaget's (1964) oft-cited comments:

> The principal goal of education is to create men who are capable of doing new things, not simply of repeating what other generations have done—men who are creative, inventive, and discoverers. The second

goal of education is to form minds which can be critical; can verify, and not accept everything they are offered. The great danger today is of slogans, collective opinions, ready-made trends of thought. We have to be able to resist individually, to criticize, to distinguish between what is proven and what is not. So we need pupils who are active, who learn early to find out by themselves, partly by their own spontaneous activity and partly through material we set up for them; who learn early to tell what is verifiable and what is simply the first idea to come to them [p. 5].

Piagetian Recommendations to Educational Practice

Piaget espouses a theoretical concept of the development of intelligence and knowledge that places a critical importance on "actions." He has constantly affirmed that it is necessary for the child to experimentally and actively manipulate objects in order to arrive at an understanding of the transformation of objects and associated relations. He criticizes pedagogy that overemphasizes showing, demonstration, or iconic representations of objects. He does not accept that the perception of objects, or of the associated transformations, is equivalent to direct action upon the objects by the learner himself. Furthermore, he contends that it is only through active-manipulation experiences with concrete materials, where the child projects and verifies hypothesis of his own invention, that true learning will occur. He states (Piaget, 1970b) that "an education which is an active discovery of reality is superior to one that consists merely in providing the young with ready-made wills . . . and ready-made truths [p. 26]." This basic principle of Piaget's theory has been emphasized by others (e.g., Almy, Chittenden, & Miller, 1966; Chittenden, 1969; Ginsberg & Opper, 1969). According to Schwebel and Raph (1973), the major difference between Piagetian-inspired teaching methodology and other current practices in education is the contrast between "actively learning" and "presentation learning."

Piaget discriminates between development and learning. He sees the development of knowledge as a spontaneous process that is formally related to the personal process of embrygenesis. Thus, it appears, the crucial factor in development is primarily biological in nature. (As we know, the biological clock cannot easily be advanced.) Learning, on the other hand, is seen as being *provoked* by situations as opposed to being a spontaneous function. But, for Piaget, it is a limited process. Learning is associated with single tasks. Thus, Piaget places the development of intellectual functions foremost. For him, they explain learning. To take the opposite viewpoint is to entertain reductionistic, associationistic, and atomistic approaches.

The principal aim of educaion for Piaget is to develop intelligence—and to "teach" how to develop it. In this context of the developing intellect, learning is projected as the "active nature of knowledge." Knowledge becomes virtually synonymous with the process of logical thinking, the essential function of intelligence.

Piaget proposes that the problem of pedagogy can only be resolved by resolving the related problem of the nature of intelligence and the epistemological problem of the nature of knowledge. Intelligence, as he sees it, derives from the coordination of actions that initially occur overtly in physical form and later occur covertly in an interiorized and reflective form. The "actions" of interiorized action are described as processes of transformation, that is, of logicomathematical knowledge.

Defining the relevance of this continuous development of action schemes (from initial sensorimotor actions to formal mental operations) for education, Piaget states that the theory provides educators with a number of sufficiently consistent elements of reference.

A critical problem facing the teacher is the reconciliation of the concept of equilibrated operation structures to classroom teaching procedures and the evaluation of learning. Piaget has always insisted that the order of development of children's thinking is invariant, though the rate of progression is variable. He accepts possible accelerations or delays that are mainly dependent upon cultural, familial, or social factors. For Piaget, cognitive development is determined by maturational, experiential, and social factors that, in turn, are coordinated and integrated by the equilibration process. Kamii and DeVries (1974), for example, state that, "equilibration, which regulates the influence of the three other factors, refers to an internal regulation process of differentiation and coordination which always tends towards increasing adaptation [15]." Piaget's concern with learning has been to emphasize the coordination of operational structures (e.g., classificatory systems, which in a coordinated or equilibrated state only become accessible to the child's thinking during the later part of the concrete-operational period). The *operation* is the essence of knowledge, and any single operation is always part of a total structure (cf. Flavell, 1963; Piaget, 1970b,c). Theoretically, once a total coordination of operations within any stage of development has occurred, the child should be able to generalize such thinking without any major limitation. This has never been demonstrated unambiguously by the Genevans or other investigators.

A major controversy related to this issue has centered on the possibility of training logicomathematical concepts. As Beilin (1971b) points out, the Genevans first became interested in training studies as a defense of the equilibration model (cf. Piaget, 1964). Piaget remains critical of current obsessions with accelerating logical thought development, though the Genevans' recent general attitude to some forms of training is more favorable. Recent training studies have been concerned with attempts to define adequately the mechanism of equilibration and also to specify transitions in development. Piaget is unwilling to go along with the implication that training may lead to the genuine acquisition of structures of operation, although reviews of neo-Piagetian training literature present certain contrary evidence (cf. Beilin, 1971b; Brainerd, 1973; Glaser & Resnick, 1972; Klausmeier & Hooper, 1974).

Such controversy, which in this case is no where near being resolved, points to an interesting phenomenon in education—that is, the teacher searching for principles to guide classroom management. Recommendations to the teacher searching for guiding principles on pedagogical method based on Piagetian theory are suitably represented by Kamii and DeVries. They claim that logicomathematical knowledge is not directly teachable since it is constructed from the relationships the child creates among objects. Subsequent relationships are always related to prior relationships, since there is a supposed tendency toward increasing adaptation. According to Kamii and DeVries (1974):

> The second characteristic of logico-mathematical knowledge is that if it is left alone to develop, or if the child is encouraged to be alert and curious about his environment, there is only one way in which it develops, and that is towards more and more coherence. All normal children will have class inclusion sooner or later without a single lesson in class inclusion [p. 167].

Such views are appropriate as opinion, but the teacher must be careful to distinguish between opinion and empirically established fact. Interpreting Piaget's theory to provide enlightenment to pedagogical methodology is not easy. He has identified schools by two general categories: the *activity* school, which he espouses, and the *traditional* school, which he criticizes. The concept of the traditional school is exemplified by a system that imposes work and where, according to Piaget (1970b), "the student's intellectual and moral activity remains heteronomous because it is inseparable from a continual constraint exercised by the teacher [p. 151]." He supposes that in a school the child is identified with the adult and that the existence of the important factor of *internal structural maturation* is denied. There is no doubt such schools exist. However, no useful purpose is served by juxtaposing such lifeless, dreary, and boring establishments as apparently the only counterpart to the idealistic activity school. In the latter school, asserts Piaget (1970b), the emphasis would be on "real activity, [and] spontaneous work based upon personal need and interest [p. 152]." Activity would be the pivot of such a school. One important aspect of activity is that process by which symbolic representation serves as the means of assimilating reality. Suitable equipment is advocated (but not specified) that provides a catalyst aiding the transformation of external active manipulative experiences into internal intellectual realities.

Activity is seen as being dependent on interest—the dynamic aspect of assimilation. Perhaps, like Dewey, Piaget's conception of interest as the motivational source of intelligent activity has been misconstrued and misreprestented by even his most ardent followers. He goes to some lengths to explain the law of interest. He likens it to Claparede's definition, which defines interest in terms of the law of functional autonomy. He warns that although the active school should treat the child as an autonomous, functionally active individual, account must be taken of the structure of the child's mentality. The objective is to find the most suitable pedagogical methodology, one that facilitates both the present intellectual reasoning power of the child's thought and its development over a period of time. Such recommendations may provide difficulties for the teacher. The problem is to balance the idea that the child forms his own intelligence through autonomous active manipulation and representation of his environment, motivated by interest, with the notion that the role of the teacher is to provide not merely a suitable learning environment but a social interaction that aids the systematization of the child's active intellectual processes. Piaget (1970b) says that "there is a necessity for a rational, deductive activity . . . and the necessity also, in order to establish such a reasoning activity in the child, for a remaining social structure entailing not merely cooperation among the children but also cooperation with adults [169]."

That Piaget demotes receptive educational methods is not surprising. That he reduces the concept to an extreme polarity from active discovery is unfortunate. He argues that receptivity denies the development of intelligence through an adaptive process, since it precludes interest.

He explains that the active school fundamentally reacts against receptive learning because such learning is synonymous with verbal pseudo-ideas that lack true meaning for the child. We argue in a later section of this chapter that receptive learning, under certain conditions, can be potentially meaningful, and that active discovery learning, under certain conditions, may be potentially a rote process.

Common Components of Piagetian School Programs

The relevance of Piaget's findings to the problem of identifying the major components common to any Piagetian educational program has been more thoroughly explicated by his followers than by Piaget himself. Aebli (1951) is cited as providing one of the best single sources of Piagetian principles for education (cf. Flavell, 1963, p. 367). Piaget provides two basic ideas to underpin a conception of an education program: (a) stable and ·enduring cognitions about the world come about only through *active* commerce with the world; and (b) interaction with peers is crucial for the child's de-egocentrism. However, neither of these can be considered explicit enough to provide clear guidelines to teachers. Statements on the application of Piaget's theory provide, in the main, controversial and divergent opinions.

Ginsburg and Opper (1969) mention six very general implications from Piaget's theory. These may be summarized briefly:

1. The language and thought of the child are qualitatively different from that of the adult, and the child may find it difficult to assimilate some sequences of ideas.
2. The young child learns more easily from concrete experiences.
3. Tasks should take into account the child's readiness for, and interest in, learning.
4. The development of curricula must take into account the invariant sequence of cognitive development.
5. Social interaction is a crucial factor in the child's development.
6. Traditional methods of instruction—that is, group lessons with a given sequence of material, transmission of materials via lecture or other verbal explanation—have grave deficiencies.

The basic pedagogical principles taken from Piaget's theory are also repeatedly reiterated by the contributors to the volume *Piaget in the Classroom* (Schwebel & Raph, 1973). They are perhaps best exemplified by Kamii (1973) who succinctly states that learning is an active process, that social interaction is important for intellectual development, and that intellectual activity is primarily based on actual experiences rather than on language per se. The underlying single basic recommendation to teachers is that the prime aim of the school is to develop the child's intelligence.

Piaget (1970b) goes to some lengths to identify principles of education and their psychological value. He speaks in terms of the *new* education, in which his basic aim is to adapt the child to the immediate social environment. The methodology of the new education is described as "encouraging this adaptation by making use of the impulses inherent in childhood itself, applied with the spontaneous activity that is inseparable from mental development [p. 151]." As we have seen, the significant principle upon which the remaining recommendations rest is that the education of the new school appeals to real activity and spontaneous work that is based on the established needs and interests of the child.

We can see that for Piaget there are two important characteristics of development: First, the human organism is *obliged* at a sensorimotor or more advanced intellectual level to accommodate to the external environment; and, second, the act of accommodation requires that the properties of things be assimilated into intelligence. However, it is important to point out here that from Piaget's point of view, the obligation for accommodative activity is created by an internally maturing potential for intellectual activity. The motivational source for learning, therefore, is primarily an internal force, aided and abetted by the environment's intrusions.

Contiguous with the above-mentioned characteristics is the insistence, although not clearly delineated, that "things" that may be translated into objects and events (subject matter) have no interest per se. They act as catalysts for the necessary activity that promotes the developing intellect. The rationale for this evaluation of objects and events involves the theoretical interpretation of assimilation in its purest form, as being synonymous with play. The functional significance of play is described in terms of forms of symbolism and fiction, but mainly it refers to the functional assimilation of intellectual realities. Piaget states that the transductive form of assimilation of early childhood gives way eventually to deductive experimentation—the salient characteristic of reason. Viewed in this way, the intelligence of the young child undergoes a necessary adaptive process by undertaking authentic work. Piaget does not spell out what form authentic work should take. Also, he stresses that the intellectual function is controlled by the law of interest (Piaget 1970b, p. 159). It remains for the teacher to demonstrate the law in pedagogic methodology. The only guideline provided is an analogous reference to the distinction between a self-imposed effort in acquiring knowledge and the acceptance of predigested knowledge. The most common misinterpretation of this admonition in educational practice is to suppose that the teacher must accommodate teaching to the idiosyncratic interests of the child. However, Piaget would have us take account of interest in the context of the autonomous child. Now, it may be contended that autonomy is not an invariant quality of the human organism. It is perhaps best viewed as a developing quality of the intelligence and cannot, therefore, be considered an invariant.

As a basic element of the developing intellect and personality of the child, autonomy can be supposed to have a special relation to each stage of development. There is a danger associated with autonomy that experience in initiating experimentation may be meaningless and arbitrary. As Erikson (1972) has warned, "if denied the gradual *and well guided* experience of the autonomy of free choice . . . the child will turn against himself all his urge to discriminate and to manipulate [p. 21; italics added]." Piaget is aware of the danger. In his view, the principal aim of education is the task of *forming* the child's intellectual and moral reasoning power. What pedagogy must do is take account of the qualitative difference between childish thought and adult thought and provide "the most suitable *methods* and *environment* to help the child . . . achieve coherence and objectivity on the intellectual plane and reciprocity on the moral plane [Piaget, 1970b, p. 160]." Piaget considers that the active practicality of the infant intelligence remains qualitatively distinct from the later-emerging conceptual intelligence, though it nevertheless constitutes the essential foundation for all subsequent cognitive growth. Whatever tasks is undertaken by the child in the concrete-operaional stage of thinking, therefore, should be aided by necessary concrete-manipulative experience. Such experience may be conceived of as an overt physical manipulation of objects and, more importantly, as a covert mental assimilative manipulation of perceived objects in the real world. It is the latter activity, supported by symbolic representation, that continues to promote intellectual development.

Conceptual intelligence is described by Piaget as proceeding from the unstructured stage of syncretic assimilation to the advanced stage of logical generalization. He warns against the danger of pseudoconcepts being formed in the earlier stages of development of the intelligence by emphasizing purely receptive learning. He does not, however, distinguish between the rote learning he refers to and a state of receptive learning that may be meaningful. This distinction is obviously a critical one and requires further explication. A potentially useful comparison between reception and discovery will be taken up later when we discuss other early childhood education programs.

Piaget would argue that any systematic application of his theory to education must conceptualize pedagogy as resting on three basic psychological points of view. First, there must be authentic, rational reasoning activity on the part of the learner. Second, such reasoning activity, by necessity, can only be established by cooperation among children and between children and adults. Third, the development of intelligence is likely to be best promoted by the influence of some sort of systematization by the adult.

Four Representative Early Childhood Education Programs

Most attempts to implement Piagetian theory in the classroom have been confined to preschool and primary grade programs. Four representative programs will exemplify the similarities and discrepancies among the attempts to apply Piaget's ideas to pedagogical practice.

Lavatelli, (1970) who studied with Piaget in Geneva, has developed the Early Childhood Curriculum: A Piaget Program (ECC). This curriculum kit is organized according to three themes: classification; number, space, and measurement; and seriation. The basic objective of the program is to lay a foundation for the emergence of concrete operations. The theme goals are stated in terms of both mental-operation and language structure models. Language is considered necessary insofar as it supports the elaboration of initial preconceptual mental structures demanding symbolic representation. The procedure suggested for using the various sets of activities within each theme is to organize short structured training sessions several times a week with groups of five to six children. It is predicted that guided interaction with concrete materials provides the necessary action which, at this stage of mental development, leads to the assimilation of new ideas. The ECC program is designed for use as a sequential series of group activities. It must be supposed that Lavatelli endorses the Genevan belief that with respect to the young child, content per se is not of prime importance, except to the degree that an array of selected materials lends itself to a concrete manipulation that is expected to result in the internalization of particular logical operations. For example, the first set of materials used for the theme of number, space, and measurement provides for the concrete manipulation of toys and pennies into one-to-one corresponding series. The aim of the activity is to promote a conservation of number when the series of pennies is recomposed into a pile; that is, for each toy there is still a penny despite the perceptual difference. The second set of materials is composed of cupcake cubes. Again, the aim is to promote conservation of number by guilding one-to-one correspondence, with and without physical correspondence. The third set deals with conservation of volume and uses liquid in containers of various shapes as its materials. Lavatelli (1970b) stresses that it is essential for the teacher to understand educational objectives of the ECC in terms of mental operations and language development. She goes on to say that there is no one right way for conducting training sessions.

Although we agree that similar learning may result from various kinds of instructional techniques, nevertheless it is important to realize that there are underlying principles that guide mental functioning. The concepts of, for example, hierarchical classification or seriation have critical attributes, and the teacher must know what these attributes are. The establishment of critical attributes of process concepts should provide guidelines for the selection of materials that can be organized into hierarchical classes or into series quantifiable on some scale. Guided learning should make provision for the identification and organization of critical attributes that lead to the acquisition of the concept. In that sense, there is a right way of selecting materials and conducting learning activities.

Early Childhood Curriculum was tested in a pilot program at the University of Illinois and public school kindergartens in University City, Missouri. Lavatelli (1970a) reports that "there were significant gains on Binet scores and on Piaget-type tests where each [test] was employed [p. 4]." It is not clear whether or not control groups were used in this research program.

However, kits such as Lavatelli's may have limited effects on learning that are not commensurate with their costs. There are a number of important questions that need to be asked of curriculum kits. For example, at what point does learning from one set of materials achieve a desired behavioral change, thus making further use unnecessary? How many sets of selected materials are necessary for the promotion of generalized ways of knowing? Can a kit of materials provide a continuum of activities and materials on an increasing scale of complexity or diversity that may be assumed necessary to test for the desired objectives of generalizability and durability of learning? Definitive answers to questions such as these are currently not available.

David Weikart and associates developed a preschool curriculum at Ypsitanti, Michigan, in 1962, The Cognitively Oriented Curriculum: A Framework for Preschool Teachers. The curriculum was partially based on the child development theories of Piaget (Silverman &

Weikart, 1973) and utilizes three basic ideas drawn from Piagetian theory: *(a)* action is a general condition of learning; *(b)* representation, as a broad system of organization, provides a conceptual tool for planning operations; *(c)* a child's rich experiences in his environment leads to verbal description and articulation. (The third idea is somewhat suspect in the context of orthodox Piagetian theory regarding the relationship of thought and language.) Weikart states that the teacher's application of Piagetian theory to activity classrooms results in the establishment of a content of education. A sequence of classificatory behaviors were selected and formed the bases of classroom methodologies. It is claimed that the intention of the Cognitive Curriculum (as it is called) is not to teach classification but to create a learning environment in which children learn from experiences created out of their own interests and interactions with peers and adults. Classification ability is considered a basic prerequisite for the later development of reading and math skills, and a number of classification goals and associated classroom procedures were identified and incorporated into the program. The model adopted for the organization of the classroom is described in Weikart (1973) as the open framework program. Within this model, both the teacher and child are seen as initiators. The teacher controls materials in interest centers (conducts the sorting, arranging, comparing, combining) and extends the child's activities through questions, suggestions, or encouragement with the child choosing interest centers and materials freely. The evaluation of the outcome of each day results in decisions for the following day's materials and classroom organization.

The relationship between evaluation, selection of learning materials, and the child's autonomous choice of activities requires clarification—which it does not receive in Weikart's paper (1973). Suggested learning goals and teacher role are clearly related to an open-framework curriculum. However, although Weikart stresses an important relationship between teacher-initiated learning and the course of intellectual development, this relationship remains an unclear facet of the teaching–learning process. This is mainly due to the fact that the concept of teacher-initiation is not fully described. And yet, initiation is expected to be a crucial variable in the learning situation. Similarly, it is stated as a given that the child will display a propensity for self-directed learning. We know that self-directed activity may take diverse courses. As in the case of initiation, terms such as this need to be defined clearly.

In the open framework program, goals for classification are clearly described—for example, "sorting all the objects in a group into two sets." The physical environment of the classroom and the arranging and sequencing of equipment and materials is described as structured. Within this structure the child can choose freely not only the materials to use but a desired result. The role of the teacher to observe, question, suggest, and encourage. Supposedly, in the open framework model the intention is not to combine the two distinct approaches of *teacher initiates* and *child responds*. One could surmise that if a child's activity is assessed by the teacher as not being conducive to the achievement of classification goals, the activity would be followed by questions, suggestions, and encouragement aimed at changing behavior in a teacher-desired direction. The teacher's role in such situations would be to *initiate*. It appears likely that the child needs to respond and would be unlikely, at such time, to initiate. As Weikart (1973) puts it, "these curricula . . . demand that the teacher create a transaction between the child and his environment to develop his abilities [p. 10]." It is unclear what might be deemed necessary interactions between the teacher as a guiding influence and the child as an autonomous learner.

Constance Kamii began her initial efforts to implement Piagetian theory in the classroom while working with the Weikart program at Ypsilanti. She considers the program's initial efforts to be derived from a misunderstanding of Piagetian theory. Her objections concern tasks aimed at teaching classification skills and the attempts to prematurely move preschool children to the stage of concrete operations (cf. Denis-Prinzhorn, Kamii, & Monoud, 1972).

Kamii and DeVries (1974) present a Piagetian curriculum for early education that spells out in some detail the theoretical foundations. They argue that the educator must understand Piaget's basic ideas about the nature of knowledge and the mechanisms of its development. These basic ideas are expressed in terms of the epistemological–biological and constructivist perspective of Piaget's theory.

Kamii and DeVries (1974) describe Piaget as an "interactionist–relativist." His emphasis in explaining development is on the internal factors. Piaget's development is primarily a spontaneous process tied to the whole process of embryogenesis. Learning, on the other hand, is associated with single tasks—an atomistic viewpoint. Piaget's interactionist view is contrasted with the "empiricist view," which emphasizes external detriments. Thus, Kamii and DeVries introduce an immediate polarity upon which all subsequent statements about the application of Piagetian theory to pedagogical methodology are based. This stance tends to weaken their position, since evidence can be produced to show that various types of curricula appear to promote similar types of learning—including the development of intelligence in a Piagetian sense. For example, Weikart (1973) established the Ypsilanti Preschool Curriculum Demonstration Project in an effort to answer the question, Does it matter which curriculum is employed? Three programs were selected and the different curriculum styles compared: Weikart's cognitively oriented curriculum based on the principles of sociodramatic play, principles drawn from Piaget's theory of intellectual development, and observation of teachers; a language-training model developed by Bereiter and Englemann (1966) using task-oriented techniques; and a unit-based program that emphasized social–emotional goals using teaching methods of the traditional nursery school. Each of the programs did unusually well on all criteria. There were uniformly high gains on IQ and uniformly high ratings on several tests of language growth, emotional growth, and social adjustment. The overall findings indicated no significant differences among the three curricula on almost all the major measures used. Weikart concluded that such factors as a consistent daily routine, commitment to program goals, efficient planning, and evaluation are perhaps more potent in influencing outcomes than particular curricula employed.

Kamii and DeVries (1974) are critical of these curriculum programs. Their main complaint is that they fall into the "empiricist school." The alternative they offer is based on seven principles of teaching in both the socioemotional and cognitive realms of Piaget's theory. Briefly summarized they describe the role of the teacher: (a) to encourage the child to be independent, curious, and courageous in his endeavors; (b) to encourage interaction among children; (c) to cooperate on an equal footing with the child; (d) to put teaching in the context of play; (e) to accept both wrong answers and correct responses; (f) to teach according to the kinds of knowledge at issue (i.e., physical, social, and logico-mathematical knowledge), and, (g) to teach to content as well as process.

They describe the relationship between the three types of knowledge as interactionism, stressing that logico-mathematical knowledge must be constructed by a process of reflecting abstraction and equilibration but that physical and social knowledge cannot be constructed outside a logico-mathematical framework. (It is clear Piaget does not subscribe to the rationalist notion of innate intellectual structures.) Logico-mathematical structures are developed by active construction via the overt and covert manipulation of objects and events in the physical world. Kamii and DeVries place learning in the broad sense of development. The development of intelligence is expressed in Piagetian terms of maturation, experience (physical, logico-mathematical), social transmission, and equilibration. Equilibration is the regulator and refers to "an internal regulatory process of differentiation and coordination always tending towards increasing adaptation [Kamii & DeVries, 1974, p. 15]." It is not surprising, therefore, that they advocate the role of the teacher as being an interpreter of a child's readiness to undertake certain tasks, not to learn the task but to experience a way of thinking so as to extend his own ideas. They emphasize that there is no reason to (a) teach Piagetian tasks; and (b) move children to the stage of concrete operations. They also take the view that "it is fruitless to try specifically to organize content [p. 58]." Content may be any situation and activity from daily living, the child development curriculum, or activities related to aspects of Piaget's theory that promote development.

Objectives are divided into long- and short-term cases. Long-term objective stress the adaptive value of attainments in intellectual, moral, and socioemotional development. Short-term objectives are expressed in rather general terms. Only two are quoted in the context of cognition: "(a) to come up with interesting ideas, problems, and questions; (b) to put things into relationships and notice similarities and differences [p. 43]."

This particular curriculum approach is still under evaluation. Formative evaluation is used and is aimed at developing activities, testing them in the classroom, and modifying them according to findings. Kamii and DeVries have no illusions about the limitations of preschool education. Summative evaluation is not considered possible "as long as children have to go to repressive, traditional schools from ages six to sixteen [p. 74]."

A preschool curriculum program, The Piagetian Preschool Educational Program (PPEP), adopting a similar general approach to that of Kamii, was subjected to a 3-year comprehensive field evaluation at the University of Wisconsin Early Childhood Study Center (Bingham-Newman, Saunders, & Hooper, 1976). The basic question examined by the program was whether a preschool curriculum based on Piagetian theory would facilitate the process of developmental change.

In keeping with orthodox Piagetian theory, the research aim was to encourage children to independently discover certain aspects of the world. The stated intention of the program was *not* to directly teach logical operations. Thus, the accent in the school setting was on the children's active manipulation of objects. The role of the teacher was to encourage such activities, to ask probing questions, and to encourage peer interaction. Children were free to respond as they wished. Correct answers were not taught if they did not occur spontaneously. The researchers declared that correct answers per se are not as important as the underlying thinking process; children need to find out about the world for themselves.

This type of statement echoes Piaget's insistence that the young child's intelligence cannot be enhanced by purely receptive educational methods (Piaget, 1970b). The problem of juxtaposing active autonomous discovery against receptive learning has already been discussed earlier in this chapter. The dimensions of learning suggested by Ausubel (e.g., Ausubel & Robinson, 1969, pp. 43–45) present an alternative theory concerning the means whereby knowledge is made available to the learner. These dimensions are reception, discovery, meaningful, and rote learning. Both reception and discovery learning may be meaningful, and conversely, depending on the circumstances, they may be rote. It is unlikely, however, that learning in the usual type of classroom setting will be at either extreme; *meaningful* and *rote* are relative terms.

The framework of the PPEP was based on a number of principles drawn directly from Piagetian theory. Briefly summarized, these include the following:

1. Intelligence is the incorporation of given data into an organized framework through the active, reciprocal process of assimilation and accommodation to various aspects of the environments.
2. Learning is an active process, subordinate to development, involving the manipulation and exploration of objects and events.
3. The development of intelligence is the necessary rapproachment between cognitive, affective, and psychomotor behavioral domains.

Four content areas were selected: logicomathematical knowledge, infralogical knowledge, knowledge of the physical environment, and knowledge of the social environment (Bingham-Newman, 1974, pp. 53–56). Specific logical concepts dealing with classification, seriation, number, and space–time relations, as well as representational and measurement skills were emphasized during the 15-minute small-group activity sessions each day.

Each week, routine formative evaluation was conducted. Summative evaluation occurred at annual intervals. Two-phase comparisons (1971–1973 an 1972–1974) were made between children in the PPEP and a group of children attending a conventional preschool nursery program. Assessment measures used included the Peabody Picture Vocabulary Test, the Raven Coloured Progessive Matrices Test, and Piagetian tasks of classification, double-series matrices, seriation, transitive inference, measurement skills, and conservation of number, length, and quantity. Final assessments showed significant gains by both PPEP children and the control subjects on the majority of summative measures. There were no significant differences in performance generally between treatment groups. Other positive evidence reported concerned the high quality of teacher and student–teacher effectiveness, the children's level of responsiveness, and the continuing interest and support of parents (Bingham-Newman, Saunders, & Hooper, 1976).

The four programs we have described all claim adherence to Piagetian developmental theory. Although they have obvious similarities, mainly concerning the style in which they endorse principles drawn from Piaget's theory, they differ significantly in their expressions of pedagogical methodology. Kamii rejects what she calls the empiricist approach to learning; that is, that knowledge comes from outside the individual through the senses. Thus, programs such as those developed by Lavatelli and Weikart would be labeled empiricist, since they set out to teach the child intellectual skills. Although both these programs include small group-learning sessions concentrating on concrete operational reasoning—for example, Lavatelli's (1970a) complementary classes using sets of planes, bricks, and cars—their authors argue that the intention is to promote rather than directly teach the development of operations. Indeed, Kamaii's critique (Kamii & DeVries, 1974) leads to the semantic problem of "what's in a word," rather than presenting results of an objective and comprehensive study of particular programs. Kamii's approach to the role of the child as learner demonstrates an affinity with a purist Piagetian theory in terms of child-centered activity. Lavatelli's program provides a polar distinction by demanding that most learning activity be initiated by the teacher. The major differences between the four programs fall somewhere along the dimensions defined by the following parameters: (a) the teaching of separate and distinct Piagetian tasks intended to promote the emergence of concrete operations, for example Lavatelli; and (b) the advocacy of an entire curriculum based on Piaget's views of *knowing* and *learning* as conceived by Kamii (c.f., Hooper & DeFrain, 1974).

Evaluation of Piagetian Programs

The evaluation of Piagetian-oriented preschool programs has been confined to a small number of projects only one of which, Weikart's, has been in existence for some years. Thus, relatively little empirical evaluation has been carried out on the various programs. Kamii's present curriculum has not undergone complete evaluation as yet since development is still proceeding. As Kamii points out, summative evaluation can occur only when the curriculum and objectives are clearly enough defined and a fairly long period of instruction has been completed. Formative evaluation of the program, however, has been thorough. The procedure adopted has been for a team of theorists and teachers to develop and test activities in the classroom. These activities have been subsequently modified according to the findings. Kamii asserts that the main objective of future evaluation will be formative rather than summative: "We will constantly assess classroom activities in terms of their harmony with the theory [Kamii & DeVries, 1974, p. 75]." Unfortunately, this approach is likely to lead to a straw man argument. It is clear that a theory demands the setting up of operational hypotheses to test its validity. Kamii, apparently, assumes the validity of the theory.

Weikart's preschool program began in 1962 with the Ypsilanti–Perry Preschool Project. This program and related programs represent a long-term effort aimed at remediating academically handicapped children. The initial program, based on traditional methods geared to social and emotional development, gave way to a "cognitively oriented" program. Both achievement tests and teacher rating scales indicated that children in the program did better in school (from kintergarten onwards) than did a control group. Initial gains in IQ scores by experimental children leveled off in the primary grades to become about equal with those obtained for control group children. These evaluative procedures were extended during the period 1967–1971 by the implementation of three distinct programs which comprised the "Curriculum Demonstration Project": (a) a structured cognitive; (b) a task-oriented language training program, developed by Bereiter and Engelmann at the University of Illinois, using drill methods and behavior modification; and (c) a traditional program emphasizing social and emotional growth.

The project was twice repeated, and no significant differences were found between the three programs in terms of gains in "intelligence," language growth, emotional growth, and social adjustment. For the researchers, these were startling results. Weikart (1973) does not report any specific task evaluation. It may well be that distinctions in intellectual development (or, for that matter, social–emotional development) were not detected because of the form of the evaluation used. Weikart and his colleagues concluded that there was no best curriculum. They made a subjective search for common elements in the three kinds of programs and came up with the following similarities: consistent daily routine, strong commitment to objectives by teachers and paraprofessionals, and daily planning and evaluation. There was one supervisor to coordinate the operation of the three programs—a feature Weikart considers of critical importance. Though each term endeavored to maintain the "purity" of its separate program, there may have been some across-program diffusion.

The PPEP curriculum at the University of Wisconsin Early Childhood Study Center was conceived as an exploratory 3-year research program. Though the experimental children made significant gains on the majority of the summative measures (standardized tests and Piagetian tasks), few of the comparisons between PPEP and the control group were significant.

The Lavatelli Early Childhood Curriculum has only received a pilot program evaluation with no controls. Lavatelli (1970a) reports significant gains on Binet scores and Piagetian tasks.

One further Piagetian preschool program, Thinking Goes to School, never became a fully developed program, only lasting from September 1970 to June 1972. The school, which was conceived by Furth and Wachs, was discontinued by the administration. A complaint by Furth and Wachs (1974) states that there was "constant pressure to show short-term results on standard reading tests, and the constant need to justify the program not on its own terms, but in terms of the traditional philosophy and of immediate results [p. 270]."

From the orthodox Piagetian viewpoint, the usual distinction made is between process and product. However, supporters of this perspective seem to overstate their case. Denis-Prinzhorn, Kamii, and Monoud (1972) criticize short-term empirical evaluation on the following grounds: "When the researcher's interest is in the teachability of a task, his attention necessarily becomes focused on the correctness of answers children give on the posttest. . . . For Piaget, the thing is the process of thinking. . . . The answer the child gives is of interest . . . insofar as it tells us something about the underlying process [p. 68]." The Piagetian programs reported here disclaim interest in the empirical evaluation of the product, insisting that knowledge is constructed during a long-term process of active manipulation of the environment. Thus, the development of intelligence cannot be adequately evaluated with a short-term task or project.

It is conceivable, however, that an investigator may be concerned with both product and process at the same time in a context where both factors have a complementary value. Ausubel, for example, has described cognitive development "in terms of a sequence of stages of increasing independence on *concrete empirical data* in comprehending the meaning of concepts and propositions and in *manipulating* these propositions mentally [Ausubel & Robinson, 1969, p. 205]." It could be hypothesized that the internalization of relatively abstract concepts and practice in performing operations upon them (that is, relating ideas of process to the exemplifying of the concepts) will facilitate developmental readiness. Lawton (1974) found that such a procedure adopted with 6- and 10-year-old children resulted in the facilitation of concrete operations in two related tasks. This approach to teaching–learning procedures would be concerned with the sequential development of intellectual skills and the acquisition of physical and social knowledge. The results of summative evaluation would be viewed in relation to data from formative short-term evaluation. It may well be that changes in the developing intelligence of the child, discovered in the short-run, may provide useful feedback information to the teacher. This, in turn, may result in changes in the learning environment and in pedagogical methodology so as to provide a greater potential for the ongoing intellectual development of the child.

Let us look at three examples that help illuminate the problem facing the teacher; that is, to distinguish between the myth of training and the undoubted metamorphosis that results from certain types of teaching procedures. First, and very briefly, as Bruner has pointed out (Bruner, Goodnow, & Austin, 1956), the human organism has "an exquisite capacity for making distinctions [p. 1]." The resolution of the problem of registering differences among objects and events—not to be overwhelmed by complexity of the discriminanda—is to categorize. For example, when stimuli are classed as "forms of the same thing," this constitutes an identity response. In addition, when discriminable things are classed as "the same kind of thing," this is the construction of an equivalence class, which may have affective, functional, or formal properties. Of the two forms of categorizing, the first might be supposed to be easier. The point Bruner makes is that whether the capacity to so categorize is innate or learned matters little. The crucial point is that the development of such competencies depends notably on learning. Lewis Carroll provides a humorous insight on such learning in these lines from "The White Knight Tells His Tale":

> And now, if e'er by chance I put my fingers into glue,
> Or madly squeeze a right-hand foot into a left-hand shoe
> Or if I drop upon my toe a very heavy weight
> I weep, for it reminds me so of that old man I used to know.

The myth of learning here would suppose that such classifying operations should have been coordinated in the later years of the concrete-operational stage (i.e., before age 9 or 10 at the latest). Yet, it is quite clear that in the adult world, much confusion exists about what constitutes an identity class. Further, as Ausubel (1966) has pointed out, intellectual development is not completely consistent; nor is there ever reached an invariant generality of behavior for a particular stage. From the Genevan perspective, learning is always subordinate to development. For young children, certainly, content per se is not seen as having any intrinsic value, except in the sense that it lends itself to the manipulation of objects and events necessary for the continuing development of logicomathematical structures. However, though the findings of secondary source investigations (e.g., Braine, 1959; Dodwell, 1960; Ervin, 1960; Lovell, 1959; Lovell & Ogilvie, 1960; Peel, 1959) have generally supported Piaget's formulations regarding stages of intellectual development, they also point to intraindividual, interindividual, intersituational, and intertask variability. Also, findings from training studies generally tend not to confirm a synchronous development of logical operations (cf. Brainerd, 1973; Klausmeier & Hooper, 1974). Indeed, Ausubel (1966), referring to criteria of developmental stages states that development is "always referable to a given range of difficulty and familiarity of the problem area. Beyond this range, individuals commonly revert (regress) to a former stage of development [p. 50]." To find a completely equilibrated structure of operation may be considered analogous to the quest for the Holy Grail. Certain sources of evidence indicate that the same types of logical operations and problem-solving strategies are employed at all age levels, and differ mainly in the degree of complexity of operations (cf. Lovell, 1968). Ausubel (Ausubel & Robinson, 1969) proposes an alternative interpretation of Piaget's account of cognitive development in the early stages, one that could have some meaning to the teacher. He states that the essential condition for learning primary concepts at the preoperational stage is that relevant concrete examples be made available to the child and that the child learn to recognize that each example contains the set of critical attributes that define the concept. The child will then be capable of understanding propositions indicating relationships between such primary concepts and "in certain necessarily restricted and concrete situations the child will be able to use such propositions in very elementary kinds of problem solving [p. 184]." Manipulation of objects and events does not necessarily have to be in direct connection with external concrete objects and events. Ausubel advocates an expository teaching–receptive learning model in which new knowledge can be meaningfully associated with general ideas already existing in cognitive structure. The accommodation would be by rote if not related, or if unrelatable, to existing knowledge. If the learner makes sense out of the new knowl-

189

edge in relating it in some authentic manner to existing knowledge in cognitive structure, then *meaningful learning* will result. *Discovery learning,* which the "new education" supposes is the prerogative of Piagetian-inspired curricula, may in fact be viewed as an alternative dimension to reception learning. The important distinction in discovery learning is that the learner discovers for himself the principal content of what is to be learned. It can be postulated that the form and extent of interaction between the assimilation and accommodation of new knowledge and existing knowledge will depend on the structure of existing ideas in cognitive structure. The degree of this complex relationship may vary considerably.

According to Ausubel, the value of expository teaching rests on the presentation of a structure of verbal propositions. These verbal propositions, providing necessary cues regarding manipulation, can guide the internal manipulation of images. It is important to recognize, however, that the very young child tends to be stimulus-bound. At the concrete-operational stage there is a move toward greater facility in dealing with secondary abstractions, for which attributes can be provided as verbal definitions so long as the child is provided with adequate concrete props. Such props are vital where the child is manipulating propositions in problem solving. The qualitative distinctions between this second stage and the final stage of development, which Ausubel terms the "abstract logical stage," is an ability to relate critical attributes of new secondary abstractions to cognitive structure without props. Ausubel poses certain educational implications stemming from such an interpretation of cognitive development. First, to avoid pedagogic (and semantic) confusion, it is necessary to distinguish between different kinds of thinking processes. For example, the young child uses a *developmental* type of intuitive process due to a lack of explicitness and an unsystematic approach to problem solving. However, an *unsophisticated* type of intuitive approach may also be used by the cognitive mature individual. This tends to occur where there is a degree of naivety with respect to the content of tasks. Though the preschool child's thinking is restricted to relatively concrete concepts (primary) in the learning of most relational propositions, Ausubel does not consider it necessary, in all probability, "that *all* relational learning during this period takes place on a non-verbal, non-problem-solving or completely autonomous self-discovery basis in order to be meaningful. Simple derivative propositions . . . correlative, superordinate and combinatorial propositions can also be learned on a reception basis [in Ausubel & Robinson, 1969, p. 203]." With such types of learning, adequate examples of concepts need to be provided, or an opportunity for the manipulation of concrete

objects, or both. Autonomous, self-discovery processes might well en-
hance learning (and provide motivation), but these are not considered
indispensable for meaningful reception learning. The metamorphosis in
such learning would be relatively long-term, dependent on a sequential
process of learning—a continuing of a reception–discovery dimension
where generalizability and durability of learning are related to the degree of meaningful association between prior and subsequent learning
events.

We have seen that certain pedagogical interpretations from Piagetian theory are in contrast to such implications. Piaget would contradict
the expected value of expository teaching, since he would expect that
for a long while the child would have little or no understanding of
hierarchical systems of concepts. However, the polarity of Piaget's
argument, when comparing the active and receptive schools, rests on
the assumption that receptive learning always implies that the child
will elaborate its concepts in an adult fashion. He says "the existence
of verbalism, that dismal scholastic fad—a proliferation of pseudo-ideas
loosely hooked onto a string of words lacking all real meaning—is
fairly exclusive proof that the workings of this mechanism are not
without their snags [Piaget, 1969, p. 164]." The essential view of the
young child as an autonomous, active, self-discovery learner, involved
in the manipulation of physical and social phenomena (in the concrete),
is perhaps the most important principle emanating from Piagetian
theory. Many open-classroom and self-discovery approaches accept
Piaget's theory as a systematic theoretical foundation. However, caution
has been urged in the acceptance of educational recommendations stemming from Piaget's theory (e.g., Beilin, 1971b; Kohnstamm, 1967;
& Sullivan, 1967). Sullivan (1969) has pointed out that "the Piagetian
contribution to the structure and sequencing of subject matter is more
apparent than real. This is not the fault of Piaget, but rather of his
educational followers. . . . The use of Piaget's stages as indicators of
'learning readiness' seems most premature and needs more careful consideration [p. 33]." Beilin (1971b) notes that there is little consensual
agreement between Piagetians and neo-Piagetians regarding the conceptual and operational definitions of operativity. He also points out
the theoretical and practical limitations of Piaget's criticism of verbal
instructional procedures:

1. The special relationship between language and logical thought
   processes remains unknown or conjectural
2. "Actions" as defined by Piaget also occur in linguistic contexts
3. Language embodies operational properties (cf. Riegel, 1970)

191

4. Language interchanges appear to be present to varying degrees in most of the successful training procedures (cf. Brainerd, 1973)

The influence of specific instruction on the acquisition of logical operations remains controversial. Lavatelli's program espouses such methodology, whereas Kamii's disavowal of such procedures represents the orthodox view of the Piagetian doctrine. Beilin (1971b) asks the important question: How much prior concurrent knowledge that can only be acquired by rote or didactic methods is essential for the acquisition of logical concepts? On the basis of evidence, it seems reasonable to predict that short-term training can effect real gains in the acquisition of logical concepts; longer programs should be based on the realization that successive steps in a varied and well-structured program should lead to wider gains. However, it still remains for a complementary educational technology to be designed and evaluated. The evidence for either an "enrichment" process or an "instructional" process leaves the issue unclear. Elkind (1973) suggests that "we do not have the longitudinal evidence yet on which to make that decision. Until the evidence is in, we can only urge that those who favor enrichment will keep open minds while those who favor instruction will not let their zeal influence their judgment [p. 120]."

The value of Piaget's theory to future pedagogical methodology is its potential as a source of important hypotheses, as yet unevaluated. We need to know more clearly the relations that exist between operativity and learning, whether levels of operativity may set the upper limits but not the lower limits of the quality of learning, and to what extent the nature of information processing and task complexity affect operativity. In the spirit of Erickson, the emphasis would be on a generativity—which makes man not only a learner but a teacher, as well.

Conclusions

It should be readily apparent to the reader at this point that there is an inherent paradox in evaluating the general worthiness of Piagetian-inspired early childhood education programs if the usual tenets of an empiricist educational philosophy are employed. From the perspective of contrasting world views or metatheories (cf. Hooper, 1973; Overton & Reese, 1973; Reese & Overton, 1970), it is unfortunately all too common to adopt the accountability criteria from one view (i.e., the mechanistic case) and apply them to their polar counterparts (i.e., the organismic case). This probably represents a case of mixing essentially irreconcilable truth criteria (Reese & Overton, 1970). For example, some of the programs reviewed (e.g., Lavatelli, 1970a) emphasize a major role for teacher-initiated inputs and the employment of *specific* behavioral objectives and associated instructional strategies, usually of a verbal didactic variety. This is clearly at variance with the usual recommendations of Piagetian theory.

In addition, there is often an imposed emphasis on short-term summative accountability in conjunction with *specific* operational assessments. It is at best a moot question if evaluation and accountability criteria of this kind should be applied to Piagetian early childhood education programs as described here.

Finally, and of greatest basic importance, many educational program designers (and critics of educational program efficacy) emphasize a conception of cognitive development as gradually progressing and distinctly *non*unitary and multidimensional in nature. This is, or course, in marked contrast to the conventional Genevan interpretation of intrastage behavioral characteristics and interstage transition processes (cf. Beilin, 1971b; Flavell, 1971; Inhelder, 1956, 1962; Piaget, 1970a,b; Pinard & Laurendeau, 1969; Wohlwill, 1973). Moreover, the adoption of one of these global orientations effectively constrains the type of research problems to be investigated and the methodologies to be employed (Hooper, 1973).

It is also clear, from the Genevan perspective, that a genuinely "valid" Piagetian early childhood education program (e.g., Kamii & DeVries, 1974) appears to have much in common with the traditional approach to nursery schools and to self-discovery learning open-classroom programs as typically described (Furth & Wachs, 1974; Hooper & DeFrain, 1974; Schwebel & Raph, 1973). As such, they are subject to the oft-cited strengths and weaknesses of these open-ended approaches to educational programming, which are themselves potential candidates for future evaluation research.

Through the 1960s the work of Piaget served to stimulate much of the research undertaken with respect to the cognitive development (and, to a lesser extent, the affective development) of the young child. No doubt, the impetus of that research will continue, though a new orientation focused on a critical analysis of stage theory and information processing is already apparent (e.g., Flavell, 1971, 1972; Lavell, 1968; Sullivan, 1969; Wohlwill, 1973; Brainerd, 1976).

The Piagetian ECE programs, as referred to above, present a pedagogical model oriented toward the self-construction of knowledge with the emphasis on the promotion of the growth of logical operations.

This approach presents quite clearly the Genevan emphasis on an interactionist orientation to logical concept acquisition: interaction between the child and his peers, the child and the physical environment, the child and the teacher.

A second system, referred to in this chapter, would endeavor to provide the child with hierarchically structured subject matter concepts and propositions along with high-order rules for manipulating such learning materials (e.g., Ausubel & Robinson, 1969; Lawton, Lewis, & Deibert, 1976). A related system, (dissimilar with respect to certain crucial elements) is that prescribed by Bruner (1965) for the transmission of cultures amplifying skills and knowledge. In teaching, an emphasis would be placed on economy of learning (the learning of hierarchical conceptual systems), transfer, and the learning of general rules. Such systems are not so much concerned with using readiness (the developmental stage) as a criterion for defining change in intellectual behavior as in seeking factors that cause that change to occur, and in asking whether it is feasible and useful to manipulate those factors.

Whether learning is viewed as primarily autonomous or as resulting primarily from an interdependency between child and adult (with the adult prescribing much of what is learned) depends on whether emphasis is given to, say, the genetic–epistemological viewpoint of Piaget or to the fundamentally psychological viewpoints of Bruner or Ausubel. Elkind (1973) sees the distinction as a conflict between what he terms *enrichment* and *instruction* (preschool) programs, though he admits that he has no answer to the question of what kind of program is best. He suggests that longitudinal evidence on which to make decisions is still required.

It is clear that we lack the essential information necessary to resolve many of the questions and issues formulated in the present discussion. Most obvious is the lacuna that exists concerning short-term and (especially) long-term evaluation of the representative Piagetian programs. In this regard it should be emphasized that the great majority of the specialized early childhood education models and associated curriculum programs have *not* undergone comprehensive longitudinal assessment. Investigations such as those of Bingham-Newman, Saunders, and Hooper (1976), Klaus and Gray (1968), Miller and Dyer (1975), Sigel, Secrist, and Forman (1973), and Weikart (1973) remain the exceptional cases that employed long-term evaluation strategies.

In a similar vein, information on program impact on parental attitudes and family-process variables is generally not available. It is possible that certain far-reaching influences of preschool programming innovation extend beyond the immediate confines of the classroom and are not measurable in terms of short-range, child-centered assessment settings. For example, little is known of the potential of university-based demonstration programs for significantly improving undergraduate teacher training programs or of their possible utilization as settings for the inservice training of professional teachers (cf. Lawton & Hooper, 1976).

Finally, the most fundamental knowledge gap concerns the lack of nonconfounded normative data on the development of logical reasoning and associated cognitive functioning during the years of early and middle childhood. Thus the question of how to best characterize the concrete-operations stage (as an essentially unitary or nonunitary developmental phenomenon, for example) remains unresolved. Moreover, evidence from training studies does not unequivocally support the long-term stability of induced logical concepts or the learning of qualitatively more complex understandings. Nor do such studies clearly indicate the degree of intraconcept and interconcept transfer of instruction. Even if it is unambiguously shown that these controlled instructional experiences are *sufficient* conditions for the attainment of higher-order logical concepts, the case for constituting *necessary* determinants is an open question (cf. Wohlwill, 1973, pp. 317–320). Additional ecological analyses of children in naturalistic settings must eventually be conducted to resolve this final question.

REFERENCES

Aebli, H. *Didactique psychologigue: Application à la didactique de la psychologie de Jean Piaget.* Neuchatel: Delachaux et Niestle, 1951.

Almy, M., Chittenden, E., & Miller, P. *Young children's thinking.* New York: Columbia Teachers College Press.

Athey, I. J., & Rubadeau, D. O. (Eds.), *Educational implications of Piaget's theory: A book of readings.* Waltham, MA: Blaisdell, 1970.

Ausubel, D. P. Stages of intellectual development and their implications for early childhood education, *Orientamenti Pedagogici,* 1966, *6,* 47–60.

Ausubel, D. P., & Robinson, F. G. *School Learning: An introduction to educational psychology.* New York: Holt, Rinehart, & Winston, 1969.

Beard, R. M. *An outline of Piaget's developmental psychology for students and teachers.* New York: Basic Books, 1969.

Beilin, H. Developmental stages and developmental processes. In D. R. Ross, M. P. Ford, & G. B. Flamer (Eds.), *Measurement and Piaget.* New York: McGraw-Hill, 1971. (a)

Beilin, H. The training and acquisition of logical operation. In M. Rosskopf, L. Steffe, & S. Taback (Eds.), *Piagetian cognitive development research and mathematical education.* Washington, D.C.: National Council of Teachers of Mathematics, 1971. (b)

Bereiter, C., & Engelmann, S., *Teaching the culturally disadvantaged child in the preschool*. Englewood Cliffs, NJ: Prentice-Hall, 1966.

Bingham-Newman, A. M. Development of logical operations abilities in early childhood: A longitudinal comparison of the effects of two preschool settings. Unpublished doctoral dissertation, University of Wisconsin, Madison, 1974.

Bingham-Newman, A. M., & Saunders, R. A. Take a new look at your classroom with Piaget as a guide. *Young Children*, 1976, in press.

Bingham-Newman, A. M., Saunders, R. A., & Hooper, F. H. *Logical operations in the preschool: The contribution of Piagetian theory to early childhood education*. Technical Report No. 354. Madison: Wisconsin Research and Development Center for Cognitive Learning, 1976.

Braine, M. D. S. The ontogeny of certain logical operations: Piaget's formulation examined by non-verbal methods. *Psychological Monographs: General and Applied*, 1959. (Whole No. 475.)

Brainerd, C. J. Neo-Piagetian training experiments revisited: Is there any support for the cognitive-developmental stage hypothesis? *Cognition*, 1973, 2, 349–370.

Brearly, M., & Hitchfield, E. *A guide to reading Piaget*. New York: Schoken Books, 1969.

Bruner, J. S. *The process of education*. Cambridge, MA: Harvard University Press, 1960.

Bruner, J. S. The growth of mind. *American Psychologist*, 1965, 20 (12), 1007-1017.

Bruner, J. S., Goodnow, J. R., & Austin, G. A. *A study of thinking*. New York: Wiley, 1956.

Bruner, J. S., Olver, R. R., & Greenfield, R. M. *Studies in cognitive growth*. New York: Wiley 1966.

Chittenden, E. A. What is learned and what is taught. *Young Children*, 1969, 25, 12–19.

Denis-Prinzhorn, M., Kamii, C., & Monoud, P. Pedagogical application of Piaget's theory. *People Watching*, 1972, 1 (2), 68–71.

Dodwell, P. C. Children's understanding of number and related concepts. *Canadian Journal of Psychology*, 1960, 14, 191–205.

Elkind, D. Preschool education: Enrichment or instruction. In B. Spodek (Ed.), *Early childhood education*. Englewood Cliffs, N.J.: Prentice-Hall, 1973.

Erikson, E. H. Eight ages of man. In C. S. Lavatelli & F. Stendle (Eds.), *Readings in child behavior and development* (3rd ed.). New York: Harcourt, Brace, Javanovich, 1972.

Ervin, S. M. Training and a logical operation by children. *Child Development*, 1960, 31, 555–564.

Evans, E. D. *Contemporary influences in early childhood education* (2nd ed.). New York: Holt, Rinehart, & Winston, 1975.

Flavell, J. H. *The developmental psychology of Jean Piaget*. Princeton, NJ: Van Nostrand, 1963.

Flavell, J. H. Staged-related properties of cognitive development. *Cognitive Psychology*, 1971, 2, 421–453.

Flavell, J. H. An analysis of cognitive developmental sequences. *Genetic Psychology Monographs*, 1972, 86, 279–350.

Furth, H. *Piaget for teachers*. Englewood Cliffs, NJ: Prentice-Hall, 1970.

Furth, H., & Wachs, H. *Thinking goes to school: Piaget's theory and practice*. London: Oxford University Press. 1974.

Ginsberg, H., & Opper, S. *Piaget's theory of intellectual development: An introduction*. Englewood Cliffs, NJ: Prentice-Hall, 1969.

Glaser, R., & Resnick, L. B. Instructional psychology. In P. Mussen & M. Rosenzweig (Eds.), *Annual review of psychology*. Palo Alto, CA: Annual Reviews, 1972.

Hooper, F. H. Piagetian research and education. In I. E. Sigel & F. H. Hooper (Eds.), *Logical thinking in children: Research based on Piaget's theory*. New York: Holt, Rinehart, & Winston, 1968.

Hooper, F. H. Cognitive assessment across the life-span: Methodological implications of the organismic approach. In J. R. Nesselroade & H. W. Reese (Eds.), *Life-span developmental psychology: Methodological issues*. New York: Academic Press, 1973.

Hooper, F. H., & DeFrain, J. *The search for a distinctly Piagetian contribution to education*. Theoretical Paper No. 50. Madison: Wisconsin Research and Development Center for Cognitive Learning, 1974.

Inhelder, B. Criteria of the stages of mental development. In J. M. Tanner & B. Inhelder (Eds.), *Discussions on child development* (Vol 1). New York: International University Press, 1956.

Inhelder, B. Some aspects of Piaget's genetic approach to cognition. In W. Kessen & C. Kuhlman (Eds.), Thought in the young child. *Monographs of the Society for Research in Child Development*, 1962, 27 (2), 19–34.

Kamii, C. P. Interactionism and the teaching of young children. In M. Schwebel & J. Ralph (Eds.), *Piaget in the classroom*. New York: Basic Books, 1973.

Kamii, C., & DeVries, R. Piaget for early education. In R. K. Parker (Ed.), *The preschool in action* (2nd ed.), Boston: Allyn & Bacon, 1974.

Kaufman, B. Will the real Jean Piaget please stand up: An epistemological critique of three Piaget-based early childhood curricula. Urbana, IL: Educational Resources Information Center, 1975.

Klaus, R., & Gray, S. The early training project for disadvantaged children: A report after five years. *Monographs of the Society for Research in Child Development*, 1968, 53, Serial No. 120.

Klausmeier, H. J., & Hooper, F. H. Conceptual development and instruction. In F. Kerlinger & J. Carroll (Eds.), *Review of educational research* (Vol. 2). Itasca, IL: Peacock, 1974.

Kohlberg, L. Early education: A cognitive-developmental view. *Child Development*, 1968, 39, 1013–1062.

Kohnstamm, G. A. *Piaget's analysis of class inclusion: Right or wrong?* The Hague: Mouton, 1967.

Lavatelli, C. *Early childhood curriculum—A Piaget program*. Boston: American Science and Engineering, 1970. (a)

Lavatelli, C. *Teacher's guide to accompany early childhood curriculum—A Piaget program*. Boston: American Science and Engineering, 1970. (b)

Lovell, K. A follow-up study of some aspects of the work of Piaget and Inhelder into the child's conception of space. *British Journal of Educational Psychology*, 1959, 24, 104–117.

Lovell, K. Systemalization of thought. In E. A. Lunzer & J. F. Morris (Eds.), *Development in human learning*. London: Staples Press, 1968.

Lovell, K., & Ogilvie, E. A study of the conservation of substance in the junior school child. *British Journal of Educational Psychology*, 1960, 30, 109–118.

Lawton, J. T. An analytical study of the use of advance organizers in facilitating children's learning. Unpublished doctoral dissertation, University of Leeds, England, 1974.

Lawton, J. T., & Hooper, F. H. *The prospects for a logical concept curriculum in the preschool and early elementary grades*. Working Paper No. 157. Madison: Wisconsin Research and Development Center for Cognitive Learning, 1976.

Lawton, J. T., Lewis, R. A., & Deibert, J. *The contribution of Ausubelian theory to early childhood education*. Working Paper No. 154. Madison: Wisconsin Research and Development Center for Cognitive Learning, 1976.

Miller, L. B., & Dyer, J. L. Four preschool programs: Their dimensions and effects. *Monographs of the Society for Research in Child Development*, 1975, *40* (5–6), Serial No. 162.

Overton, W. F., & Reese, H. W. Models of development: Methodological implications. In J. R. Nesselroade & H. W. Reese (Eds.), *Life-span developmental psychology: Methodological issues*. New York: Academic Press, 1973.

Peel, E. A. Experimental examination of some of Piaget's schemata. *British Journal of Educational Psychology*, 1959, *29*, 89–103.

Piaget, J. Psycho-pédagogie et mentalité enfantine.. *Journal de Psychologie. Normale et Pathalogigue*, 1928, *25*, 31–60.

Piaget, J. Le dévelopment de l'esprit de solidarité chez l'enfant. In *Troisième cours pour le personnel enseignant*. Geneva: Bureau International d'Education, 1930. (a)

Piaget, J. La notion de justice chez l'enfant. In *Troisième cours pour le personnel enseignant*. Geneva: Bureau International d'Education, 1930. (b)

Piaget, J. Introduction psychologique à l'education internationale. In *Quatrième cours pour le personnel enseignant*. Geneva: Bureau International d'Education, 1931.

Piaget, J. Remarques psychologiques sur le self-government. In *Le self-government à l'école. Geneva*: Bureau International d'Education, 1934.

Piaget, J. Remarques psychologiques sur le travail par équipes. In *Le travail par équipes à l'école*. Geneva: Bureau International d'Education, 1935.

Piaget, J. The right to education in the modern world. In *UNESCO, freedom and culture*. New York: Columbia University Press, 1951.

Piaget, J. Development and learning. In R. Ripple & V. Rockcastle (Eds.), *Piaget rediscovered*. Ithaca, NY: Cornell University Press, 1964.

Piaget, J. *The child's conception of time*. London: Routledge and Kegan Paul, 1969.

Piaget, J. Invited seminar. Catholic University of America, Washington, D.C., June 6, 1970. (a)

Piaget, J. *The science of education and the psychology of the child*. New York: Viking Press, 1970. (b)

Piaget, J. *Structuralism*. New York: Basic Books, 1970. (c)

Piaget, J. *To understand is to invent: The future of education*. New York: Viking Press, 1973.

Pinard, A., & Laurendeau, M. "State" in Piaget's cognitive-developmental theory: Exegesis of a concept. In D. Elkind & J. H. Flavell (Eds.), *Studies in cognitive development: Essays in honor of Jean Piaget*. New York: Oxford University Press, 1969.

Reese, H. W., & Overton, W. F. Models of development and theories of development. In L. R. Goulet & P. B. Baltes (Eds.), *Life-span developmental psychology: Research and theory*. New York: Academic Press, 1970.

Riegel, U. F. The language acquisition process: A reinterpretation of selected research findings. In L. R. Goulet & P. B. Balles (Eds.), *Life-span developmental psychology: Research and theory*. New York: Academic Press, 1970.

Schwebel, M., & Raph, J. (Eds.), *Piaget in the classroom*. New York: Basic Books, 1973.

Sigel, I. E. The Piagetian system and the world of education. In D. Elkind & J. H. Flavell (Eds.), *Studies in cognitive development: Essays in honor of Jean Piaget.* New York: Oxford University Press, 1969.

Sigel, I. E., Secrist, A., & Forman, G. Psycho-educational intervention beginning at age two: Reflections and outcomes. In J. C. Stanley (Ed.), *Compensatory education for children, ages two to eight: Recent studies of educational intervention.* Baltimore, MD: Johns Hopkins University Press, 1973.

Silverman, C., & Weikart, D. *Open framework: Evolution of a concept in preschool education.* Michigan: High Scope Educational Research Foundation Report, Ypsilanti, 1973.

Strauss, S. Inducing cognitive development and learning: A review of short-term training experiments. *Cognition,* 1972, *1,* 329–357.

Sullivan, E. V. *Piaget and the school curriculum: A critical appraisal.* Toronto: The Ontario Institute for Studies in Education, 1967.

Sullivan, E. V., Piagetian theory in the educational mileau: A critical appraisal. *Canadian Journal of Behavioral Science,* 1969, *3,* 1.

Wallace, J. G. *Concept growth and the education of the child.* The Mere, Upton Park, Slough Bucks: National Foundation for Educational Research in England and Wales, 1965.

Weikart, D. P. Development of effective preschool programs: A report on the results of the High/Scope-Ypsilanti preschool projects. Paper presented at the High/Scope Educational Research Foundation Conference: Using the High/Scope cognitive approach to learning in infant, preschool and early elementary education. Ann Arbor, Michigan, May, 1973.

Wohlwill, J. F. *The study of behavioral development.* New York: Academic Press, 1973.

9

Conceptualization of Children's Logical Competence: Piaget's Propositional Logic and an Alternative Proposal

ROBERT H. ENNIS

University of Illinois at Urbana–Champaign

This essay draws upon material from two articles that I have previously published:

"Children's ability to handle Piaget's propositional logic." *Review of Educational Research* 45: 1–41, 1975. Copyright 1975, American Educational Research Association, Washington, D.C.

"An alternative to Piaget's conceptualization of logical competence." *Child Development* 47: 903–919, 1976. Copyright 1976, Society for Research in Child Development, Chicago, Illinois.

I am grateful to the organizations listed for permission to adapt and incorporate parts of these articles.

Helpful suggestions were made by Joe Burnett, Lindley Darden, Stephane Dausse, J. A. Easley, Jr., Helen Ennis, Walter Feinberg, Lucia French, William Gardiner, L. L. Gross, W. R. Kenzie, Thomas Knapp, Lawrence Kohlberg, Jana Mason, Ellen Markman, Robert Monk, Richard Morrow, Daniel Osherson, Dieter Paulus, Lucille Ringel, James Roberge, Robert Rumery, Barbara Moor Sanner, Sydney Shoemaker, Edward Smith, Patrick Suppes, Thomas Tomko, Eric Weir, and Lauren Weisberg.

The writings of Jean Piaget seem to be a first place to turn for information about children's (deductive) logical competence[1] since he dominates the literature and is so frequently cited when the topic is under discussion. Unfortunately, my search of Piaget's work in that area was unrewarding, yielding no substantial information (apart from the verbatim accounts of children's talk). His logical principles look unsatisfactory; his generalizations seem defective; and his basic categories and theorizing in this area appear to be devoid of empirical interpretation.

In this essay I shall try to elaborate and substantiate these claims and propose an alternative conceptualization of the area.

The first part of the essay is concerned with presenting a few essential features of propositional logic and then exhibiting a defect in many contemporary, symbolic, propositional-logic systems, a defect that may have motivated Piaget's development of his own system of logic. This is followed by a description of Piaget's system, including his "combinatorial system" and a delineation of some fundamental flaws in his system, flaws that make it unsuitable as either a guide to logical reasoning or as a structure for describing how children, adolescents, and adults actually do reason: As a guide, it is bad; as a description, it is false.

Following this is an examination of possible interpretations of Piaget's claim that children ages 11–12 and under "cannot yet handle" propositional logic (in the context of his views that older adolescents can handle it and that children from 7–8 to 11–12 can handle class

---

[1] The discussion of logical competence throughout this paper employs the ordinary sense of the word "competence." This contrasts with what appears to be a technical sense of the word as used by Flavell and Wohlwill (1969). Competence in their sense seems to consist only of knowledge of the rules governing some subject matter (pp. 71–75), whereas in the sense used in this paper, it is broader, incorporating both knowledge of rules and the ability to use them in various standard circumstances. The latter sense appears to be more in accord with standard usage. Just as a pilot is not competent at instrument flying unless, in addition to knowing the rules and principles, she or he can actually keep track of the variety of things on the instrument panel and coordinate these things with control pressures, so as to keep the airplane on the appropriate course within tolerances, it would seem odd to say that someone is competent in logic even though that person gets mixed up in dealing with premises from which she or he has withheld belief or even though an irrelevant premise regularly causes the person to make mistakes. In order to avoid misinterpretation by the consumers of research and others, I use "competence" in the broad, standard sense. This distinction between two senses of the word "competence" is not an attempt to make a theoretical point but merely an attempt to facilitate communication.

logic). I argue that the claim is either false, untestable (and therefore useless), or not about deductive logic, depending on the interpretation under consideration. A key problem that Piaget does not resolve is that of making a distinction between propositional logic and class logic. What is the difference between the deductive logic that children supposedly can handle and that which they supposedly cannot yet handle? Alternatively, what logic is it that older adolescents supposedly can handle but that children 11–12 and under supposedly cannot handle? The lack of an even moderately clear answer to these questions is a conceptual problem for Piaget's approach.

On the assumption that these logical and conceptual difficulties exist, then an alternative to Piaget's conceptualization of the field is needed. The one I propose does not try to accomplish all that Piaget was trying to accomplish. Rather, it is an alternative in the sense that it attempts to provide (*a*) a correct formulation of logical principles and a plausible grouping of them; (*b*) a basic empirical vocabulary that will enable investigators to organize data at a fairly low theoretical level in the form of meaningful propositions that others can test and supplement, propositions that also can serve as tests of higher-level hypotheses and bodies of theory; and (*c*) a dimensional analysis of logical competence that seems appropriate on the basis of existing research and my experience teaching logic and investigating logical competence. The proposed dimensions of logical competence, the logical principle dimension, the content dimension, and the complexity dimension, will be elaborated in the last third of this essay.

Clarity of presentation requires an introduction to standard propositional logic. Readers familiar with the standard logical concept of a proposition and the paradoxes of material implication and disjunction can proceed directly to page 207.

Standard Propositional Logic

Propositional logic is generally taken to be one basic kind of deductive logic, one that is exemplified by the following valid argument, using content from an Inhelder–Piaget example (1958):

Example 1

Premises:

   1. *If this rod is thin, then it is flexible.*
   2. *This rod is thin.*

Conclusion:

   3. *This rod is flexible.*

The argument is called "valid" because the conclusion follows necessarily from the premises. An invalid argument is one in which the conclusion does not necessarily follow from the premises.

Basic Units and Logical Operators

In the argument there are two different simple propositions involved, which remain essentially unchanged throughout the argument. The propositions are "this rod is thin" and "this rod is flexible." Using the labels, p and q: let p = "this rod is thin"; and let q = "this rod is flexible."

In standard propositional logic the basic units are propositions (like "this rod is thin" and "this rod is flexible") that can stand alone (as in Lines 2 and 3 of Example 1) or can be joined or modified by logical operators (like "if" and "then" in Line 1) but that remain essentially unchanged throughout the course of an argument. The shift from "it is flexible" in Line 1 to "this rod is flexible" in Line 3 is not regarded as an essential change since the two mean exactly the same in the context of this argument. In Line 1 the word "it" is not free to refer to anything but this rod.

The argument in Example 1 can be symbolized as follows:

Example 2
> 1. *If p, then q*
> 2. *p*
> 3. *Therefore, q*

Often one finds $p \supset q$ or $p \rightarrow q$ used to represent "If p, then q." Piaget uses $p \supset q$.

In the compound proposition "If p, then q," the stated relationship between p and q is called implication because of the words "if" and "then." Piaget uses that name. Other standard logical operators are "not," "and," and "or," with the associated labels negation, conjunction, and disjunction (or alternation). Later, I shall draw a distinction between alternation and disjunction.

Propositional logic is ordinarily concerned with the validity of arguments utilizing propositions standing alone or under the influence of one or more of these four logical operators. There are a variety of systems for judging validity. One primary difference among them consists in their stance toward the paradoxes I am about to elaborate.

The Paradoxes of Material
Implication and Disjunction

Material implication is that interpretation of the implication relationship that holds "if *p*, then *q*" to be equivalent by definition to this
negajunction (that is, this negated conjunction): "not both *p* and not
q"; regards the latter (and thus the former) as shown true by either
showing the truth of *q* or the falsity of *p*; and regards them as shown
to be false by the combination of the truth of *p* and the falsity of *q*.
Thus, the conditional "If this rod is thick, then it is flexible" would be
judged equivalent to "It is not the case both that this rod is thick and
that this rod is inflexible." Both would therefore be shown to be true
by showing either one of the following:

1. *This rod is flexible (q).*
2. *This rod is not thick (not p). (Here p represents "this rod is
   thick.")*

In Case 1, showing that rod is flexible (*q*) shows that not both of
the following are true (since the second is not true): "The rod is thick"
and "The rod is inflexible." In Case 2, showing that the rod is thin
(and thus not thick, i.e., not *p*) shows that not both are true since the
first, "the rod is thick," is not true. Putting it only in terms of letters,
if *q* is true, then it must also be true that not both *p* and not *q*. If *p*
is false, then not both *p* and not *q*. The falsity of either negajunct
proves the negajunction.

A number of people have balked at this sort of result because, for
example, showing that a rod is thin does not by itself seem sufficient to
prove that if it were thick, it would be flexible. Defenders of the result
might note that in putting the challenge I changed from the indicative
"is" to the subjunctive "were" and hold that the odd result does not
matter, anyway, since, by assumption, the rod is in fact thin. Thus, they
would hold, no mistaken conclusion can be drawn from the result "if
the rod is *thick*, then it is flexible." They also note the elegance achiev-
able by incorporating the given equivalence into the system.

The following non-Piagetian example puts more strongly the case
against so defining implication:

Example 3

If we depart after 5 p.m., the airplane will get ice on the wings.

On a particular day this winter we were going to and did depart
before 5 p.m. Imagine yourself to be in that situation: about to depart

before 5 p.m. on the day in question. The antecedent in Example 3 is false. That is, it is not the case that we depart after 5 p.m. By the material-implication definition of implication, that we depart before 5 p.m. establishes the claim made in Example 3. This is an unacceptable result since the claim made in Example 3 is about a relationship between our departure time and wing icing, something that must be substantiated by the weather conditions not by our departing before 5 p.m.

In this example there is no shift to the subjunctive, and it does make a difference whether the supposed establishing of the claim of Example 3 is legitimate. If it were, then a pilot might, as he is departing before 5 p.m., justifiably say to a passenger who was expecting and hoping for a later departure, "If we depart after 5 p.m., the airplane will get ice on the wings."

This wing icing example does not argue against the elegance defense. In fact, the material-implication definition of implication does contribute to the building of an elegant logical system. Unfortunately, the price is distortion.

Such results are called the "paradoxes of material implication." These paradoxes are absent from the logic propounded by Piaget and from the set of logical principles presented later in this essay; they are discussed in detail in philosophical literature (including Lewis, 1912; Strawson, 1952; Russell, 1960; Faris, 1962; Clark, 1971; and Young, 1972).

Parallel paradoxes, less widely discussed, hold for disjunction when defined (as it is in contemporary elegant presentations) roughly as follows: "p or q" means same as "at least one of the two propositions, p and q, is true." In a way that shows more clearly the elegance-achieving connections among conjunction, negation, and implication, the definition can be put as follows: "p or q" means the same as "It is not the case that both not p and not q." According to this interpretation, a disjunction is established by establishing one of the disjuncts, whatever the other may be. Thus, to use the plane departure situation again, the departure before 5 p.m. would establish the following claim:

Example 4

Either we depart before 5 p.m. or the plane will get ice on the wings.

Again we have a paradoxical result, one whose similarity to the results in implication is evident. This similarity is not surprising in view of the interlocking series of definitions employed by elegant systems in order to achieve simplicity. These elegant systems are often called "truth-functional."

Although there is much more to say than the presentation of these examples, it is best not said in an essay focusing on Piaget's approach to logical competence and an alternative. The examples must at least give pause to one who accepts a contemporary elegant logical system (e.g., Neimark, 1970; Taplin, Staudenmayer, and Taddonio, 1974).

To the defender of elegant systems one response is still open: that these systems are constructed for purposes of simplicity and elegance; they are artificial and make no pretense of reflecting natural language patterns. In reply, people interested in children's logical competence should say that we *are* interested in natural language patterns, and we want to judge children's competence by these standards, not by some artificial ones. Perhaps that was Piaget's motivation for constructing his system. In any case he spoke with pride of his having avoided the pitfalls of material implication (Piaget, 1967, p. 273). His so doing is the first of my three reasons for presenting the preceding discussion of the paradoxes; the material-implication paradoxes might explain why Piaget went to the trouble of constructing his novel system. My other two reasons are these: To understand most contemporary elegant systems, one must grapple with these paradoxes; finally, their existence explains why in the latter part of this essay I will present a system that is less elegant than those encountered in most logic texts.

That completes this brief exposition of propositional logic. One might find further enlightenment in one or more standard logic texts. In order of increasing difficulty, texts by Ennis (1969), Fisk (1964), and Strawson (1952) are some that attempt to avoid the paradoxes; and (again in order of increasing difficulty) texts by Black (1952), Beardsley (1966), Copi (1961), and Quine (1960) incorporate the paradoxes at least to some extent. Incidentally, the standard use of truth tables (which I shall not explain but which are explained in the last four works mentioned) does embody the paradoxes of material implication and disjunction.

Piaget's Propositional Logic

In some respects, Piaget's propositional logic is like the elegant system. He does use the standard notation of the propositional calculus developed by logicians within the last century. (See pp. 293–303 of *Growth of Logical Thinking from Childhood to Adolescence*, Inhelder & Piaget, 1958, which will henceforth be referred to as *GLT*.) He uses the letters p, q, r, etc. He represents implication by $p \supset q$, disjunction by $p \lor q$, negajunction (which he calls "incompatibility") by p/q, and negation by an overbar. (For example, $\bar{p}$ is the negation p.) These are standard symbolizations. He treats "if p, then q" as equivalent to "not p, or q" (*GLT*, p. 298), a standard equivalence in propositional logic.

Furthermore, he treats both "if p, then q" and "not p, or q" as equivalent to the combination, $p \cdot q \vee \bar{p} \cdot q \vee \bar{p} \cdot \bar{q}$ (*GLT*, pp. 296 and 297), as is done in elegant propositional logic. This last is a crucial equivalence, bearing further scrutiny—particularly of the meaning that Piaget attaches to the combination $p \cdot q \vee \bar{p} \cdot q \vee \bar{p} \cdot \bar{q}$ and to others like it. But before looking at Piaget's meaning for such combinations, we should examine his general combinatorial system and his method of generating the total set of 16 of these combinations. This set also fits into the tradition of elegant propositional logic (even though his interpretation, as I shall later show, does not).

The Combinatorial System of Sixteen Binary Operations

Piaget's combinatorial system of 16 binary operations is a crucial feature of his propositional logic. What is this system? It is best explained by showing how it is generated, building with the letters p and q.

There are four different ways in which the symbols p, q, $\bar{p}$ and $\bar{q}$ can be combined in pairs without repeating either symbol (or either letter) in a pair:

a. $p \cdot q$ b. $p \cdot \bar{q}$ c. $\bar{p} \cdot q$ d. $\bar{p} \cdot \bar{q}$

Following Piaget, let us call each of these four pairs an "element."

These elements can nonredundantly be joined together by the symbol $\vee$ in 16 different ways if we count single appearances of an element and the absence of any element. Each of these 16 combinations is a "binary operation." Using the order used by Piaget in his presentation in *GLT* (pp. 293–303), Table 9.1 presents the 16 binary operations that are possible, starting with two letters. (Starting with three letters, there are 256; with four letters, 65,536. The formula is 2^{2^n}.) These combinations, which he calls "operations," make up his combinatorial system.

In this binary operation system the equivalences going across the lines are the standard ones of elegant propositional logic (e.g., in Line 7, treating $p \supset q$ as equivalent to the combination $p \cdot q \vee \bar{p} \cdot q \vee \bar{p} \cdot \bar{q}$ and calling it "implication").

The crucial difference between Piaget and the elegant system is in the meaning and justification of the *combinations* in Column 2. Since implication is so basic, I shall concentrate heavily on the combination for implication in my exposition of Piaget's approach to the meaning and justification of these combinations.

Meaning and Justification of Combinations

In elegant propositional logic $p \cdot q \vee \bar{p} \cdot q \vee \bar{p} \cdot \bar{q}$ means that *at least one* of the three conjunctive elements ($p \cdot q$, $\bar{p} \cdot q$, and $\bar{p} \cdot \bar{q}$) is true, producing the material implication situation in a somewhat different form, but again the truth of q or the falsity of p establishes the truth of the whole. Consider the first alternative, the truth of q. The truth of q establishes (if p be true) the first element or (if p be false) the second element. Since p must be either true or false (a standard assumption in this sort of logic), then either the first or second element is established by the truth of q. Since the truth of any of the elements establishes the whole, the truth of q establishes the whole—and therefore establishes its equivalent, "if p, then q." Similarly, the falsity of p establishes the whole—and thus also the implication, "if p, then q." Thus, we have material implication built into the crucial equivalence on the elegant interpretation of combinations.

But Piaget does not interpret them that way, thus avoiding material implication and its paradoxes. For him, the way to show that $p \cdot q \vee \bar{p} \cdot q \vee \bar{p} \cdot \bar{q}$ is true is to show that *all three* elements, not just any one, hold and that the fourth possibility, $p \cdot \bar{q}$, does not hold. Now this is impossible if we continue to treat p and q as propositions since the first conjunctive element holds p to be true, and the second holds it to be false. Either this rod is thin, or it is not thin. It cannot be both.

But Piaget does not treat p and q as propositions in the sense defined on page 204. He does not treat them as able to stand alone. Instead, he treats p and q as sentences (call these sentences "propositional functions") containing variables for which one may substitute references to different objects (e.g., "rod x is thin," "rod x is flexible"). These propositional functions cannot meaningfully stand alone since "rod x" does not have a referent. There is no way to tell whether the propositional function "rod x is thin" is true (when it stands alone) since we do not know what rod is rod x.

However, Piaget's propositions, although unable to stand alone meaningfully, can be made meaningful by adding either "for any x . . ." or "there exists an x such that . . ." In contemporary logic these additions are called, respectively, the "universal quantifier" and the "existential quantifier." I shall illustrate the use of each.

Example 5
Assuming the domain of rods
1. *For any x, rod x is thin (meaning, "All rods are thin").*
2. *There exists an x, such that rod x is thin (meaning, "There is at least one thin rod").*

Propositional functions can meaningfully stand together in sentences like the following:

Example 6
1. *For any x, if rod x is thin, then rod x is flexible (or in other words)*
2. *If a rod is thin, then it is flexible.*

Example 6 is a generalization about all rods within the realm under consideration. Thus, it is basically different from the conditional of Example 1, which is about one rod only. It incorporates a universal quantifier to make a generalization. Piaget's implications are generally of this form.

Furthermore, his combinations (like $p \cdot q \vee \bar{p} \cdot q \vee \bar{p} \cdot \bar{q}$) have an implicit existential quantifier attached to each element so that the appearance of an element means that the existence of at least one of the indicated sort of case is claimed. For example, the appearance of the element $p \cdot q$ in the above combination amounts to a claim that there is at least one case such that p and q, or in terms of our example there is at least one subject such that it is a thin rod and it is a flexible rod. Or, less awkwardly, there is at least one thin, flexible rod. Similarly, to include the element $\bar{p} \cdot q$, in terms of our example is to claim that there is at least one thick (nonthin), flexible rod; and the element $\bar{p} \cdot \bar{q}$, that there is at least one thick, inflexible rod. Thus, all three elements can hold since they are about different cases. The inconsistency that one would face in standard propositional logic by asserting all three elements does not exist for Piaget since he makes existential claims using propositional functions. And the elements can stand alone since they have an implicit existential quantifier attached.

There are two other crucial features of Piaget's combinations: (*a*) on the simplest reading, the $\vee$ that joins the elements in a combination is to be read "and" rather than "or"; and (*b*) there is, in addition to the presented combination, an implied denial of the existence of any unmentioned kind of case; in the implication combination a denial of any case fitting the description $p \cdot \bar{q}$, or in our example, a denial of the existence of any thin rods that are not flexible.

Thus, the combination for the implication in Example 6 is to be read as follows:

Example 7

> *There is at least one rod that is thin and flexible* $(p \cdot q)$*; and there is at least one rod that is thick and flexible* $(\bar{p} \cdot q)$*; and there is at least one rod that is thick and inflexible* $(\bar{p} \cdot \bar{q})$*; and there are no rods that are thin and inflexible* (no $p \cdot \bar{q}$s).

When Piaget says "$(p \supset q) = (p \cdot q) \vee (\bar{p} \cdot q) \vee (\bar{p} \cdot \bar{q})$" (Piaget, 1949, p. 233; also *GLT*, p. 297), he is implying that Example 6 (either 1 or 2) is equal to Example 7.

We now have the means to interpret any Piagetian propositional logic formula: If it is in operator form as found in the right-hand column in Table 9.1 (e.g., $p \supset q$), we convert it to its combination form in the second column of Table 9.1 (e.g., $p \cdot q \vee \bar{p} \cdot q \vee \bar{p} \cdot \bar{q}$). Then, using the strategy just outlined, we can say that the formula implies the existence of at least one of each of the kind of cases described in each element (e.g., $p \cdot q$) of the combination *and* implies the nonexistence of any cases coming under any one of the four possible elements ($p \cdot q$, $p \cdot \bar{q}$, $\bar{p} \cdot q$, $\bar{p} \cdot \bar{q}$) that are not mentioned in the combination.

Furthermore, we have the means to prove and disprove Piagetian propositional logic formulas. By establishing the content of Example 7, for example, we prove (in Piagetian logic) the implication relationship

TABLE 9.1

Piaget's System of Sixteen Binary Operations

Piaget's name and number	Constructed combination	Piaget's logical shorthand
1. Complete affirmation	$p \cdot q \vee p \cdot \bar{q} \vee \bar{p} \cdot q \vee \bar{p} \cdot \bar{q}$	$p * q$
2. Negation of complete affirmation	Nothing	0
3. Conjunction	$p \cdot q$	$p \cdot q$
4. Incompatibility	$p \cdot \bar{q} \vee \bar{p} \cdot q \vee \bar{p} \cdot \bar{q}$	p/q
5. Disjunction	$p \cdot q \vee p \cdot q \vee \bar{p} \cdot q$	$p \vee q$
6. Conjunction negation	$\bar{p} \cdot \bar{q}$	$\bar{p} \cdot \bar{q}$
7. Implication	$p \cdot q \vee \bar{p} \cdot q \vee \bar{p} \cdot \bar{q}$	$p \supset q$
8. Nonimplication	$p \cdot \bar{q}$	$p \cdot \bar{q}$
9. Reciprocal implication	$p \cdot q \vee p \cdot \bar{q} \vee \bar{p} \cdot \bar{q}$	$q \supset p$
10. Negation of reciprocal implication	$\bar{p} \cdot q$	$\bar{p} \cdot q$
11. Equivalence	$p \cdot q \vee \bar{p} \cdot \bar{q}$	$p = q^{a}$
12. Reciprocal exclusion	$p \cdot \bar{q} \vee \bar{p} \cdot q$	$p \text{ vv } q$
13. Affirmation of p	$p \cdot q \vee p \cdot \bar{q}$	$p \ [q]$
14. Negation of p	$\bar{p} \cdot q \vee \bar{p} \cdot \bar{q}$	$\bar{p} \ [q]$
15. Affirmation of q	$p \cdot q \vee \bar{p} \cdot q$	$q \ [p]$
16. Negation of q	$p \cdot \bar{q} \vee p \cdot \bar{q}$	$\bar{q} \ [p]$

[a] He also uses "$p \supseteq q$" for "equivalence."

specified in Example 6. And by showing that one or more of the conditions specified in Example 7 fails, we show (in Piagetian logic) that the implication relationship in Example 6 does not hold. These methods for proving and disproving play a significant role in judging and describing children's logic in *GLT*.

Accuracy of Interpretation

Does Piaget really mean that the assertion of a combination means that there is at least one case of each of the mentioned elements and that there are no cases of the unmentioned elements? I believe so, both because his detailed interpreters say so and because a number of things he says in *Traité de Logique* and *GLT* indicate this interpretation.

The presented interpretation of combinations is given to Piaget's propositional logic not only by Charles Parsons, a hostile critic and a logician (1960, pp. 76–77) but also by John Flavell, a friendly summarizer (1963, p. 215), by Seymour Papert, an interpreter and defender (1963, pp. 109 and 117), and by Herbert Ginsburg and Sylvia Opper (1969, pp. 181–196).

Then a number of things that Piaget says strongly support the interpretation. He defines implication in *Traité de Logique* (1949) in a way that makes any other interpretation implausible:

> *Implication:* $(p \supset q)$—if the conjunctions $(p \cdot q)$; $(\bar{p} \cdot q)$ *and* $(\bar{p} \cdot \bar{q})$ are true, while $p \cdot \bar{q}$ is false, there is then implication in the sense (asymmetric) "p implies q":
> $$(p \supset q) = (p \cdot q) \vee (\bar{p} \cdot q) \vee (\bar{p} \cdot \bar{q}).$$
> In terms of classes, implication corresponds with inclusion $P < Q$, which leaves empty the class $(P\bar{Q})$.

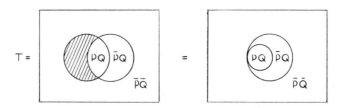

[1949, p. 233; my translation]

The word "and" in the first sentence of the passage suggests that all three must hold (although he did not say "if and only if"). Otherwise, why should he say "and"? And how else can all three hold unless there is at least one case of each? Furthermore, the example he presents right after the quoted words fit the interpretation. In his example *P* stands for being a mammal, and Q stands for being a vertebrate. There is at least one thing that fits each of the three classes, PQ, $\bar{P}Q$, and $\bar{P}\bar{Q}$; and nothing that fits the class $P\bar{Q}$.

Piaget's exposition in *Traité de Logique* is the place to which he and Inhelder refer us for a more detailed explanation than one finds in *GLT* (*GLT*, p. xxiv). Hence, this definition of implication is particularly significant. It is also troublesome for someone trying to see in Piaget a distinction between propositional and class logic because Piaget here says that the two "correspond" and uses a class-inclusion example to exemplify implication, which is supposedly a propositional-logic operation. The question "What logical thing is it that adolescents supposedly can do but children cannot do?" inevitably occurs to one who reads this item in *Traité de Logique*. But let us put that question aside temporarily.

The interpretation is also supported by a number of things he says in *GLT*. He illustrates complete affirmation with a case in which he holds that the subject learns that "all four possible associations occur [p. 293]." The only plausible interpretation of "all four possible associations occur" appears to be "There is at least one case of each of the four pairs of propositional functions, $p \cdot q$, $p \cdot \bar{q}$, $\bar{p} \cdot q$, and $\bar{p} \cdot \bar{q}$."

In discussing the possibility of integrating the expression $p \cdot q$ into larger combinations, like the one for implication, he speaks of the "occurrence of $p \cdot q$" (p. 294). The phrase "the occurrence of $p \cdot q$" seems to mean the occurrence of at least one case fitting the description $p \cdot q$.

In discussing incompatibility, he speaks of the *presence* and *absence* of the "characteristics denoted by p and q [p. 295]." If p and q denote characteristics, then they are class terms, or at least terms for propositional functions.

He says that "observing three associations" establishes an implication (p. 305). For some reason he does not at this point mention the lack of the fourth association, $p \cdot \bar{q}$, but he must include this idea, so presumably he just forgot to say it here. The important thing is that "observing three associations" (plus denying the fourth) establishes an implication. To observe an association is to have seen at least one case fitting the description.

Finally, he makes a statement about nonimplication that is puzzling unless one accepts the total interpretation. The statement is that someone in Stage III, before deciding that he has found an example of nonimplication, makes sure that everyone of the other elements is "eliminated." These eliminated elements include $p \cdot q$ (p. 299). Why must one eliminate $p \cdot q$ in order to establish nonimplication $p \cdot \bar{q}$? Why is observing $p \cdot \bar{q}$ not enough? The answer lies in the formula for interpretation of combinations: There must be at least one case of each of the mentioned elements *and no cases of the unmentioned elements*. Since the element $p \cdot q$ is unmentioned in the one-element combination $p \cdot \bar{q}$ (which is defined as nonimplication), the subject has to eliminate $p \cdot q$.

Although the previous quotations and cited testimony by other interpreters make a strong case for the interpretation I have presented of Piaget's propositional logic, Piaget's style does not readily lend itself to precise interpretation. Sometimes he says one thing, sometimes another; and often his language is vague. For example, he (or perhaps Inhelder; they do not specify) suggests on page 17 that each of the three elements in an implication must be shown to be *possible*, not that each must have an example. This alternative interpretation has difficulties, but it is a different interpretation from the one I have given. I will consider both interpretations.

Piaget's Propositional Logic: Some Problems

I have gone to some length to establish the given interpretation because of the problems engendered by this logic. One wants to be confident of an interpretation that results in the difficulties I am about to enumerate, which come under two headings: (*a*) some paradoxes of Piagetian logic; and (*b*) the lack of safeguards against overgeneralization. Parsons (1960) perceived a number of these difficulties, but his discussion has not received due notice I believe, because of its compactness and the typographical errors in the published version.

PARADOXES

Some paradoxes of Piagetian logic are (*a*) the specified requirement of the existence of mentioned cases and nonexistence of unmentioned cases, (*b*) the incompatibility between "if p, then q" and "if q, then p", and (*c*) the incompatibility between the affirmation of p and the affirmation of q. These paradoxes, which I shall elaborate, do not destroy his system. In can still be self-consistent. But the system, whether we treat it as normative or descriptive, is not about the implication, etc., that we (and children and adolescents) know.

Requirements of the Positive and Nonexistent Cases. Although the case-existence problem crops up in a variety of places, I shall focus on its appearance in the implication combination $p \cdot q \vee \bar{p} \cdot q \vee \bar{p} \cdot \bar{q}$. The problem is that it is unreasonable to require the existence (I shall consider possibility later) of at least one of each of the three kinds of case. This is most clear for the second kind, symbolized by $\bar{p} \cdot q$. It does not make sense to require that there be at least one *thick* (nonthin), flexible rod for it to be the case that if a rod is thin, it is flexible. There might not be any thick, flexible rods. But that should not falsify the implications "If a rod is thin, it is flexible."

Next consider the requirement of the first kind of case $(p \cdot q)$ for the implication statement "If anyone grabs those two wires, that person will be shocked." Because of my rudimentary electrical knowledge, I know that generalization to be true of two wires in my house, but there is no case of $p \cdot q$, that is, of a person who has grabbed the two wires and was shocked. And there might never be such a case. According to the given (existence, not possibility) interpretation of Piaget's combinations, the lack of such a case shows that the implication is mistaken. This should not be.

With respect to the requirement of a case of $\bar{p} \cdot \bar{q}$ consider the statement "If a body has inertia, then it is in principle detectable." Let $p =$ "body x has inertia" and $q =$ "body x is in principle detectable." Let the domain be bodies. Now the statement represented by "if p, then q" might be true, and it might be false. I am inclined to accept it. But the fact that there are no bodies that do not have inertia (and thus no cases of the first half of the element $\bar{p} \cdot \bar{q}$—and thus no cases that satisfy the whole element) should not prove it wrong. The requirement of a case fitting $\bar{p} \cdot \bar{q}$ is thus mistaken.

The requirement that there be no cases of the unmentioned elements is all right for implication but not for nonimplication. Earlier I noted that Piaget required the nonexistence of any case fitting $p \cdot q$ in order that we have a case of nonimplication, $p \cdot \bar{q}$ (GLT, p. 299). In the pendulum experiment described in GLT an increase in weight does not imply an increase in the period of the pendulum. This is what we would ordinarily call a case of nonimplication. And we would call it that on the ground of a clear case of an increase of weight without a change in the period of the pendulum.

We would do this even though we did have a case of $p \cdot q$, that is, a case of an increase in weight that *was* accompanied by an increase in the period. This could easily happen if the length of the pendulum were increased at the same time that the weight was increased. Thus, the requirement of no $p \cdot q$s is inappropriate for nonimplication in the ordinary sense of "nonimplication."

Now the specification of the four requirements enables Piaget to avoid the paradoxes of material implication and their analogues. Unfortunately, however, his requirements are themselves paradoxical.

On the interpretation that he requires *possibility of existence* rather than *existence* of the cases, the problems remain. With respect to the element $\bar{p} \cdot q$, it seems unreasonable to require that it be possible for there to be a thick, flexible rod in order that it be true that if a rod is thin, it is flexible. More strikingly, it seems unreasonable to require that it be possible for there to be a case of an increase in the period of a pendulum without an increase in length in order that it be true (at a given point on this earth) that if the length is increased (p), the period is increased (q). Certainly, none of their pendulum subjects in *GLT* could have shown such possibility, yet some were credited justifiably with inferring to the generalization "if the length is increased, the period is increased."

With respect to the element $p \cdot q$, it seems unreasonable to require the possibility of someone's grabbing both wires in order that it be true that if anyone grabs the two wires, that person will be shocked. The wires might be deliberately placed 20 feet apart because we realized that if anyone grabs both, he will be shocked. Placing them 20 feet apart makes it impossible to grab them both. If, in reply, someone makes the assumption that it is possible for a person to develop who has a 20-foot reach, then the counter is that, on this interpretation of possibility (logical possibility), anything is possible, and the Piagetian requirement under the possibility interpretation becomes empty.

It is similar with the element $\bar{p} \cdot \bar{q}$. I do not think it possible for there to be a body without inertia. This does and should not stop me from believing that if a body has inertia it is, in principle, detectable.

Under the possibility interpretation applied to nonimplication, the requirement of the nonexistence of a case of $p \cdot q$ would remain: that the element(s) not mentioned never occurs. The difficulty shown in the pendulum experiment would still obtain. A case of an increase in weight accompanied by an increase in the period does occur, as was shown by the subjects in the experiment, even though the appropriate conclusion was that an increase in weight does not imply an increase in the period.

Thus, the requirements remain paradoxical under the possibility interpretation as well as the existence interpretation of the Piagetian elements of combinations. In developing a system that avoids material implication and its analogues, Piaget introduced problems that are at least as serious.

Clash between "If p, then q" and "If q, then p." According to the given interpretation of Piaget's combinations, "If p, then q" requires the existence of at least one case of $\bar{p} \cdot q$; but "If q, then p" requires the nonexistence of any case of $q \cdot \bar{p}$, which is equivalent to $\bar{p} \cdot q$. Thus, not both implications can be true. In terms of our example, it would be logically impossible for both to be true:

1. *If a rod is thin, then it is flexible.*
2. *If a rod is flexible, then it is thin.*

The first conditional requires the existence of a thick, flexible rod. The second requires that there be no flexible rods that are thick (i.e., no thick, flexible rods).

This is not necessarily an inconsistency within his system, but it is not in accord with the way people use the word "if" in their everyday valid reasoning. I should not like to have students judged for their reasoning prowess according to his idiosyncratic use of "if." And on the view that takes Piaget as only describing children's reasoning, one must respond that children (and adults, too) often do take those two implications as equivalent—but never incompatible (O'Brien & Shapiro, 1968; Ryoti, 1972; Ennis, Finkelstein, Smith, & Wilson, 1969; Ennis & Paulus, 1965).

Piaget does not recognize this inconsistency between one-way implication and other-way implication (he calls them "reciprocals" of each other), saying in *Traité de Logique* (p. 234) and implying in *GLT* (p. 302) that both can be true.

Since his allowing implication to be true each way is inconsistent with the basic structure of his system, it appears that here is an aberration that must be resolved. He can do so by simply declaring that implication, as he means it, is incompatible with its converse, and both are incompatible with two-way implication. Thus, his "if p, then q" would mean something like "if, but not only if, p, then q," etc.; and the compatibility claims mentioned in the previous paragraph would just be about ordinary implication, not Piagetian implication. This resolution would be idiosyncratic, making his system useless for the study of logical competence (it would judge right answers wrong and wrong answers right), but the system would then be internally consistent.

Clash between the Affirmation of p and the Affirmation of q. The affirmation of p is defined as $p \cdot q \vee p \cdot \bar{q}$, which requires that there be no cases fitting $\bar{p} \cdot q$. The affirmation of q is defined as $p \cdot q \vee \bar{p} \cdot q$, which requires that there be a case fitting $\bar{p} \cdot q$. In terms of an example, to affirm that people are mortal ($p = $ "x is a mortal") is inconsistent with the affirmation that people are vertebrates ($q = $ "x is a vertebrate") when the population under consideration is people. The first affirmation requires the nonexistence of immortal vertebrates; the second affirmation requires the existence if immortal vertebrates. This paradoxical result also arises under the possibility interpretation. I do not see how to resolve this paradox other than by requiring that only one generalization be affirmed.

LACK OF OVERGENERALIZATION SAFEGUARDS

The lack of safeguards against overgeneralization is a problem, especially since the subjects' reasoning described in *GLT* is inductive reasoning from evidence to generalizations. The Piagetian logic that I have sketched out might well be regarded as an inductive logic since it takes us from observation of cases to generalizations. For example, the inference to "If a rod is thin, then it is flexible" from the examination of individual cases is inductive. How does the invitation to overgeneralization arise? Consider this short, simple list of steps in generalizing from data—without commitment to the order in which the steps are presented:

I shall call Step 1 the process of observing cases. Step 2 consists in checking cases against the generalization to see whether they contradict it or are instances of it. Step 3 consists in judging whether the cases selected are typical or representative of all the cases covered by the generalization. If they are typical or representative, we can generalize.

In the immediate preceding discussion, I suggested problems with Piaget's approach to Step 2, noting that he had too many necessary conditions. The problem here is in Step 3.

It is an old problem: how to justify the inductive leap from observed data to a conclusion that goes beyond the data. In terms of our example, the problem is how to justify the leap from the observation of a small number of cases of rods to the generalization "If a rod is thin, then it is flexible." One way to handle the problem is to deny that the generalization goes beyond the data—to claim that the generalization is only about the data that have so far been gathered. This approach effectively eliminates the leap but makes the generalization relatively useless. It does not give any indication of what to expect of the next thin rod we encounter nor even what to expect of already examined thin rods the next time they are examined. If Piaget choses this resolution, he is talking about a relatively useless process. That he does not choose this resolution is suggested by his expressed concern about implication and its legitimate generalization "to all cases" (p. 59). It appears that he is talking about reasoning to generalizations to go beyond the data. How else can we explain his use of the phrase "to all cases"?

Here the crucial phrase in his definition of implication is that stating the fourth necessary condition: In *GLT* (p. 16) it is specified as the requirement that a person show $p \cdot \bar{q}$ to be false in order that $p \supset q$ be true; in *Traité de Logique* (p. 233) it is specified as "while $p \cdot \bar{q}$ is false." Does that mean that in all the *examined* cases there are no cases fitting $p \cdot \bar{q}$ (this is the more likely interpretation and the one offered by interpreters Ginsburg & Opper, 1969, pp. 187, 188, 191, 193, and 194), or does it mean that in all examined *and unexamined* cases there are none fitting $p \cdot \bar{q}$ (the less likely interpretation)?

If it means that the set of *examined* cases must contain none fitting $p \cdot \bar{q}$, then we have a condition that can be satisfied by observation, but the formula for the meaning of implication becomes a generator of overgeneralizations. Consider the following argument produced by the anti-feminist political sage who claims that United States presidents will always be males. Put in the language of implication between propositional functions, this claim becomes, "If x is a United States president, then x is a male (for every x)."

According to Piaget's definition of implication in terms of a combination, that claim would be made true by the following facts:

1. *There is a case of a president who is male* (George Washington).
2. *There is a case of a nonpresident who is male* (Alexander Hamilton).
3. *There is a case of a nonpresident who is not male* (Martha Washington).
4. *There is no case of a president who is not a male.* (There are none at the time of writing.)

All these conditions are satisfied. But surely that does not prove the antifeminist correct.

The Piagetian combination gives us a set of conditions that are presented as jointly sufficient and separately necessary for an implication. The fourth condition leads us into difficulty when we take all four as sufficient. On the examined-cases interpretation, the condition leads us to produce overgeneralizations.

This invitation to overgeneralization is apparently accepted by Piagetian interpreters, Ginsburg and Opper (1969). Using the examined-cases interpretation, as I indicated earlier, Ginsburg and Opper characterize the "adolescent's conclusions [as] certain and necessary, . . . since the experiments have been designed properly [p. 188]." That even properly designed experiments lead to conclusions that are certain and necessary should be anathema to any experimenter, especially in view of the fact that Piaget–Inhelder adolescents spent not more than an hour or so on their experimental work with pendulums.

On the *examined-* and *unexamined*-cases interpretation, the fourth condition holds that there must be no cases of $p \cdot \bar{q}$, past, present, and future. Thus, an inductive leap must already be made in order that one be able to satisfy the fourth condition of the formula. Yet the formula for implication ($"p \cdot q \vee \bar{p} \cdot q \vee \bar{p} \cdot \bar{q}$, and no case of $p \cdot \bar{q}"$) appears to be an inductive guide for going from data to generalizations. It appears to be a formula for induction, yet to satisfy the formula one must already have performed a crucial part of the induction. Since Inhelder and Piaget's subjects in *GLT* did not observe all past, present, and future cases (a physical impossibility), this is an unlikely interpretation, leaving us with the examined-cases interpretation.

One crucial feature of the inductive leap from examined to unexamined cases is the judgment that the examined cases are typical. Piaget's logic neglects the problem of typicality in extending the examined cases to cases not found in the experimental setup contrived by Inhelder. Yet the conclusions discussed cover cases not found in those experimental setups. "If a rod is thin, then it is flexible" covers more than the rods Inhelder provided. It covers the aerial to my television set and a glass stirring rod in my chemistry laboratory. And it covers Inhelder's rods in circumstances different from those she provided.

I could go on conceiving of possible alternative interpretations since Piaget's style is not conducive to clear understanding, but the evidence I have put forward adequately supports, I believe, the interpretation I have offered. Alternatives are open to someone who does not accept this interpretation, but one must stop somewhere. A person who seeks to offer another interpretation is obligated to defend it textually and to see whether what Piaget says, under *that* interpretation, is defensible. The types of problems that I have raised with the interpretation I have offered are among those that should be considered. The basic question is this: Does Piaget's logic commit us to conclusions to which we should not be committed, and does it prevent us from drawing conclusions that we are entitled to draw? On the interpretations I have offered, Piaget's logic fails on both counts.

Piaget's Logic: A Descriptive or Normative System?

It might be urged, in reply to my criticisms of Piagetian logic as a system of logic, that he was only using the symbolism of logic but was not attempting to offer a way of judging the validity of reasoning: that Piaget's system is a descriptive system, not a normative one. Ginsburg and Opper (1969) suggest this approach: "Piaget's major question is not whether the adolescent can come up with the 'right' answer. Rather the issue is whether and how his thought differs from that of the younger child [p. 182]."

It is true that Piaget is attempting to offer a descriptive system. But his descriptions involve statements about the presence or absence of traits that Piaget judges normatively by his logic. For example, in his descriptions he uses such words as "inadequate" and "solution" (p. 287); "temptation" and "conclude too quickly" (p. 294); "know," "verify . . . truth . . . falsehood," and "counterproof" (p. 304). These are evaluative terms when applied by Piaget to his subjects.

Thus, his system is an attempt to describe, to state empirical truths, but the empirical statements are about ability to do what Piaget construes as good or bad logic. His claims about children's ability to handle propositional logic thus have both normative and descriptive dimensions. Having dealt with the normative dimension, let us now turn to the descriptive dimension.

Testability and Significance of Piaget's Claim That Children 11–12 and Younger Cannot Handle Propositional Logic

In *GLT* is is claimed that concrete-stage children "from 7–8 to 11–12 years . . . cannot yet handle . . . propositional logic [p. 1]," although they apparently are believed able to handle class logic (p. xxiii, 273–274). It is also suggested (pp. xxii, 1, 43, 104, 296, and others) that adolescents (especially Stage III-B subjects who are 14–15 and older) can handle propositional logic.

Although the authorship of some of these claims is not explicitly attributed to Piaget or to Inhelder, I shall speak as if it is Piaget. The thoughts expressed are in accord with his writings elsewhere and are the sort of thing for which Piaget is very well known. Finally, all people to whom I have talked about the matter take the views expressed to be Piaget's.

In his explicit assertion that children "from 7–8 to 11–12 . . . cannot yet handle . . . propositional logic" and his suggestion that propositional logic facility develops with the onset of Stage III, which appears to start at 11–12 (*GLT*, p. 1), there is a vagueness since it is not clear what he is saying about children who *are* either 11 or 12. Perhaps he is allowing for individual differences, in which case the vagueness seems appropriate, at least in the early-development stages of this theory.

Be that as it may, the problem that I want to raise is about the *meaning* of "handle propositional logic" regardless of how he deals with the loose boundary. A rough indication of a boundary somewhere around 11 or 12 will enable us to consider this meaning problem, which is more fundamental than the question of the location of the boundary.

Since the claim about those 11–12 and below is initially more clear than the one about children 11 through 15 and above, and since my ultimate concern is whether he is saying anything in this key quotation (and others like it), I shall focus on the more explicit claim, that children 11–12 and younger "cannot yet handle . . . propositional logic."

Given the previous analysis of Piaget's propositional logic, it is tempting to say that we are glad that children do not handle his propositional logic and hope and believe that adolescents and adults as well do not exercise their alleged capacity since the logic is so implausible. So we should ignore the claim and get on with our work. But the problem is not that simple.

For one thing, the logic is correct in some respects. (E.g., the following two principles are correct and implicit in his logic: (a) there must be no cases fitting $p \cdot \bar{q}$ for p to imply q,[2] and (b) the implication "if p, then q," does not imply the implication "if q, then p.") It would be useful to know whether children 11–12 and under act in accord with these correct principles if Piaget's claim gives this sort of information. Furthermore, if adults and children over 11–12 actually do operate in accord with the principles of Piaget's propositional logic, strange as this way of thinking may be, then it would be valuable to know that about them, and it would be valuable to know that children 11–12 and under are different in this respect.

Some Initially Puzzling
Features of Piaget's Claim

In my experience persons who are acquainted with the propositional logic tradition are puzzled when first faced with this claim of Piaget's. If "handle propositional logic" means to master the propositional calculus as taught in most contemporary logic courses, then the question is why should Piaget have picked on such young children as lacking this ability and indicated that adolescents can handle propositional logic; for most college students cannot handle propositional logic in that sense. If, on the other hand, the claim is that practically no children can reason in accord with any of the principles of propositional logic, then those who also have current or recent acquaintance with children feel that the claim is just false. This feeling is substantiated by a variety of studies, including ones by Burt (1919), Donaldson (1963), Ennis and Paulus (1965), Ennis, Finkelstein, Smith, and Wilson (1969), Hill (1961), O'Brien and Shapiro (1968), Roberge (1970b), Ryoti (1973), and Shapiro and O'Brien (1970).

These studies as a group also show that children are considerably worse at making judgments about invalid forms of arguments than about valid forms. But adolescents also are considerably worse at making judgments about invalid forms than valid forms (Carrol, 1971; Ennis & Paulus, 1965; Flener, 1974; Gardiner, 1966; Howell, 1965; Mar-

---

[2] Interpreting p and q as propositional functions.

tens, 1967; Miller, 1968; Paulus, 1967; Roberge, 1970b; Ryoti, 1973; Shapiro & O'Brien, 1970). Table 9.2 depicts a variety of valid and invalid argument forms. Valid arguments are those in which the conclusion follows necessarily; in invalid arguments, it does not follow necessarily.

What is it then that children allegedly cannot do that adolescents can do? Both have ability to reason in accord with at least some of the principles of propositional logic, and both have considerable trouble with logical fallacies.

Perhaps one might expect (on the basis of Piaget's claim) that there is some quantum jump in propositional logic ability from childhood to adolescence. This is a difficult suggestion to evaluate for both logical and practical reasons: The logical ones are the vagueness of the boundary line to which I referred earlier and the vagueness of the size of the difference needed to count as a quantum jump. A significant practical difficulty is that of gathering data on a large enough representative sample, data generated by using the same (or quite comparable) test (or other evaluation method) with each child repeatedly over a period of approximately 10 years—longitudinally from, perhaps, age 7 to 17. The reason that the data should be gathered longitudinally is that the alleged quantum jump might occur at somewhat different ages for different children—"11–12" is vague. To group the children cross-sectionally by ages or grades could partially mask such jumps. No study exists that satisfies this practical problem, and Piaget has left us rather in the dark about the logical problems.

Two already-mentioned studies by the Critical Thinking Project, with which I am associated, illustrate these difficulties but also show in some detail why one should wonder what logical thing it is supposed to be that children cannot do that adolescents can do. (See Table 9.3.) In these studies, which were in the tradition of testing for mastery of specific logical principles, no quantum leaps are apparent, although one should remember that they are cross-sectional studies. The test used with the older ones was a group paper-and-pencil test (see Ennis & Paulus, 1965) using items of the following form (modeled after a description by Roberge (1970b):

Suppose you know that
If ——, then ——.
Another premise (or two)
then would this be true?
Proposed conclusion

223

TABLE 9.2
Logical Principle Forms

Part I: Relational Logical Principles: Principles of Conditional, Class, and Alternation Logic

	Conditional logic		Class logic	Alternation logic	
	Propositional logic	Propositional-function logic		Propositional logic	Propositional-function logic
			A. Formally Valid Moves		
1. *Detachment*	If p, then q[a]	(For all x) if x is an A, then x is a B[a]	All As are Bs	Either p or q[c]	(For all x) either x is an A, or x is a B[c]
	p	n is an A[a]	n is an A	Not p	n is not an A
	——[b]	——	——	——	——
	q	n is a B	n is a B	q	n is a B
2. *Particular transitivity*	If p, then q	(For all x) if x is an A, then x is a B	All As are Bs	Either p or q	(For all x) either x is an A, or x is a B
	If q, then r	(For all x) if x is a B, then x is a C	All Bs are Cs	Either not q or r	(For all x) either x is not a B or x is a C
	p	n is an A	n is an A	Not p	n is not an A
	——	——	——	——	——
	r	n is a C	n is a C	r	n is a C

	If-then form	(For all x) conditional	All As	Disjunctive	(For all x) either
3. Full transitivity	If p, then q If q, then r ——— If p, then r	(For all x) if x is an A, then x is a B (For all x) if x is a B, then x is a C ——— (For all x) if x is an A, then x is a C	All As are Bs All Bs are Cs ——— All As are Cs	Either p or q Either not q or r ——— Either p or r	(For all x) either x is an A, or x is a B (For all x) either x is not a B, or x is a C ——— (For all x) either x is an A, or x is a C
4. Particular contraposition	If p, then q Not q ——— Not p	(For all x) if x is an A, then x is a B n is not a B ——— n is not an A	All As are Bs n is not a B ——— n is not an A	Either p or q Not q ——— p	(For all x) either x is an A, or x is a B n is not a B ——— n is an A
5. Full contraposition	If p, then q ——— If not q, then not p	(For all x) if x is an A, then x is a B ——— (For all x) if x is not a B, then x is not an A	All As are Bs ——— All non-Bs are non-As	Either p or q ——— Either q or p	(For all x) either x is an A, or x is a B ——— (For all x) either x is a B, or x is an A
6. Biconditionality[d]: a. Forward positive detachment	p if and only if q p ——— q	(For all x) x is an A if and only if x is a B n is an A ——— n is a B	All and only As are Bs n is an A ——— n is a B	p or q, but not both Not p ——— q	(For all x) x is an A, or x is a B, but not both n is not an A ——— n is a B

TABLE 9.2 (continued)

	Conditional logic			Alternation logic	
	Propositional logic	Propositional-function logic	Class logic	Propositional logic	Propositional-function logic
A. Formally Valid Moves					
b. Reverse positive detachment	p if and only if q q ——— p	(For all x) x is an A if and only if x is a B n is a B ——— n is an A	All and only As are Bs n is a B ——— n is an A	p or q, but not both Not q ——— p	(For all x) x is an A, or x is a B, but not both n is not a B ——— n is an A
c. Forward negative detachment	p if and only if q Not p ——— Not q	(For all x) x is an A if and only if x is a B n is not an A ——— n is not a B	All and only As are Bs n is not an A ——— n is not a B	p or q, but not both p ——— Not q	(For all x) x is an A or x is a B, but not both n is an A ——— n is not a B
d. Reverse negative detachment	p if and only if q Not q ——— Not p	(For all x) x is an A if and only if x is a B n is not a B ——— n is not an A	All and only As are Bs n is not a B ——— n is not an A	p or q, but not both q ——— Not p	(For all x) x is an A, or x is a B, but not both n is a B ——— n is not an A

B. *Formally Invalid Moves*

7. *Particular conversion*	If p, then q q ——— p	(For all x) if x is an A, then x is a B n is a B ——— n is an A	All As are Bs n is a B ——— n is an A	Either p or q q ——— Not p	(For all x) either x is an A, or x is a B n is a B ——— n is not an A
8. *Full conversion*	If p, then q ——— If q, then p	(For all x) if x is an A, then x is a B ——— (For all x) if x is a B, then x is an A	All As are Bs ——— All Bs are As	Either p or q ——— Either not q or not p	(For all x) either x is an A, or x is a B ——— (For all x) either x is not a B, or x is not an A
9. *Particular inversion*	If p, then q Not p ——— Not q	(For all x) if x is an A, then x is a B n is not an A ——— n is not a B	All As are Bs n is not an A ——— n is not a B	Either p or q p ——— Not q	(For all x) either x is an A, or x is a B n is an A ——— n is not a B
10. *Full inversion*	If p, then q ——— If not p then not q	(For all x) if x is an A, then x is a B ——— (For all x) if x is not an A, then x is not a B	All As are Bs ——— All non-As are non-Bs	Either p or q ——— Either not p or not q	(For all x) either x is an A, or x is a B ——— (For all x) either x is not an A, or x is not a B

TABLE 9.2 *(continued)*

Part II: Nonrelational Logical Principles: Principles of Negajunction, Conjunction, and Disjunction

	Negajunction		Conjunction		Disjunction	
	Propositional logic	Propositional-function logic	Propositional logic	Propositional-function logic	Propositional logic	Propositional-function logic
			A. Formally Valid Moves			
11. *Detachment*	Not both p and q p | ^{e} q ———— Not q | Not p	(For all x) it is not the case both that x is an A and x is a B n is an A | n is a B ———— n is not a B | n is not an A	p and q ———— p | q	(For all x) x is an A, and x is a B ———— n is an A | n is a B	p v q | Not q Not p | ———— ———— | p ^{e} q	(For all x) x is an A v x is a B n is not an A | n is not a B ———— n is a B | n is an A
12. *Addition*	Not p | Not q ———————— Not both p and q	(For all x) x is not an A | (For all x) x is not a B ———— For all x it is not the case both that x is an A and x is a B	p q ———— p and q	(For all x) x is an A (For all x) x is a B ———— (For all x) x is an A, and x is a B	p | q ———— p v q	(For all x) x is an A | (For all x) x is a B ———— (For all x) x is an A v x is a B

13. Illicit detachment	Not both p and q		(For all x) it is not the case both that x is an A and x is a B		p v q		(For all x) x is an A v x is a B	
	Not p	Not q	n is not a B	n is not an A	p	q	n is an A	n is not a B
	q (or not q)	p [or not p]	n is a B (or n is not a B)	n is an A (or n is not an A)	Not q (or q)	Not p (or p)	n is not a B (or n is a B)	n is not an A (or n is an A)

[a] p, q, and r stand for propositions; x is a variable term; n is a term referring to some particular thing. A, B, and C are class names or designators.

[b] The short horizontal line separates the premise(s) and the conclusion in each idealized argument form.

[c] Roberge has urged that "Either not p or q" may be used here and elsewhere in this column (with a corresponding change in the other premise, if any) because "Either p or q" is logically equivalent to "If not p, then q" rather than "If p, then q." He has a significant point, but I chose to use "Either p or q" because that is the most natural form of alternation. If one wants, one can think of p in "Either p or q" as standing for "not p," in "Either not p, or q," which is equivalent to "If p, then q." Alternately, one can think of the p in "If p, then q." in order to achieve a Roberge-suggested equivalence with "Either p or q." Similar comments apply to "(For all x) either x is an A or x is a B." To save space, the clause "but perhaps both" is omitted from each alternation except in the sixth row (a, b, c, and d), in which the clause is inappropriate.

[d] To show parallelisms, biconditionality principles are grouped together.

[e] To save space, pairs of principles are combined in the same row, the second premise and conclusion pairs (or just premise pairs—row 12) being separated by vertical lines.

[f] v is used for the disjunctive compound. To say that "p v q" holds is to say that at least one of "p" and "q" holds regardless of what the other is.

TABLE 9.3

Percentages of Students Satisfying the Criterion for Mastery of Certain Conditional-Logic Principles

	Grade[a]						
	1	2	3	5	7	9	11
N	30	28	29	102	99	80	78
Mean CA (years:months)	6:5	7:6	8:5	10:9	12:9	15:4	16:11
Mean IQ[b]	107.1	109.7	106.8	108	117	110	109
Principle							
Validity Principles							
1. Detachment[c]				51	56	66	62
2. Particular transitivity	13	29	45	26	52	53	58
3. Full transitivity				25	45	40	58
4. Particular contraposition	40	64	62	30	41	35	35
5. Full contraposition				34	40	35	33
6. Biconditionality				23	40	26	40
Fallacy Principles							
7. Particular conversion	0	11	7	2	3	4	3
8. Full conversion				2	5	11	19
9. Particular inversion	20	43	31	3	6	5	12

[a] The test used for Grades 1–3 is different from that used for Grades 5–11. Intertest comparisons of absolute percentages (rather than trends) are not warranted. Grades 1–3 from Ennis *et al.* (1969, pp. 23c, 54a). Grades 5–11 from Ennis and Paulus (1965, pp. V-16 and V-18).

[b] *Wechsler Intelligence Scale for Children* for Grades 1–3. *Lorge Thorndike* or *California Test of Mental Maturity* for Grades 5–11.

[c] The logical form of these principles appears in the conditional logic columns of Table 9.2. In these studies the two conditional-logic columns were used interchangeably. In reasoning from implication statements, it does not logically matter whether a principle is in propositional or propositional-functional form; there might well be an empirical difference, however, and we did not check for that in these studies.

The possible responses that the students could select were "A. Yes," "B. No," or "C. Maybe." The meaning of these possible answers was explained to the students as follows:

> This is what the possible answers mean:
> 1. YES: It must be true.
> 2. NO: It cannot be true.
> 3. MAYBE: It may be true, or it may not be true. You were not told enough to be certain whether it is "YES" or "NO."

A judgmentally derived operational definition was used (Ennis, 1964): at least five correct out of the six items illustrating a principle was treated as a sufficient condition for mastery. Table 9.3 gives the percentages of students at each of the grade levels tested (5, 7, 9, and 11) who satisfied this criterion for each listed principle. The oldest students did not do very well. Perhaps Piaget would say that our criterion was too strict, for they are supposed to be able to handle propositional logic. A marked difference between the validity principles (Lines 1–6) and the fallacy principles (Lines 7–9) is evident here and not readily explainable by Piaget's claim. Furthermore, no quantum jump from fifth to seventh grade (mean CAs, 10–9 and 12–9) is apparent. There is a fairly large jump between these two grades in the pair of transitivity principles but not in the other seven principles studied.

The study with the younger children used an individually administered interview-type test that asked children to reason with statements they were given about some physical objects in front of them. The criterion of mastery was the same (at least five out of six), and a verbal justification judged adequate by the interviewer was required for an answer to be considered correct. Only four principles were examined in this study, but certain things do stand out: that among these younger children (mean CAs ranging from 6–5 to 8–5), there are a considerable number who show competence in three of the four principles (including one invalidity principle, particular inversion—Line 9). Another notable feature of this compilation of data is the apparent great leap backward from Grade 3 to Grade 5, presumably a spurious result of the different tests that were used. This anomalous result does focus our attention on the practical difficulties involved in testing claims about long-term development. Extraneous features can so easily creep in and misdirect our attention.

But in any case these data appear to conflict with Piaget's views: The sizable percentages of third graders (mean CA, 8–5) who met the criterion for three of the four principles tested (45, 62, and 31%) together with the fact that adolescents also did quite poorly on the fourth principle suggest that Piaget's claim about children's inability to handle propositional logic is false. The percentages exhibited by the oldest ones (mean CA, 16–11) do not on the face of it suggest that they *can* handle propositional logic. The lack of any obvious quantum leap and the vast differences between the fallacy and validity principles are not readily explicable by Piaget's claims. In sum, the claims appear false, but perhaps they have been misinterpreted. If so, then one must look further in the search for the logical thing that adolescents can do but children cannot do.

Knifong (1974), after working with the original Ennis *et al.* (1969) data, attempts to provide what he regards as a Piagetian explanation of the successes young children have on particular transitivity and contraposition (see the conditional logic columns of Lines 2 and 4 of Table 9.2 and the same lines in Table 9.3), suggesting that their thinking could be interpreted as *transduction* rather than *deduction*. He also feels that this would explain their poor performance on the invalidity principles. The explanation appears to be that transduction is biconditional reasoning. So viewed, successes on the validity principles and failures on the invalidity principles are to be expected, he holds. He represents the biconditional as $p \rightleftarrows q$.

There are three difficulties. One is that biconditional reasoning *is* propositional (or propositional-functional, using Piaget's p and q) deduction, and Knifong's explanation holds that children this age do transduction, one of the defining characteristics of which is that it is not deduction and certainly not Piagetian propositional deduction, however that might be construed. They therefore cannot be doing both transduction and biconditional reasoning.

A second difficulty is that sizable percentages of the young children did well on particular inversion (Line 9 of Table 9.3). Knifong's explanation predicts that they would not. ("If p, then q," interpreted as "$p \rightleftarrows q$," together with "not p," yields "not q." These children did not accept that this conclusion necessarily followed. They should have, according to Knifong's explanation.)

A third difficulty is that, as was seen in Table 9.3, adolescents do poorly on the invalidity principles and much better on the validity principles. Since Knifong calls this pattern transduction for children, why not also call it transduction for adolescents? On what ground can a pattern be called transduction when children do it but not when adolescents do it? If one is willing to call it transduction when adolescents do it, then we are back to the standard problem: What is the disinctive logical thing that adolescents can do but that children cannot do?

*A Holistic Quality: Working
within the Combinatorial Systems*

I mentioned these studies and Knifong's attempt for the benefit of those who think, as I once did, that such empirical research has a bearing on Piaget's claims. I do not now think that it does because my close reading of Piaget suggests that the quality supposedly distinguishing adolescents and children and equivalent to ability to handle propositional logic is quite elusive.

This quality, a holistic one, seems to be the ability to work within the combinatorial system that I described in some detail earlier. I say this because of his many expressions of an essential or equivalence relationship between the two. That is, he speaks of the "combinatorial system which constitutes propositional logic" (*GLT*, p. 55) and indicates in a variety of ways a very close connection or identity between handling propositional logic and using the complete combinatorial system (*GLT*, pp. 42, 43, 54, 55, 93, 104, 254, and 296).

Since in these cited pages he says a variety of explicitly different things about the significance of the combinatorial system for handling propositional logic, for convenience I shall use the phrase, "working within the combinatorial system," letting that refer to whatever it is about the combinatorial system that Piaget equates to handling propositional logic. However, it is still unclear what Piaget is saying children cannot do because it is not clear how to tell whether children are working within the combinatorial system.

*Working within the Combinatorial
System: Possible Criteria*

Since the phrase "working within the combinatorial system" does not have an immediately obvious meaning, one must cast about for possible criteria for its application. In my search I came up with four candidates, but as I shall try to show, none rendered Piaget's claim about children useful to someone interested in children's deductive logic competence. It is, of course, open to any Piaget interpreter to come up with some other criterion, but I could find no others with any degree of plausibility.

The following four possible criteria for telling whether someone is working within the combinatorial system can be found discussed by Piaget in *GLT*: (*a*) the use of the language of propositional logic; (*b*) suppositional reasoning; (*c*) distinguishing one operation from another; and (*d*) isolating the variables.

233

THE USE OF THE LANGUAGE
OF PROPOSITIONAL LOGIC

One's first impulse might be to look at the language children use and understand to see whether they express themselves in terms like "if . . . then," "either . . . or," "implies," "not both," etc., and can reason correctly with propositions containing such terms since these terms have direct translations into the symbolism of the combinatorial scheme of 16 binary operations. This was and is my impulse. It is followed in the earlier-mentioned research that some might think conflicts with Piaget's claim. But Piaget explicitly rejects this as a way of telling whether a child is working within the combinatorial system, holding it to be useless to employ a verbal or linguistic criterion exclusively and denying that the use of the words "if . . . , then" shows that a statement is an implication (*GLT*, p. 279). He goes on to say on the next page that one can always state propositional relationships in class language, and *vice versa* (*GLT*, p. 280). This is reminiscent of his definition of implication in *Traité de Logique* (p. 233), in which he exemplified the implication relationship with a class-inclusion situation (mammals and vertebrates) and used a circle class-inclusion diagram to make it more clear.

On the other hand, Piaget or Inhelder (they do not identify), in one of the places in which an attempted connection between what children do and their working within the combinatorial system appears most clearly, apparently makes use of this linguistic criterion. An attempt is made to show, for a subject referred to as *GOU*, that each of the 16 binary functions can be discovered in his dialogue (*GLT*, p. 103). Piaget says elsewhere that Stage III subjects are able to distinguish a combination from the other 15 combinations (*GLT*, p. 296). But the person doing the distinguishing here is Piaget/Inhelder, not *GOU*. In treating each binary operation, Piaget/Inhelder shows to his/her own satisfaction that *GOU*s protocol for each binary operation either contained the wording of the binary operation, or it contained a thought that Piaget/Inhelder expressed in the language of that binary operation. In this demonstration Piaget/Inhelder did not refer to *GOU*'s reasoning suppositionally, nor even to *GOU*'s distinguishing each operation *from* all fifteen others, nor to *GOU*'s isolation of the variables. To show that GOU used the binary combination, the linguistic criterion apparently was used exclusively.

Incidentally, Bynum, Thomas, and Weitz (1972) have contended that the GOU protocol contained only 8 of the 16 binary operations. What Piaget/Inhelder see, other people do not see when looking at the same data. Such radical disagreement lends support to the desire to get some fairly clear and plausible categories and concepts to use in describing children's logical competence.

If the linguistic criterion were used to identify propositional logic, then Piaget's claims appear false, even about his own kind of experiments. Weitz, Bynum, Thomas, and Steger (1973), using a strictly linguistic criterion for identifying the binary functions, replicated the magnetism experiment from which the *GOU* protocol springs. They found no significant difference in the extent of use of the binary functions among 9-, 12-, and 16-year-olds; and found that all three groups used the same five operations and that no one used more than five. The five they found were conjunction, implication, disjunction, converse implication, and nonimplication. Futhermore, "of these five, only two were used with any regularity: conjunction and implication. . . . The more developed reasoner used the *same* operations as the less developed reasoner, but the former used those operations in a more complex and sophisticated manner [p. 283]."

Piaget's rejection of the linguistic criterion insulates him against such results but makes one wonder what would count as a test of his theory. As Piaget/Inhelder showed in the analysis of the *GOU* protocol, the linguistic criterion for identifying cases of propositional logic is attractive. When deprived of this criterion, one must look elsewhere for some interpretation of the claim that children can handle class but not propositional logic.

By disregarding the distinction between propositions and propositional functions, Piager has made the problem of distinguishing class and propositional logic more difficult for himself. Class inclusion statements (e.g., "Thin rods are flexible") are, in contemporary systems, formulated in terms of propositional functions (e.g., "For all rods, if rod x is thin, then it is flexible"); whereas propositional statements (e.g., "If this rod is thin, then it is flexible") are not formulatable in terms of propositional functions. (These examples were explained on pages 204 and 209.) By merging propositions and propositional functions, while retaining the symbolic trappings of propositional logic, Piaget gives extra impetus to the need for his proposing a clear criterion for distinguishing the two types of logic.

SUPPOSITIONAL REASONING

Shortly following his rejection of the linguistic criterion, Piaget offers a semilinguistic criterion that I shall call the suppositional-reasoning criterion. He asserts that the use of condition-contrary-to-fact implication statements (e.g., "if x were the case, then y would be the case") implies that propositional logic is in use (*GLT*, p. 279).

This criterion is also presented in his *Judgment and reasoning in the child* (1928/1959), although there it is offered as a characteristic of the possibly broader trait, formal reasoning ability: "The child cannot reason from premises without believing in them. Or even if he reasons implicitly from assumptions which he makes on his own, he cannot do so from those which are proposed to him. Not till the age of 11–12 is he capable of this difficult operation [p. 252]." The suppositional trait is that of being able to reason from that which the reasoner believes to be untrue, or at least does not believe to be true. Perhaps this is the mark of ability to work within the combinatorial system or to handle propositional logic.

There are two problems here. First of all, many children under 11–12 do have this trait (Ennis, 1971); thus, his view would be false if this criterion were used. Second, even if children under 11–12 did not have this trait, there is no reason to think that the trait is connected with the ability to work within Piaget's combinatorial system. What could be the connection?

DISTINGUISHING ONE OPERATION FROM ANOTHER

Piaget offers the subject's ability to distinguish one operation *from* the 15 others as the way to tell whether the subject is working within the combinatorial system (*GLT*, pp. 293, 296, 298).

However, this criterion is not helpful because Piaget does not tell us how to determine whether someone is *distingishing* one operation from the 15 others; thus, untestability is again suggested. It is somewhat ironic that Piaget/Inhelder in commenting about *GOU*'s protocol (reported earlier) did not check to see whether *GOU* distiguished each from the 15 others but showed that Piaget/Inhelder could do the distinguishing.

A seemingly plausible way to tell whether people are distinguishing each from the others would get us back to the verbal criterion explicitly rejected by Piaget: We would look to see whether they reason correctly from and to statements that contain such term as "if . . . then" and "either . . . or." If, for example, they conclude "If a rod is thin, then it is flexible" rather than "Either a rod is thin, or it is flexible" when the former is the appropriate conclusion, then we judge them to have successfully distinglished, given that both were alternatives that were presented to them. Similarly, when given a particular-contraposition kind of argument (see Table 9.2, Line 4, conditional column), if they draw the correct conclusion, then we can be fairly sure that they treated the "if . . . then" statement as an "if . . . then" statement rather than an "either . . . or" statement. Again, there is evidence of distinguishing. But this approach depends on the rejected verbal identification of the different propositional statements.

The ability to isolate variables and hold all but one constant in making an empirical inquiry is offered by Piaget as a sure sign of the combinatorial system (*GLT*, pp. 279–288). His reasoning, although difficult to explicate, seems to go like this (reconstructed from the discussion in *GLT*, pp. 284–288): The base associations or elements (of which there are four for two variables: $p \cdot q$, $p \cdot \bar{q}$, $\bar{p} \cdot q$, and $\bar{p} \cdot \bar{q}$) are not rich enough to interpret the results of separating variables and holding some constant. One also needs combinations of these base associations (e.g., $p \cdot q \vee \bar{p} \cdot q \vee \bar{p} \cdot \bar{q}$, the combination for implication). Let r mean "rod x is made of brass" and p and q mean "rod x is thin" and "rod x is flexible," respectively. By holding r constant, one might get a case of $p \cdot q$, a case of $\bar{p} \cdot q$, a case of $\bar{p} \cdot \bar{q}$, and no cases of $p \cdot \bar{q}$, although, had r not been held constant, one might have obtained a case of $p \cdot \bar{q}$ (a thin rod that did not bend because it was made of glass). Thus, one would be entitled by virtue of the fact that r was isolated and held constant to conclude "if p, then q," other things being equal. The strategy of isolating and holding variables constant can only make sense if one is striving to ascertain the truth of such combinations as the one for implication rather than uncombined base associations of elements. Hence, separating variables implies a combinatorial system.

If this explication of his argument is correct, then his crucial assumption is that the strategy of isolating and holding variables can only make sense if one is striving to ascertain the truth of a *combination* (like the Piagetian implication combination). That isolating the variables implies choosing the implication combination from the total number of possible ones depends on whether that combination truly represents implication. I argued earlier that it does not.

That the base associations are by themselves inadequate (*GLT*, p. 287) is correct since one must take account of context, existing knowledge, reasonableness of attempts to falsify, sampling procedures, etc. But the Piagetian combinations are also inadequate for at least these reasons. Furthermore, the base associations *do* represent all possible combinations of the variables under consideration.

One must be careful in dealing with this aspect of Piagetian argument not to indulge in an ambiguous use of the term *possible combination*. There are the possible combinations of variables (e.g., a thin, flexible rod evidences one combination of variables) and the possible combinations of the Piagetian elements ($p \cdot q \vee \bar{p} \cdot q \vee \bar{p} \cdot \bar{q}$ is one of the

combinations). The four base associations represent all the possible combinations of the variables p and q (assuming, as Piaget does, only two
values for each variable). A subject's thinking of all four base associations as the possible combinations (of variables) is not the same as a
subject's thinking of the 16 possible combinations of Piagetian elements.
That a subject thinks of the possible combinations of variables, as one
might well do who isolates the variables for purposes of varying them
one at a time, could suggest, by trading on an ambiguity, that the
subject is thinking of the possible combinations of Piagetian elements.
Thinking of the possible combinations of Piagetian elements could then
perhaps be taken as working within Piaget's combinatorial system.
Thinking of the possible combinations of variables would be evidenced
by isolating the variables. There is thus a danger of trading on an
ambiguity in inferring from someone's isolating the variables to someone's working within the combinatorial system.

The result of this discussion is that even if ability to isolate variables is a characteristic limited to children over 11–12 (a limitation
denied in a study by Anderson, 1965), there is no reason to believe
that from this it follows that working within the combinatorial system
is limited to children over 11–12. There appears to be no connection
between isolating variables and working within the combinatorial system. Hence, even though Piaget offers isolation of variables as a
criterion for the presence of the combinatorial system, there is no
reason to accept it as a criterion. One could with as much reason offer
it as a criterion for the presence of class reasoning, which Piaget assigns to children between 7–8 and 11–12.

Of course, one can insist that it is Piaget's theory and that he has
a right to interpret his terms any way he chooses. The result, then,
could be that Piaget *is* talking about isolating the variables when he
uses the phrase "handle propositional logic." There is an Alice in
Wonderland air about such a way of thinking, but if we accept it, we
must still remember that he would not then be talking about what
we are interested in when we express an interest in children's deductive-
logic ability.

Piaget's Treatment of Some
Apparent Counterexamples

Based on the foregoing analysis of Piaget's theory,[3] it appears that
the claim that children 11–12 and under cannot handle propositional

---

[3] I have not considered having Piaget's INRC structure as a possible interpretation of working within the combinatorial system or handling propositional logic

logic is a false, untestable, or otherwise defective claim. Piaget's response to a comment made in 1965 by Patrick Suppes at a Paris conference fails to modify this impression. Suppes presented Piaget with some logical problems that children successfully solve. In conditional logic he mentioned a propositional detachment problem and a particular contraposition problem (see Table 9.2 for these forms) with which Suppes said untrained children "show . . . remarkable facility." (Piaget, 1967, p. 277). The content of these propositional problems was the everyday experience of children in school: "If John is in school, then Mary is in school."

Piaget suggested in reply that Suppes' situations are "relatively simple" (1967, p. 277), but one wonders how that serves as a defense of his view. That is, there is no place in the combinatorial binary operations system for distinguishing simple from complex situations. Implication is defined in terms of its Piagetian combination $p \cdot q \vee \bar{p} \cdot q \vee \bar{p} \cdot \bar{q}$, and there is no mention of simplicity. What could be the connection between the combinatorial system and simplicity?

Piaget also said that the children's reasoning "seems precocious" (p. 278). This feature of Piaget's reply suggests untestability. Does he believe that children who appear to go against his theory are just precocious?

If Piaget did not mean to avoid the counterexample impact of Suppes' examples by attributing simplicity to the situations or precociousness to the children, then the third facet of his reply would hopefully be relevant: "One must . . . dissociate that which comes from language and that which language permits the imagination to evoke concretely. . . . " ("Ce que le language permet comme evocation concrete par l'imagerie en general" is how Piaget put this last phrase.) "Does [the child] reason by means of situations that he can evoke, or imagine, or does he reason by means of combinations of terms [Piaget, 1967, pp. 277–278, translation mine]?" In this, the third facet of his reply, Piaget draws a distinction two ways (presumably the same distinction but does not apply it to Suppes' cases. Piaget only states the distinction and then goes on to other things.

Perhaps Piaget here means that one could misinterpret the reasoning that occurred. Piaget's distinction would then be called upon to show how what might appear to be one thing was really something

---

because having that structure for implication, for example, seems only to require distinguishing and relating $p \supset q$ (I) from and with $p \cdot \bar{q}$ (N), $q \supset p$ (R), and $\bar{p} \cdot q$ (C), rather than the 15 other combinations (Beth & Piaget, 1966, pp. 181–183), thus neglecting the important $p \vee q$, $p \cdot q$, and p/q. Lunzer (1965, p. 30) has noted other problems with Piaget's applying the INRC structure to children's thought.

else, for Suppes' two examples are propositional logic in the standard sense of "propositional logic," and these examples were handled by children well under the age of 11–12. Whether or not Piaget was skirting the counterexamples by calling the situations simple and the reasoning precocious, application of his distinction might also be a way of dealing with them.

The distinction appears on the face of it to be one between reasoning by means of language and combinations of terms and reasoning by means of images. Although Piaget does not here specify which side of the distinction applies to children 11–12 and under, presumably they are the ones who reason by means of concrete images, reasoning by means of language and combination of terms being reserved for adolescents.

Applying the distinction to Suppes' examples, a first inclination is to think that Piaget meant that although Suppes' children might appear to be reasoning by means of language and combination of terms, they were only reasoning by means of concrete images—and thus they fit Piaget's theory. Testability questions on this interpretation immediately arise, for one wonders how Piaget would know that these children were reasoning by means of concrete images without assuming his theory to be correct in the first place.

Perhaps Piaget meant that Suppes' children were working with images, though not reasoning. The testability-or-falsity problem would arise here, for one wonders what right he has to say that these children were not reasoning. My associates' experiences (Ennis et al., 1969) with 6–9-year-olds, including interviews and observations of their justifications of their conclusions, strongly suggest that many do reason—and reason correctly—with "if-then" statements.

On the other hand, one wonders what it is that these children were not doing. What have they failed to do? What would they do differently with these or other logic examples if they were reasoning by means of language and combinations of terms? Piaget does not tell us.

Perhaps "reasoning by means of language" is reasoning that operates through an understanding of the *meaning* of the language used and, in particular, of an understanding of the *meaning* of the logical operators involved—in Suppes' two cases, "if-then" and "not." One wonders on what ground Piaget can deny this description to Suppes' children (if he does so). Age is a ground that makes the theory look untestable.

In sum, then, Piaget's simplicity-of-situation response appears irrelevant to the propositional-logic question. His precociousness response, if he means it the way it sounds, pushes his claim toward untestability. If he means his precociousness response some other way, then his distinction between reasoning with images and reasoning with language and combinations of terms fails to allay the impression of untestability. Perhaps there are other interpretations, but the only ones that occur to me are implausible.

After Piaget's responses to Suppes' question, Anatol Rapoport (Piaget, 1967, p. 280) attempted a defense of Piaget by suggesting that children would not be successful with examples with similar content but in which nothing necessarily followed. He offered an example of the particular conversion form. (See Line 7, Column 1, in Table 9.2.) Rapoport suggested that many children would get this sort of problem wrong. His suggestion is supported by the data on Line 7 of Table 9.3 and other studies mentioned earlier.

Rapoport's comment is relevant in that he specifies a type of example for which children do not show "remarkable facility." Thus, one might argue, here is something that children would do differently if they were reasoning by means of language and combinations of terms. Hence, the Suppes-mentioned successes would be misleading.

The trouble with this defense is that adolescents also do poorly on this sort of problem. (Again see Line 7 of Table 9.3 and other studies mentioned earlier.) If inability to handle the invalidity principles is to count against a person's reasoning by means of language and with combinations of terms, then the Stage III-B adolescents (covered in the right-hand column of Table 9.3), who are supposed to be able to handle propositional logic, also lack the specified ability. Rapoport's example would make Piagetian theory testable at one level at the cost of making it false at another.

But Rapoport's point does advance the discussion by focusing it. Piaget's response leaves me with a strong impression of untestability. An untestable theory does not tell us anything and cannot be a basis for predictions.

An Alternative to Piaget's Conceptualization of Logical Competence

In view of the difficulties in Piaget's conceptualization of logical competence the development of an alternative seems needed. The one I am about to present does not try to accomplish all that Piaget was trying to accomplish. Rather, it is an alternative in the sense that it attempts to provide a correct formulation of logical principles; a basic empirical vocabulary for describing logical competence; and a three-dimensional analysis of logical competence consisting of the logical-principle dimension, the content dimension, and the complexity dimension. Each dimension is in turn made up of parts.

There is room within the confines of this alternative approach for refinement, adjustment, and supplementation. I hope that it will serve as a step in the right direction.

Logical-Principle Dimension

A person is proficient on the logical-principle dimension to the extent that she or he can (with understanding) operate in accord with elementary principles of deductive logic. An arrangement of principles is to be found in Table 9.2. Each complete column entry (or "box") in the table may be regarded as specifying a logical principle. Since there are many boxes in Table 9.2, the question of parsimony of course arises and will presently be examined.

VALIDITY

For those boxes in Parts IA and IIA, "Formally Valid Moves," the principle for each box is that adherence to the form given in the box guarantees a valid argument (an argument in which the conclusion follows necessarily from the premises). The moves in the boxes IB and IIB are formally invalid moves: For each box the principle is that an argument that adheres to the forms in these boxes is invalid unless it is somehow saved by its content.[4]

COLUMN AND ROW SEPARATION AND GROUPING IN TABLE 9.2, PART I

Conditional and Class Logic. The three left-hand columns of Table 9.2, Part I, present standard elementary principles of conditional and class logic. This distinction between class and conditional logic is widely used, although, as I argued earlier, it is not clear how Piaget makes and applies this distinction.

The first and third columns are readily interpretable. That is, considering the first premise form in the first column, one can substitute a proposition for p and one for q and come up with an idiomatically acceptable compound proposition, for example, "If Mike is a dog, then

---

[4] For example, an argument of the propositional particular-conversion form (Row 7, first column) becomes valid if the appropriate content is supplied. The content of the second premise ("q") might be the conjunction, "r implies p" and "r." Then the argument becomes valid (though one premise would be irrelevant).

Mike is an animal," p being "Mike is a dog" and q being "Mike is an animal." Furthermore, in the first premise of the third column (class reasoning), "All As are Bs," one can substitute a class term for A and one for B and come up with an idiomatically acceptable class proposition, for example, "All dogs are animals," A being dog and B being animal.

For the second column (Propositional-function logic) literal interpretation is stilted. Using the same assignment as before for A and B and letting x range over things, an example of the first premise form is: "(For all things) if a thing is a dog, then that thing is an animal." This is an awkward way of saying that all dogs are animals, but for systematic reasons many contemporary systems employ this way of interpreting class-inclusion propositions.

The chief reason for incorporating all three columns instead of combining the second and third, as many contemporary systems might do, or combining the first and second, as Piaget seems to have done, is to avoid prejudging possible differences among the three columns. The empirical evidence for merging any pair of columns is not yet sufficient.

There is a logical reason for not merging the first two columns, exemplified by the important difference between "If this rod is thin, then it is flexible" and "(For any rod) if that rod is thin, then that rod is flexible." The first is a specific statement about one particular rod; the second is a generalization about all rods. The first is of the form of the standard premise of the first column; the second, of the second column. One of the problems of Piaget's logic is that it does not recognize this difference, as I indicated earlier.

A reason for not merging the second and third columns, although they are logically isomorphic, is that two different forms of speech ("If . . . , then . . ." and "All . . . are . . . .") are preserved by this distinction. By reducing either form of speech to the other, we would be eliminating a natural way of expressing some generalizations. Some general statements are more naturally expressed in if-then form, others in "all" form. "If vinegar is added to baking soda, then the soda bubbles" is an example of the former. "All dogs are animals" is an example of the latter. Second, one might argue, following Strawson (1952), that there are differences between the two columns in implied commitments to existence of the classes involved.

Furthermore, it might be that reasoning is more difficult that commences with one rather than the other of these logically isomorphic forms. One interpretation of the question of which, if either, is more difficult, class or propositional logic, can be put in terms of this distinction between the second and third columns. Having these two columns separate enables us to ask this question, so interpreted.

Logical similarities between class and conditional reasoning can be seen by reading across Rows 1–10 in the first three columns. These similarities suggest investigatable questions about empirical similarities and differences between class and conditional reasoning as well as those between the two types of conditional reasoning, propositional and propositional functional.

Alternation. The last two columns of Table 9.2, Part I, present principles of alternational logic. Any attempt to present rules for reasoning using the word "or" must face at least two issues about the ordinary use of the word. The first is whether the affirmation of one alternant implies the denial of the other. The problem is usually resolved by judging "or" to be ambiguous, with a strong and a weak sense. In the strong sense, the affirmation of one alternant implies the denial of the other; in a weak sense, it does not. The weak sense is depicted in Table 9.2 (Rows 1–10, fourth and fifth columns). Sydney Shoemaker and Robert Monk (personal communication) argue that the strong sense does not exist and that the implication supposedly attributable to it (when such an implication exists) is instead attributable to contextual features. I am inclined to agree with them and have accordingly placed among the formally invalid moves the alternation moves involving the affirmation of an alternant (Rows 7–10). If there is a strong sense of "or," then principles governing it would appear in the fourth and fifth columns of Row 6 ("biconditionality") if the then-redundant "but not both" were removed.

Whether or not there actually is a strong sense of "or," contextual features that would justify "but not both" are present so often that in my experience many people tend to assume that the features are there. Hence, in evaluations of a person's competence it seems only fair to establish whether the strong assumption (or sense) is being employed. In presenting a problem to someone, one can do this by using one or the other of the following locutions for the alternation premise: "Either . . . or . . . , but not both" (the strong assumption); and "Either . . . or . . . , but perhaps both" (the weak assumption).

The other issue about the use of "or" is whether, in the proper interpretation of the weak "or," an either-or proposition is established by the establishment of one of its parts. Does the truth of p imply the truth of "p or q"? The standard contemporary answer in logic is affirmative, but I am inclined to think that the weak "or" is ambiguous: that in some contexts the answer is affirmative and in some (remember Example 4: "Either we depart before 5 p.m., or the airplane will get ice on the wings") it is negative. In order to accommodate this ambiguity, I have distinguished between "alternation" (following Strawson, 1952, p. 90) and "disjunction," using the latter term, as is commonly done, for those either-or propositions that are establishable by establishing one of the parts, whatever its relationship to the other part(s). In Table 9.2 principles of alternation appear in Part I and those of disjunction in Part II. Ambiguity can be avoided in testing situations by signaling disjunction with "At least one of the followng is true." This disambiguation is needed only when one is reasoning toward an "or" statement, not when reasoning from an "or" statement.

The inclusion of the alternation principles in the same rows as the conditional and class principles can be roughly defended as follows: The alternation first premise is generally considered to be logically equivalent to a corresponding conditional first premise. For example, "p or q" is generally considered to be logically equivalent to "if not p, then q." Furthermore, implication and alternation have a similar intuitive feel: A person is focusing on the first part in uttering alternation and conditional statements and licensing (or authorizing) the inference to the second part on the basis of something about this first part. For example, the following seem quite similar:

1. *If we do not depart before 5 p.m., then the airplane will get ice on the wings.*
2. *Either we depart before 5 p.m., or the airplane will get ice on the wings.*

They are, of course, dissimilar in that the first clause of each is the negation of the first clause of the other.

This inclusion of alternation with conditional and class logic in the same rows needs empirical investigation. That is, we should find out whether the different parts of the same rows behave similarly developmentally, whether they correlate similarly with other variables experimentally and nonexperimentally, and whether they are equally difficult for various groupings, chronological and otherwise. One wonders to what extent the logical isomorphism has empirical manifestations.

Several of the alternation principles probably are not elementary, at least not so elementary as those in Rows 1, 4, 5, 6, 7, and 9. In particular, the transitivity principles and the full conversion and inversion principles do not appear elementary in the alternation columns. They are included to show the result of transforming each of the conditional and class principles into their logical isomorphs in alternation. Perhaps the negations in the alternation principles introduce a complexity that makes these principles more difficult and rarely applicable. The topic bears further investigation. Negation as a complexity factor will be discussed later as an element of the second dimension.

The Rows in Part I, Table 9.2: Some Finer Distinctions. Generally, the rows are labeled in a manner that employs commonly used logical terms and/or that expresses hypothesized similarities between some rows. Names are based primarily on class and conditional reasoning and extended for previously indicated logical reasons across the rows. Although, as I shall show, there has been some cross-row research, more is needed.

Row 1 is labeled "detachment" because these moves essentially consist of the legitimate detaching (and affirming) of the second part of the main premise (or an instance of it) on the basis of the affirmation (or denial in the case of alternation) of the first part of the main premise (or an instance of it). Detachment in conditional logic is sometimes called "affirming the antecedent," or "*modus ponens.*"

Rows 2 and 3 are transitivity rows because of the transitive relations expressed therein. Row 2 is called "particular transitivity" because the conclusion is a particular proposition (e.g., *r*). Row 3 is labeled "full transitivity" because the conclusion is a full compound proposition (e.g., "If *q*, then *r*").

As can be seen in Table 9.3, the results of a study by the Critical Thinking Project (Ennis and Paulus, 1965) suggest that particular and full transitivity develop empirically in fairly similar pattern, thus supporting grouping them together under one label, "transitivity." More study is needed, however.

Rows 4 and 5 are labeled "particular contraposition" and "full contraposition," although only the conditional-logic part of full contraposition has traditionally been called "contraposition." Because of the basic similarity between the two rows, shown in the first three columns as an implication occasioned by a denial of the second part of the main premise, the former, which is often called "denying the consequent," or "*modus tollens,*" is here called a kind of contraposition, "particular contraposition," using the distinction between "particular" and "full" explained previously. As can be seen in Table 9.3, conditional-logic particular and full contraposition turned out to be empirically quite similar in that study, thus supporting their being grouped together. More work is needed on the empirical relationship between the two.

Row 6, "biconditionality," gives in abbreviated form the principles for a two-way implication. The first part of the main premise (or an instance of it) is a necessary and sufficient condition for the second part (or an instance) except in alternation, in which there is also a negation involved. Sometimes the relationship expressed by the main premise in conditional propositional logic here is called "equivalence." Piaget uses this name. Such a name seems misleading and probably should be avoided, for the two parts usually are not equivalent in the standard sense of the term. They simply imply each other.

The invalidity rows (7–10) present conversion and inversion in particular and full versions. Common labels for the conditional propositional particular moves are "affirming the consequent" and "denying the antecedent." These four rows depict the standard logical fallacies.

The data shown in Table 9.3 suggest that a grasp of the full conversion principles of conditional logic begins to develop before that of particular conversion. One wonders why. Full inversion was not included, so no comparison can be obtained for it. Further investigation is needed.

The Biconditional and Parallel Interpretations of the Fallacy Principles. One possible objection some might have to the list of logical principles is that the if-then relationship is treated as a one-way conditional instead of a biconditional (an "if-and-only-if" statement), while many people, so the objection would go, interpret if-then statements as biconditionals. A similar objection may be leveled at the interpretation of class-inclusion and alternation statements.

This issue has arisen in the literature in the form of discussions about the best way to account for people's frequent fallacy errors. The "atmosphere effect" explanation offered by Sells (1936) and others see reasoners as adhering to the atmosphere of the premises. (That is, negative premises yield negative conclusion, etc.) An alternative explanation suggested by Ceraso and Provitera (1971), Chapman and Chapman (1959), Taplin, Staudenmayer, and Taddonio (1974), and others, which I shall call the "biconditional-interpretation" explanation, sees people as interpreting if-then sentences as biconditionals. Similarly, class-inclusion statements are held to be interpreted as statements of class equivalence. Extended to alternation, alternation statements would be interpreted as strong alternations ("either p or q, *but not both*," which is equivalent to "p, if and only if, not q"). Thus, the so-called fallacy errors would not be logical errors at all.

I suspect that both explanatory factors (as well as others) are operative in the masses of data that have accrued showing that children and adolescents get higher scores on the basic validity moves than on the basic invalidity moves. But if one accepts the biconditional-interpretation explanation (and its parallels for class and alternation logic) for at least some of the cases, it appears that one could no longer automatically say that someone has made a mistake who accepts as valid what are here called invalid arguments, although responses could still be classified. I shall discuss the problems in terms of the if-then relationship; similar comments apply to class statements and, with reservations, to alternation statements.

The approach I propose looks on the conditional relationship as depicted in the set of principles as embodying the correct way to interpret if-then sentences and the biconditional interpretation as an incorrect way (unless the context implies otherwise). Then one might want to argue about whether the correctness is of reasoning or of linguistic knowledge. It is difficult to distinguish the two at this point; perhaps we can settle for some compromise solution, like calling a fallacy error a logicolinguistic one. But our calling it an error seems important, for a person without the one-way conditional-relationship concept as a mental tool is in trouble in this world. That is, a person should interpret an if-then statement as a one-way conditional unless there is good reason to think otherwise. For example, people should realize that the assertion "If someone was a Soviet Communist at the time of the Vietnam war, then that person was opposed to what the United States was doing there" does not imply "If someone was opposed to what the United States was doing in the Vietnam war, then that person was a Soviet Communist." The biconditional interpretation of the original assertion would so imply.

Since the "strong 'or'" interpretation of alternation statements is perhaps defensible (though I would not at the moment defend it), I have reservations about applying the above approach to alternation statements. Pending further study and discussion, I shall let it stand, however.

LOGIC OF NONRELATIONAL COMPOUNDS

In contrast to the main premises of Part I of Table 9.2, all of which claim a relationship between the parts, the compound sentences of disjunction, conjunction, and negajunction (presented in Part II of the table) do not imply the existence of a relationship between the parts. A crucial result of this nonrelationality is that a disjunction and a negajunction can be established on the basis of one part only, regardless of what the other part is. Although there are parallels among implication, alternation, negajunction, and disjunction, this crucial difference is the reason for the tabular separation between implication-alternation and negajunction-disjunction.

Negajunction and Disjunction. The two elementary valid moves in reasoning from a negajunction and from a disjunction are presented in the same line, labeled "detachment." The same line is used to save space since the two parts of each compound can be treated in the same manner. That is, an affirmation of either negajunction implies the denial of the other, and a denial of either disjunct implies the affirmation of the other.

The derivation on the negajunction and disjunction compounds is presented in Row 12, labeled "addition." When one defines implication in terms of negajunction, and alternation as disjunction, it is these derivations that produce the paradoxes of implication and disjunction. But without those elegance definitions, the derivations are acceptable.

Some formally invalid moves that are in some respects parallel to the valid detachment moves are presented in Row 13, labeled "illicit detachment." Again, pairs of possibilities are joined in the same line because of the similar logic roles of the two parts of the compound sentences. Furthermore, under each prospective conclusion is placed an alternate in parentheses because it (the denial of the given conclusion) could be the attractive one. To my knowledge, empirical evidence is not available to indicate the overwhelming attractiveness of one or the other conclusion. For example, the subject-selected conclusion to "Not both p and q" and "Not p" could be "q," but it could be "Not q."

Conjunction. The valid conjunction principles (detachment and addition, Lines 11 and 12) seem not to be principles of inference at all. That is, it does not seem to require an inference to claim that Mary is in school, given that Mary is in school and John is in school.

I list these principles partly because they are standardly found in expositions of logic and partly because in complex proofs the steps represented by these principles are useful for purposes of keeping things in order. But I do not, by their inclusion, mean to suggest that mastery of these principles should be counted as contributing to logical competence.[5]

I have not listed any invalid conjunctive principles because there do not seem to be any errors that are tempting. And I have omitted some moves that are controversial. For example, can one conclude just anything (e.g., r), given "p and q" and "not p" (or given "p and not p")? According to Aristotle, nothing has been said when a contradiction has been uttered. According to contemporary logic, anything and everything follows from a contradiction.

Another issue: Does "p and q" follow from "q and p" in any context, or are contextual features required also? Does "They had a child and got married" follow from "They got married and had a child,"

---

[5] In a previous presentation of this three dimensional system these principles were simply omitted (Ennis, 1976).

to use an example of Strawson's (1952, p. 80)? Most systems give an affirmative answer, but Strawson, with at least some point, objects.

COMPREHENSIVENESS

A possible objection to the list is that the areas selected are not comprehensive enough—that ordinal logic (serial relationships), modal logic, more "only if" relationships, partial-inclusion relationships, and necessary and sufficient condition language should be incorporated as well. There is justice in this objection. I leave the list open-ended, intending that it be supplemented by other principles. No one has yet provided a satisfactory comprehensive taxonomy of logic. In any case, the principles emphasized would certainly be prime candidates for elementary logical principles.

PARSIMONY AND ELEGANCE

One might well be struck by the large number of principles. Must there be so many? More elegant and parsimonious systems of principles exist, systems from which the presented ones can be derived, as can be seen by consulting most contemporary elementary logic textbooks. However, there are logical, practical, and empirical reasons for not adopting such systems.

The logical reason is that the systems that are parsimonious enough to provide definitional equivalences among implication, alternation, disjunction, and negajunction do so at the expense of faithful adherence to the meaning of the logical operators, especially "if . . . , then . . ." and the alternation sense of "or," as employed in reasoning by competent people. This I tried to show earlier in this essay.

As I have indicated, Piaget objected to the paradoxical material-implication definition of implication (1967, p. 273), and that objection might have been his motive for developing his system of logic, which, although it has other difficulties, does not incorporate this paradox. To my knowledge, he has not registered an objection to the comparable paradoxical definition of alternation as disjunction. Instead, he appears on occasion to have accepted it (GLT, p. 242).

The objections I have made against elegant propositional-logic systems also apply to a popular and convenient propositional-logic validity-testing method that employs a truth-value matrix called a "truth table." Because this method embodies the elegant definitional equivalences that I have challenged, there is no point to expounding it here. It can be seen in most contemporary logic textbooks. But it is interesting that Piaget does not promote this system, in spite of his proclivity for such things. The explanation presumably is that he rejects the material-implication interpretation that is built into the method.

Wason and Johnson-Laird (1972, p. 90) object to the feature of truth tables that generates one implication paradox (that a false proposition implies any proposition). They constructed an alternative that avoids this particular paradox, but theirs still contain another paradoxical result: that any two true propositions imply each other, no matter what they are. In my proposed conceptualization truth tables and other correlatives of the elegant parsimonious systems are simply abandoned.

There is much more on both sides to be said about the issue, but it should be remembered that the conceptualization of logical competence proposed here is partly based on the assumption that the critics, including Lewis (1912) and Strawson (1952) are essentially correct in their objections to the use of the elegant parsimonious systems as model for judging reasoning. The falsity of this assumption would weaken the motivation for the proposed conceptualization, but it would not destroy the motivation, for there are empirical and practical supports as well.

First of all, it has turned out, as is shown by Roberge's (1972, p. 199) summary and by data presented in Table 9.3, that there are sizable developmental differences among the principles that have been separately tested for. Propositional logic and class logic are not all-or-nothing affairs. Some principles are easier than other principles.

Second, because of the widespread interest in Piaget's claim that class-logic competence precedes propositional-logic competence, it is desirable in this system to preserve the distinction between class and propositional-function logic. In elegant parsimonious systems, the third column of Part I of Table 9.2 would not exist because it is regarded as logically isomorphic with the second column.

Third, the state of knowledge, developmental and otherwise, about the logical competence of people seems to call for the development of a broad base of well-accepted facts about things that are important. To the extent that each box represents an important principle, a base of facts about competence involving each box could be practically useful (e.g., so that educators can know what to expect of different kinds of children). And such a base could also be useful for the purpose of suggesting and testing hypotheses and higher-level theories.

A BROAD VIEW OF EMPIRICAL RESULTS
UTILIZING THE PROPOSED CONCEPTUALIZATION
OF LOGICAL PRINCIPLES

The most striking result of empirical study of the differences between principles is the repeatedly found disparity between the validity and invalidity principles, the invalidity principles being much more difficult

(Carroll, 1971; Ceraso & Provitera, 1971; Donaldson, 1963; Ennis & Paulus, 1965; Gardiner, 1966; Howell, 1965; Martens, 1967; Miller, 1968; O'Brien & Shapiro, 1968; Paulus, 1967; Roberge, 1970b; Ryoti, 1972; Sanner, 1974; Shapiro & O'Brien, 1970; Taplin et al., 1974). See Table 9.3 for typical figures showing this difference, which suggests that it is better not to treat class, conditional, and propositional logic as unitary wholes (attained at a certain stage), as stage theorists seem inclined to do. The validity principles are better attained at the studied levels (ages 6 through the late teens) than the invalidity principles. This tendency even shows up in the study in which the easiest validity principle, detachment, was not tested (Ennis et al., 1969).

Differences among the validity principles and among the invalidity principles reinforce the suggestion that it is better not to treat class and propositional logic as unitary wholes. For example, as can be seen in Table 9.3, different percentages of students met what was judged to be a sufficient condition for mastery of the different conditional-logic principles (Propositional and propositional-functional logic were not distinguished for purposes of those studies). For the oldest students (mean age 16–11) detachment was apparently the easiest, followed by transitivity, biconditionality, and contraposition, in that order. This situation does not support a unitary view of conditional logic, nor of propositional logic if Flener (1974) is correct in his finding that propositional and propositional-functional logic are about equal in difficulty.

Another set of disconfirming evidence is the different course of development taken by transitivity and contraposition. Broadly speaking, there is little development of contraposition over the years tested but more development of transitivity, which for the younger ones was slightly more difficult than contraposition but less difficult for the older ones. Roberge's (1970b) results also fit this picture.

One wonders how to explain this differential development of contraposition and transitivity (assuming that such differential development is sustained in replications). One speculative explanation is that transitivity is essentially detachment (which develops slowly but which is easier than contraposition) with some complexity added to make it more difficult, that this complexity-induced difficulty decreases as children get older, that transitivity ability thus improves as children get older, but that contraposition ability, which is essentially different from detachment, improves more slowly than complexity-handling ability over the age range tested. This speculative explanation, even if correct at its depth, leaves unexplained why detachment and (especially) contraposition develop so slowly. Perhaps contraposition is an interaction between negation and detachment. This is an area ripe for further research.

Class and conditional logic have been compared empirically and seem to be similar developmentally, although class logic might be somewhat easier. In the cross-sectional study mentioned earlier, Ennis and Paulus (1965) found class logic to be slightly easier than conditional logic and found both types to improve gradually with age (ages 10–19 were studied). Roberge (1970b), in a more tightly designed (but also cross-sectional) study, found little difference between the difficulty levels of class and conditional logic and also found comparable common patterns of growth in transitivity, the fallacies, and contraposition.

Using the interpretation of the words "class logic" assumed in Table 9.2 and accepting Flener's findings that propositional and propositional-functional logic are equal in difficulty, then findings comparing class and conditional logic should be relevant to claims about stage-related differences between class and propositional logic. This is so since conditional logic comprises the most significant parts of propositional and propositional-functional logic in everyday reasoning and since the parts of conditional logic that are propositional-functional are equal in difficulty (assuming Flener's findings) to the parts that are strictly propositional.

But the evidence is sketchy, and Piagetian stage theory is flexible. Hopefully, the methodical employment of the conceptual scheme proposed here will enable us to formulate and test a variety of hypotheses bearing on these developmental questions.

Roberge (1972, p. 199) has attempted to draw together the results of several studies, but there are formidable difficulties in such an attempt, some of which the proposed conceptualization is attempting to overcome. There is widespread lack of congruence over the names of logical moves, over what is important, over what is to count as success in logic, over test items, and even over what is valid. Hence, I do not attempt here to bring together the numerous results in the literature that confound attempts to theorize in a sophisticated way, or even to summarize.

Content as Viewed by the Reasoner

The content-dimension conceptualization springs from Wilkins' (1928) specification of the various types of content variables that appeared to influence decisions about conclusions. Here they are somewhat revised in the light of the literature, my research and teaching, and the experience and criticisms of colleagues. The elements, the names of which are for the most part self-explanatory, are as follows: (a) believed premises versus hynothetical premise versus unsurprising disbelieved premise versus surprising disbelieved premise; *(b)* prior commitment about conclusion versus no prior commitment conclusion; *(c)* symbolic variable versus lack of symbolic variable; *(d)* familiar content versus unfamiliar content; and *(e)* concrete content versus abstract content.

The first element, dealing with the reasoner's belief in the premises, distinguishes among sets of completely believed premises, sets of premises containing at least one member neither believed nor disbelieved by the reasoner (this last being the situation in which people deduce the implications of hypotheses up for test, for example), sets of premises containing at least one member believed to be false (although not surprising) by the reasoner, and sets containing at least one member believed false and surprising by the reasoner. An example of an unbelieved although unsurprising premise would be that the empty beaker in front of us contains a white powder (assuming it would not be surprising to the reasoner for the beaker to contain a white powder). An example of an unbelieved and surprising premise would be that elephants can fly (assuming that it would be quite surprising to the reasoner if elephants could fly). Whether this suggested ordering is empirically correct is a question yet to be researched. But, as I indicated earlier in considering suppositional reasoning (see page 236) it does seem that Piaget's claims (1928/1959, p. 252) about children's inability to reason suppositionally needs some adjustment. The whole area is ripe for research based on carefully defined categories of premises.

Another part of an argument about which people can have prior beliefs is the conclusion. Generally, the research does not distinguish between the first two elements of the content dimension. It shows that prior beliefs about conclusions and/or premises tend to interfere when the beliefs are in conflict with the direction of the argument (Ennis & Paulus, 1965; Gordon, 1953; Henle & Michael, 1956; Janis & Frick, 1943; Kane, 1960; Miller, 1968; Morgan & Morton, 1944; Roberge & Paulus, 1971; Thistlethwaite, 1950; Thouless, 1959; Wason & Johnson-Laird, 1972; Wilkins, 1928).

Materials containing a symbolic variable have generally been more difficult, as has unfamiliar and abstract content (Ennis & Paulus, 1965; Miller, 1968; Roberge & Paulus, 1971; Wason & Johnson-Laird, 1972; Wilkins, 1928). Abstract content is here separated from unfamiliar content, for although they often co-occur, this is not always so. For example, *responsibility* and *entropy* are abstract concepts familiar to me. Whether abstractness empirically adds to difficulty beyond the difficulty supplied by unfamiliarity has not to my knowledge been investigated.

Complexity

In apparent conflict with Piaget, Burt (1919) held complexity to be the major factor determining difficulty of logical problems: "All the elementary mechanisms essential to formal reasoning are present before the child leaves the infants' department, that is, by the mental age of 7. . . . The difficulty of a test depends on its complexity" (p. 127). Weitz *et al.* (1973, p. 283), made a similar suggestion. That complexity is a factor in logical competence is consistent with my experience in teaching logic.

Complexity explains why transitivity is more difficult than detachment since transitivity involves more connections than detachment. Somewhat speculatively, as I suggested earlier, it could help explain why contraposition developmentally behaves differently from transitivity, since transitivity involves the complexity factor, number of connections, while contraposition does not. The complexity factor in contraposition, negation, perhaps develops more slowly than number of connections.

Furthermore, the complexity dimension, assuming negation to be a matter of complexity, embodies the probable greater difficulty of material containing negation (found by Evans, 1972; Hill, 1961; Roberge, 1969; Wason & Johnson-Laird, 1972 [though not Paulus, 1967; Ryoti, 1972]). Excepting negation, aspects of the complexity dimensions are relatively unstudied. In any case, a provisional specification goes as follows: (*a*) number of connections; (*b*) intricacy of the argument; (*c*) unrelatedness of content (as perceived by the reasoner); (*d*) extent of nonstandard order of parts of the argument; (*e*) extent of inclusion of irrelevant material; and (*f*) extent of inclusion of negatives.

The first three elements of this dimension are derived from Burt's discussion. Statements 1 and 2 illustrate the distinction between number of connections and intricacy:

1. *If this thermometer is put in that liquid; then if the temperature is 20°C, the thermometer will read 20.*
2. *If this thermometer is put in that liquid, then it will read 20; and if the thermometer reads 20, you will find it comfortable.*

Statement 1 is symbolized as "$p \to (q \to r)$." Statement 2 is symbolized as "$(p \to r)$ and $(r \to s)$." Statement 1 is more intricate because an implication is implied, although it has only two connections (two arrows). Statement 2 has three connections (two arrows and a conjunction). I realize that the notion *intricacy* requires further explication but shall leave it at that for now.

The fourth and fifth elements are suggested by my logic-teaching experience and my colleagues. The idea for the last factor, extent of inclusion of negation, has many roots, including the study of negation mentioned above.

There have been a few studies of complexity aspects other than negation. Roberge (1970a) found that reversing the premise order in two-premise conditional arguments had no effect, although more study is necessary. On the assumption that the use of words "only if," as opposed to just "if," requires a transformation, such use is thus an intricacy factor. These words have been found by Wason and Johnson-Laird (1972) to increase difficulty. Kodroff and Roberge (1975) did not find that relatedness made a difference. But the matter needs more study, as does the whole complexity dimension.

This list of aspects of complexity does not include the fourth of Burt's suggested complexity factors: number of connections to be supplied by the reasoner. I avoided including this because it seems to be an assumption-finding task, which goes hand in hand with deduction in determining what an argument is but is not part of judging a deduction or even of suggesting validly derived conclusions (Ennis, 1961).

Summary

In the first sections of this chapter I have tried to explain the elements of propositional logic; to demonstrate some significant flaws in elegant contemporary systems, flaws that might well have motivated Piaget's development of his own logic; to explain Piaget's system and show some severe difficulties with it; and to evaluate for their meaningfulness Piaget's views about children's and adolescents' abilities to handle propositional and class logic. Finding no deductive-logic skill possessed by adolescents and not by children and finding no way to tell in Piaget's system whether someone can handle propositional logic, I suggest that his claims in the area are false, untestable, or not about deductive logic.

In view of the deficiencies of Piaget's system I have proposed an alternative way of conceptualizing the area, the basis of which is a three-dimensional analysis of logical competence. It is open-ended, leaving room for amendment and refinement. But it offers correct logical principles (with reservations about alternation); it provides a vocabulary on which higher-level theories can be built; and it makes possible the testing of theories, including the grouping theories sketched above.

The logical-principle dimension consists of two parts—relational and nonrelational—both split into valid and invalid moves. The relational principles are detachment, transitivity, contraposition, conversion, and inversion; and cover conditional and alternation logic, both propositional-functional and propositional, and class logic. The nonrelational principles involve negajunction, conjunction, and disjunction and include propositional-functional and propositional versions. The lack of parsimony in the system is defended.

The content dimension provisionally consists of five elements: premise disbelief, conclusional commitment, symbolization, unfamiliarity, and abstractness. A person is proficient on this dimension to the extent that she or he overcomes these barriers.

The complexity dimension provisionally consists of six elements: number of connections, intricacy of argument, unrelatedness of content, nonstandard order, irrelevant material, and negation. Again, proficiency on this dimension is present to the extent that these barriers are overcome.

There is room for addition to, subtraction from, and modification and refinement of this conceptual scheme. It is rough in some spots and vague in others, but it gives us a basis for communication, it incorporates matters of practical interest in our attempts to improve people's thinking (argued in Ennis, 1962), it accommodates a variety of existing research results, and it can serve as a partial basis for further theory, explanation, and prediction.

REFERENCES

Anderson, R. C. Can first graders learn an advanced problem-solving skill? *Journal of Educational Psychology*, 1965, *56*, 283–294.

Beardsley, M. *Thinking straight* (3rd ed.) Englewood Cliffs, NJ: Prentice-Hall, 1966.

Beth, E. W., & Piaget, J. *Mathematical epistemology and psychology.* Dordrecht-Holland: D. Reidel, 1966.

Black, M. *Critical thinking* (2nd ed.). Englewood Cliffs, NJ: Prentice-Hall, 1952.

Burt, C. The development of reasoning in school chidren. *Journal of Experimental Pedagogy*, 1919, *5*, 68–77; 121–127.

Bynum, T. W., Thomas, J. A., & Weitz, L. J. Truth-functional logic in formal operational thinking: Inhelder and Piaget's evidence. *Developmental Psychology*, 1972, *7*, 129–132.

Carroll, C. A. Low achievers' understanding of four logical inference forms: An analysis of difficuties and of the effect of instruction (Doctoral dissertation, Columbia University, 1970). *Dissertation Abstracts International*, 1971, *31*, 4377A. (University Microfilms No. 71–651).

Ceraso, J., & Provitera, A. Sources of error in syllogistic reasoning. *Cognitive Psychology*, 1971, *2*, 400–410.

Robert H. Ennis

Chapman, I. J., & Chapman, J. P. Atmosphere effect re-examined. *Journal of Experimental Psychology*, 1959, 58, 220–226.

Clark, M. Ifs and hooks. *Analysis*, 1971, 32, 33–39.

Copi, I. *Introduction to logic* (2nd ed.). New York: Macmillan, 1961.

Donaldson, M. *A study of children's thinking*. London: Tavistock, 1963.

Ennis, R. H. A concept of critical thinking. *Harvard Educational Review*, 1962, 32, 81–111.

Ennis, R. H. Assumption-finding. In B. O. Smith & R. H. Ennis (Eds.), *Language and concepts in education*. Chicago: Rand McNally, 1961.

Ennis, R. H. Operational definitions. *American Educational Research Journal*, 1964, 1, 183–201.

Ennis, R. H. *Ordinary logic*. Englewood Cliffs, NJ: Prentice-Hall, 1969.

Ennis, R. H. Conditional logic and primary children. *Interchange*, 1971, 2, 127–132.

Ennis, R. H. An alternative to Piaget's conceptualization of logical competence. *Child Development*, 1976, 47, 903–919.

Ennis, R. H., Finkelstein, M., Smith, E., & Wilson, N. *Conditional logic and children*. Ithaca, NY: Cornell Critical Thinking Project, 1969. (ERIC Document Reproduction Service No. ED 040 437).

Ennis, R. H., & Paulus, D. H. *Critical thinking readiness in grades 1–12 (Phase 1, deductive reasoning in adolescence)*. (Cooperative Research Project No. 1680) Ithaca, NY: Cornell Critical Thinking Project, 1965. (ERIC Document Reproduction Service No. ED 003 818).

Evans, J. St. B. T. Reasoning with negatives. *British Journal of Psychology*, 1972, 63, 213–219.

Faris, J. A. *Truth-functional logic*. New York: The Free Press of Glencoe, 1962.

Fisk, M. *A modern formal logic*. Englewood Cliffs, NJ: Prentice-Hall, 1964

Flavell, J. H. *The developmental psychology of Jean Piaget*. Princeton, NJ: Van Nostrand, 1963.

Flavell, J. H., & Wohlwill, J. F. Formal and functional aspects of cognitive development.. In D. Elkind & J. H. Flavells (Eds.), *Studies in cognitive development*. New York: Oxford University Press, 1969.

Flener, F. O. A comparison of reasoning with general and singular propositions by fifth, seventh, and ninth grade students (Doctoral dissertation, University of Illinois at Urbana-Champaign, 1973). *Dissertation Abstracts International*, 1974, 34, 547A. (University Microfilm No. 74-05567).

Gardiner, W. L. An investigation of understanding of the meaning of the logical operators in propositional reasoning (Doctoral dissertation, Cornell University, 1965). *Dissertation Abstracts*, 1966, 26, 6179. (University Microfilms No. 66-04109).

Ginsburg, H., & Opper, S. *Piaget's theory of intellectual development*. Englewood Cliffs, NJ: Prentice-Hall, 1969.

Gordon, R. L. The effect of attitude toward Russia on logical reasoning. *Journal of Social Psychology*, 1953, 37; 103–111.

Hill, S. A. A study of logical abilities in children (Doctoral dissertation, Stanford University, 1961). *Dissertation Abstracts*, 1961, 21, 3359. (University Microfilms No. 61-1229).

Howell, E. N. Recognition of selected inference patterns by secondary school mathematics students (Doctoral dissertation, University of Wisconsin, 1965). *Dissertation Abstracts*, 1965, 26, 5292. (University Microfilm No. 65-14886).

Inhelder, B., & Piaget, J. *The growth of logical thinking from childhood to adolescence*. New York: Basic Books, 1958.

Janis, I. L., & Frick, F. The relationship between attitudes toward conclusions and errors and judging logical validity of syllogisms. *Journal of Experimental Psychology*, 1943, *33*, 73–77.

Kane, R. B. Some effects of beliefs about conclusions of arguments on the ability to judge the validity of the argument (Doctoral dissertation, University of Illinois at Urbana-Champaign, 1960). *Dissertation Abstracts*, 1960, *21*, 1139. (University Microfilms No. 60-3936).

Knifong, J. D. Logical abilities of young children—two styles of approach. *Child Development*, 1974, *45*, 78–83.

Kodroff, J. K., & Roberge, J. J. Developmental analysis of the conditional reasoning abilities of primary-grade children. *Developmental Psychology*, 1975, *11*, 21–28.

Lewis, C. I. Implication and the algebra of logic. *Mind*, 1912, 522–531.

Lunzer, E. Problems of formal reasoning in test situations. In P. H. Mussen (Ed.), European research in cognitive development, *Monographs of the Society for Research in Child Development*, 1965, *30*, 1946.

Martens, M. A. Use of selected rules of logical inference and of logical fallacies by senior high students (Doctoral dissertation, University of Wisconsin, 1967). *Dissertation Abstracts*, 1967, *28*, 4535. (University Microfilms No. 67-16980).

Miller, W. A. The acceptance and recognition of six logical inference patterns by secondary students. (Doctoral dissertation, University of Wisconsin, 1968). *Dissertation Abstracts*, 1968, *29*, 1685A. (University Microfilms No. 68-13651).

Morgan, J. J., & Morton, J. T. The distortion of syllogistic reasoning produced by personal conviction. *Journal of Social Psychology*, 1944, *20*, 39–59.

Neimark, E. D. Development of comprehension of logical connectives: Understanding of "or". *Psychonomic Science*, 1970, *21*, 217–219.

O'Brien, T., & Shapiro, B. The development of logical thinking in children. *American Educational Research Journal*, 1968, *5*, 531–541.

Papert, S. Sur la logique Piagetienne. In L. Apostel, J. B. Grize, S. Papert, & J. Piaget, *Etudes d'Epistémologie Génétique, vol. 15: La filiation des structures.* Paris: Presses Universitaires de France, 1963.

Parsons, C. Inhelder and Piaget's "The growth of logical thinking, II: A logician's viewpoint." *British Journal of Psychology*, 1960, *51*, 75–84.

Paulus, D. H. A study of children's ability to deduce and judge deductions (Doctoral dissertation, Cornell University, 1967). *Dissertation Abstracts*, 1967, *28*, 2101A. (University Microfilms No. 67–16365).

Piaget, J. *Judgment and reasoning in the child.* Patterson, NJ: Vittlefield, Adams, 1928/1959.

Piaget, J. *Traité de logique.* Paris: Libraire Armand Colin, 1949.

Piaget, J. *Logic and psychology.* Manchester, England: University of Manchester Press, 1953.

Piaget, J. Logique formelle at psychologie génétique including discussion by Piaget, J. F. Richard, P. Suppes, M. Reuchlin, A. Rapoport, P. Fraise, H. Simon, & F. Restel). In *Les modeles et la formalization du comportement Proceedings of the International Colloquium of the National Center for Scientific Research*, Paris, July 5–10, 1965. Paris, 1967, 269–283.

Quine, W. V. O. *Methods of logic* (rev. ed.). New York: Holt, 1960.

Roberge, J. J. Negation in the major premise as a factor in children's deductive reasoning. *School Science and Mathematics.* 1969, *69*, 715–722.

Roberge, J. J. The effect of reversal of premises on children's deductive reasoning ability. *Journal of Psychology*, 1970, *75*, 53–58. (a)

Roberge, J. J. A study of children's abilities to reason with basic principles of de-

Robert H. Ennis

ductive reasoning. *American Educational Research Journal*, 1970, 7, 538–595. (b)

Roberge, J. J. Recent research on the development of children's comprehension of deductive reasoning schemes. *School Science and Mathematics*, 1972, 70, 197–200.

Roberge, J. J., & Paulus, D. H. Developmental patterns for children's class and conditional reasoning abilities. *Developmental Psychology*, 1971, 4, 191–200.

Russell, L. J. Formal logic and ordinary language. *Analysis*, 1960, 21, 25–34.

Ryoti, D. E. Student responses to equivalent inference schemes in class and conditional logic. (Doctoral dissertation, University of Illinois at Urbana–Champaign, 1972), *Dissertation Abstracts International*, 1973, 34, 624A. (University Microfilms no. 73–17395).

Sanner, B. M. A study of the ability of fifth graders to handle conditional logic. (Doctoral dissertation, University of Illinois at Urbana–Champaign, 1974), *Dissertation Abstracts International*, 1974, 35, 111A. (University Microfilms No. 74–14609).

Sells, S. B. The atmosphere effect. *Archives of Psychology*, 1936, No. 200.

Shapiro, B. J., & O'Brien, T. C. Logical thinking in children ages six through thirteen. *Child Development*, 1970, 41, 823–829.

Strawson, P. F. *An introduction to logical theory.* London: Methuen, 1952.

Taplin, J. E., Staudenmayer, H., & Taddonio, J. L. Developmental changes in conditional reasoning: Linguistic or logical? *Journal of Experimental Child Psychology*, 1974, 17, 360–373.

Thistlethwaite, D. L. Attitude and structure as factors in the distortion of reasoning. *Journal of Abnormal Social Psychology*, 1950, 45, 442–458.

Thouless, R. H. Effect of prejudice on reasoning. *British Journal of Psychology*, 1959, 45, 442–458.

Wason, P. C., & Johnson-Laird, P. N. *Psychology of reasoning.* Cambridge, Ma.: Harvard University Press, 1972.

Weitz, L. J., Bynum, T. W., Thomas, J. A., & Steger, J. A. Piaget's system of 16 binary operations: An empirical investigation. *Journal of Genetic Psychology*, 1973, 123, 279–284.

Wilkins, M. C. The effect of changed material on ability to do formal syllogistic reasoning. *Archives of Psychology*, 1928, No. 102.

Young, J. J. Ifs and hooks: A defense of the orthodox view. *Analysis*, 1972, 33, 56–63.

Index

Index

A
B
C   8
D   9
E   0
F   1
G   2
H   3
I   4
J   5